The Economic Consequences
of American Education

**CONTEMPORARY STUDIES IN
ECONOMIC AND FINANCIAL ANALYSIS, VOLUME 73**

Editors: Professors Robert J. Thornton and J. Richard Aronson,
Lehigh University

Contemporary Studies in Economic and Financial Analysis

An International Series of Monographs

Edited by **Robert J. Thornton** and **J. Richard Aronson**

The Economic Consequences
of American Education

Edited by: **ROBERT J. THORNTON**
ANTHONY P. O'BRIEN
Lehigh University

 JAI PRESS INC.

Greenwich, Connecticut   *London, England*

Library of Congress Cataloging-in-Publication Data

The Economic consequences of American education / Edited by Robert J.
Thornton, Anthony P. O'Brien.
     p.   cm. — (Contemporary studies in economic and financial
analysis ; v. 73)
    Includes bibliographical references and index.
    ISBN 1-55938-755-6
    1. Education—Economic aspects—United States.   2. Education—
Social aspects—United States.   3. Educational change—United
States.   4. Education and state—United States.   I. Thornton, Robert
J.   II. O'Brien, Anthony Patrick.   III. Series.
LC66.E253   1994
370.19'0973—dc20   93-40944
                                          CIP
                                          Rev.

CONTENTS

CONTRIBUTORS

Samuel B. Bacharach	New York State School of Industrial and Labor Relations Cornell University
Nicholas Barr	Department of Economics London School of Economics and Political Science
Raymond Bell	Department of Counseling Psychology School of Psychology and Special Education Lehigh University
John Bishop	Institute for Labor Market Policy and Center for Advanced Human Resource Studies Cornell University
Gary Burtless	Economic Studies Program The Brookings Institution
Elliott Dubin	U.S. Advisory Commission on Intergovernmental Relations
Howard Glennerster	Department of Social Administration London School of Economics and Political Science
David Honeyman	U.C.E.A. Center for Educational Finance University of Florida
Henry Levin	School of Education-CERAS Stanford University

Dennis Leyden

Department of Economics
University of North Carolina
    at Greensboro

David Lipsky

New York State School of Industrial
    and Labor Relations
Cornell University

Judith McDonald

Department of Economics
Lehigh University

Vincent Munley

Department of Economics
Lehigh University

Anthony P. O'Brien

Department of Economics
Lehigh University

Joseph Shedd

Department of Educational
    Administration and Supervision
Syracuse University

Robert J. Thornton

Department of Economics
Lehigh University

Jimmy Weinblatt

Department of Economics
Ben Gurion University

George White

Department of Leadership,
    Instruction and Technology
Lehigh University

Acknowledgments

The papers in this volume resulted from the conference entitled "The Consequences of American Education," held at Lehigh University, October 19-20, 1990. The conference was sponsored by the Department of Economics and the Martindale Center for the Study of Private Enterprise at Lehigh University. Special thanks should be given to the Warren V. Musser Entrepreneurship Fund, the Iacocca Institute, and the Lehigh University College of Education for financial assistance. There are many individuals who also deserve special acknowledgment for the success of the conference and/ or the production of this volume, among them: Richard Aronson, Richard W. Barsness, Edward Donley, Elliott Dubin, Robert Ebel, Donna Kish-Goodling, Diane Oechsle, Rene Hollinger, Rosemary Krauss, Alden Moe, and Vincent Munley.

Introduction

Much media attention has been recently directed to the "decline" in the quality of education in the United States today. That such a problem exists is undeniable, and it is one that has manifested itself in numerous forms ranging from declining SAT scores to widespread illiteracy. Evidence now exists that the performance of students in the United States lags behind that of students in many other countries at every grade level, in nearly every subject, and at every stratum of ability.

That students in a nation as advanced as the United States should experience such poor performance levels is more than just a matter of national embarrassment. It also has profound implications for the ability of the United States to continue to compete successfully in the global marketplace. And if the future competitiveness of the United States is in jeopardy, so also is its ability to sustain its high standard of living and its influence on world affairs.

The growing public awareness of the problems surrounding American education has spawned several study commissions and reports, beginning in 1983 with *A Nation at Risk*. But while most of the studies and commissions have focused on the problems of schools, teachers, and students and have suggested various educational policy prescriptions, attention must also be focused on the consequences of the problems to the American economy—the consequences of allowing the quality of American education to continue to erode and the consequences of the various policy prescriptions that have been recommended. This was one of the primary focal points of the conference held at Lehigh University on October 19-20, 1990, at which the papers presented in this volume were given.

SUMMARY OF PAPERS

The Conflict of Expectations

In "The American System of Education: A Status Report," Ray Bell paints the backdrop for the rest of the volume by giving a brief overview of the major developments in education since 1950 while he examines the current expectations of the various constituencies. He notes that the debate over the past few years which intensified with the publication of *A Nation at Risk* was not really a new one; for even as far back as the Eisenhower administration there was concern over what was taught in the schools and how it related to the national interest. At that time, however, the focal point of the concern related to the Cold War and the matter of U.S. national security. Then, as now, the credibility of schools and teachers was called into question. The difference today, however, is that many additional problems—such as crime, violence, youth suicide, sexually transmitted diseases, and teen pregnancy—have been added to the educational agenda. At the same time the effectiveness of schools in preparing students for the world of work has been increasingly questioned, especially by the corporate world. Bell argues that this conflict of expectations has created great difficulty for the education sector. It lacks the time and the resources to meet the reality of the classroom, the home, and the street as well as the expectations of the boardroom, the personnel office, and the White House. Moreover, the results of the seven years of school reform attempts since *A Nation at Risk* have been far from encouraging, even when it is recognized that the United States is not alone among the nations of the world in its predicament.

As for the future, Bell cautiously predicts that the continuing pressure on schools will result in some real reform—perhaps in the form of a national system of assessment, or greater state control of curriculum, or even radical changes in the school day or the school calendar. In any case, says Bell, choices need to be made and resources allocated in what he refers to as a major test of "national will."

The Problem of Undereducation

In "The Economic Consequences of Undereducation," Henry Levin notes the multitude of recent reports recommending educational reforms. He claims that all the reports have two things in common: they decry the present state of American education, and they predict dire consequences for the economy and society unless change comes about. Levin's paper brings both of these concerns together by analyzing the costs of undereducation.

He first notes that no single definition of undereducation exists. Rather undereducation is a relative term—relative to the society in which it exists and relative to the jobs to which it pertains. After discussing the definitional problems, Levin uses the admittedly arbitrary criterion of less-than-a-high-school education as signifying a person lacking sufficient education to fully participate in the U.S. economy. Using this definition, Levin would classify the undereducated as consisting disproportionately of blacks, hispanics, and minorities. The heavy incidence of minorities who have not completed high school is particularly ominous because these groups represent a substantial and increasing proportion of school enrollments.

What are the economic implications of a high and growing number of at-risk students? First, it will reduce the quality of the U.S. labor force, and employers will suffer in terms of lagging productivity, higher training costs, and competitive disadvantages. Second, the cost and quality of higher education will be affected as many students will leave high school with learning deficits which will preclude them from participating in college and university education. This is not to mention the costs of remedial instruction, the possible watering down of the overall curriculum, and the psychological costs to students of not being able to "make it." Finally, there will occur rising costs of public services as more people rely on public assistance.

Levin then proceeds to analyze the existing cost-benefit studies on educational investments. The results suggest that investments in at-risk students are likely to have very high payoffs to society, with the benefit-cost ratios ranging from 3:1 to 6:1.

What's Wrong with American Secondary Schools?

In "What's Wrong with American Secondary Schools: Can State Governments Fix It?," John Bishop analyses the reasons behind the poor performance of American students. Bishop believes that because American high school students are not required to take comprehensive achievement tests, the amount they have learned is difficult to assess. He argues that most colleges base their admissions policies on a combination of relative measures of achievement, such as grade point average or rank in class, and scores on the SAT, which measures aptitude rather than knowledge.

As a result American high school students have little incentive to learn. According to Bishop, the rewards to learning as seen by students and their parents are low and the costs, such as foregone TV time or harassment by other students, are high. It is hardly surprising, therefore, that when American high school students take achievement tests that are also administered to students in other industrialized countries, the scores of the American students are at or near the bottom. Scoring well on achievement tests is crucial to students in other industrialized countries if they wish to attend the best colleges and compete successfully for the best jobs. Doing well on these tests is unimportant to American students.

Bishop believes the performance of American high school students would be greatly improved if American colleges were to place much more emphasis on achievement tests, such as the Advanced Placement examinations, in the admissions process and if employers would require from job applicants proof of competency in math, science, writing, and so forth.

Teacher Bargaining and Education Reform

In "Collective Bargaining Amidst Education Reform," Samuel Bacharach, David Lipsky, and Joseph Shedd (B-L-S) note that teacher unions have played an important role in the reform debate. Moreover, they see collective bargaining as increasingly recognized as a vehicle for reform itself, with the very meaning of collective bargaining changing as a consequence.

To see where collective bargaining in public education may be headed, B-L-S claim that it is necessary to understand where it came from. Most features of education bargaining were "borrowed" from the private sector—for example, district-wide bargaining units, fixed-period agreements, bread and butter concerns, and formal grievance procedures. These bargaining features were ones which had been invented specifically for industrial unionism and labor management relations in America's factories. Moreover, these structures and processes supported nicely the top-down managerial ideology that existed in most school systems when teacher unions first won recognition in the 1960s and 1970s, just as they "fit" the factory management systems in the 1930s. However, this same management ideology is now under severe attack both in public education and in other sectors of the economy as employers are becoming increasingly dependent upon their employees' detailed knowledge of work processes and client needs. And debates over how schools should be managed today almost always hinge on the tensions between the need to allow teachers discretion and the need to coordinate their individual efforts. The dilemma is to satisfy both needs simultaneously.

What will be the future of collective bargaining in education? B-L-S claim that future collective bargaining agreements in education will reflect the structure of the overall labor-management relationship in public education, just as the structure of industrial union contracts reflected the relationships which produced them. They foresee that teachers will insist on a more active role in setting educational policies and programs, while administrators will decide that fixed-term collective bargaining contracts are inappropriate vehicles for addressing these issues. In all likelihood there will be longer collective bargaining intervals, fewer restrictions in master agreements, and more explicit procedures for securing "waivers" of contract provisions. Many observers also expect that changes will occur in the structure of the teaching profession itself, although B-L-S do not expect the often-discussed "career ladders" to catch on. The reason is that career ladders, with their more formal differentiation of teaching duties, would be a step closer to—not farther from—the rapidly-becoming-obsolete industrial bargaining model, with its detailed rules on who performs what duties.

In conclusion, B-L-S claim that changes in public expectations of school systems and changes in the way school systems are being managed are undermining the bases of teacher unionism. The question is whether unions will be able to develop strategies that allow them to meet the challenges of these changing expectations. If they can, teacher organizations will have created a new form of union that has the potential of being every bit as vigorous, powerful, and appropriate to its setting as the old industrial unions were to theirs.

The School Finance System

Most of the papers in the volume offer proposals as to how the strengthening of public education might help the United States in its efforts to increase productivity and improve its competitive position. Vincent Munley's paper, "The Structure of K-12 School Finance in the United States," examines the constraints which the existing school finance system imposes on these proposals and how the system might thereby influence—and perhaps restrict—reform efforts.

Munley first reviews the economic justification for public schools and the financing structure which supports them. He notes that public K-12 education has characteristics of both a private good and a public good, providing as it does benefits to students, their parents, the immediate community and society in general. This being the case, no single structure for organizing public education can be considered to be the "best," and it is not surprising that substantial diversity exists in both the economic and the political institutions which govern the provision of education in the United States.

Munley then proceeds to describe the financing schemes which are currently in place in order to discuss their general implications for educational reform proposals. He notes in particular the movement toward increased equity in school district spending patterns over the past few decades and the consequently greater centralization in the public sector provision of K-12 education.

Among the general implications which the current school finance systems hold for education reform proposals, Munley first notes that increased centralization may promote efficient resource allocation from the perspective of the public good characteristics of education. At the same time, however, centralization exacerbates the inefficiency associated with the collective provision of a service that has a high private good component. Will the spending changes associated with greater centralization have an influence on the quality of education? Munley thinks not, noting that there is much skepticism as to whether increased spending influences the quality of education.

This suggests in turn that the pursuit of equity in school finance and the pursuit of educational excellence may be at odds. What is more, our equity based system must be taken as a "given," even though there is need to examine precisely what equity in educational opportunity actually entails. Does it compel states to ensure that all school districts can provide *adequate* educational services? Or does it require the provision of exactly *the same* educational services? The latter "strict" definition of equity, if accepted, may affect the viability of several prominent proposals for school reform, such as magnet schools and decentralized decision-making on the part of school management.

The education reform proposal that has received the most attention is that of parental choice. According to this concept, students' parents are free to select the public school which their children will attend. Such a policy forces schools to become more efficient and to produce a superior "product." Furthermore, it is not as prone to the type of equity problems faced by the magnet-school and school-based-management reform proposals. Of course, parental choice schemes can only work when there are actual alternatives in a school district; and Munley notes with concern that the majority of U.S. school districts have fewer than 10 schools within their boundaries. To enhance choice options in such districts, therefore, the logical solution is to allow inter-district transfers, with state governments providing additional aid to the "importing" districts.

Foreign Perspectives

The next two papers in the volume take a foreign perspective on various issues in education today. In "European School Systems and Financing: Lessons for the United States," Nicholas Barr and Howard Glennerster turn the focus to the higher education sector and discuss proposals for financing higher education with so-called income-contingent loans. Under one version of this proposal, a student entering into such a contract would bind himself to having withheld and forwarded to the lender a certain fraction of his annual income for the remainder of his working life. The system would operate in a fashion similar to withholding for social security taxes. A program of this sort would make loans more widely available, because a student without collateral would be able to obtain an income-contingent loan, whereas he might be unable to obtain a conventional loan. The program is also appealing because those students who profit the most from education would end up paying the most for their education.

Under a proposal currently being considered in the United Kingdom, students would be offered income-contingent loans bearing a real interest rate of 3 percent to be repaid from an addition to the student's National Insurance Contribution, with the repayment ending once the student had repaid the principle of the loan plus interest. The authors argue that by ending repayment at the point where the loan plus interest has been paid off, this proposal reduces the problem of adverse selection whereby only those students who consider themselves poor risks will join the program.

In "The Canadian Educational System," Judith McDonald compares and contrasts the Canadian educational system with that of the United States. She notes that the Canadian educational system is administered and financed at the provincial level. In contrast with the United States, local school boards in Canada have little control over administrative matters and no control over financial matters. As a result, there is less variation in per pupil expenditures in Canada. McDonald suspects that equality in per pupil expenditures may help explain the better performance of Canadian students on standardized tests.

Post-secondary education in Canada is almost entirely funded and run by the provincial and territorial governments. Because these governments have been under tight budgetary constraints in recent years, funding for colleges and universities has suffered. McDonald observes that since 1977 real expenditures per student have fallen in nearly every province. As a result, college and university enrollments have increased, teaching staffs have been cut back, and purchases of new equipment have declined.

Overall, McDonald sees the Canadian system as beset by many of the same problems of insufficient funding and declining quality that plague the U.S. system. While Canadian students appear to be more knowledgeable than U.S. students, McDonald worries that this advantage may disappear as insufficient funding erodes the quality of the education Canadian students receive.

Evaluating Current Proposals

In "Current Proposals for School Reform," Gary Burtless assesses some of the most well-known education reform proposals which have been put forward to date. He begins by summarizing the evidence on the links between the amount and quality of schooling and the subsequent performance of students. He finds that the financial benefit to individuals from extra years of schooling is large and growing. This appears to reflect a link between the years of schooling an individual receives and how productive he/she is.

Burtless considers the possibility that schooling does not greatly improve the "human capital" of workers, but instead merely signals to employers that persons who have obtained certain levels of schooling are likely to possess certain desirable innate characteristics. If this view is correct, then the apparent correlation between increased investment in education and increased productivity might be spurious. But he notes that no statistical test has yet been proposed to distinguish between the human capital and signaling theories.

At one time the quality of measurable inputs into the education process— such as the length of the school year, the level of teacher salaries, and the size of the student-teacher ratio—seems to have had an important impact on educational achievement, but Burtless claims that this no longer appears to be the case. He notes that it is surprisingly difficult to pin down the reasons why some teachers and schools seem to do a better job than others of educating students. It appears that certain difficult-to-measure characteristics of teachers and schools may be most important in explaining differing student achievement. To Burtless, this observation suggests that education reform should take advantage of the knowledge that school principals possess about the relative effectiveness of their teachers. Burtless advocates greatly expanding the authority of principals to hire, promote, and discharge the teachers on their staffs. He would compensate teachers with increased pay for the decline in their job security.

Burtless believes that increasing the authority of principals would be most effective if a voucher system of funding education were instituted. Under this system parents would receive a voucher that could be redeemed for tuition at any public and most private schools. This market discipline would provide the motivation necessary for principals to make good use of the increased authority he proposes giving them.

THE OUTLOOK

In the end the United States is confronted with two distinct education problems. The first is the weak performance of even our better students who are enrolled in good high schools. In general our high schools today seem to be turning out students who, as a group, know somewhat less than their predecessors did twenty years ago and who know markedly less than their contemporaries in other industrial countries. The explanations offered for the intergenerational decline are numerous and include a relaxation of standards and expectations, a less rigorous curriculum, and so on. On the other hand, the gap between the knowledge of U.S. students and those in other countries may have always existed; and it is not clear that it has increased markedly in recent years. In any case, this first problem has probably not had a substantial effect on the relative economic performance of the United States in the past, and there is no good reason to expect that it will in the near future.

The other American education problem may, however, have severe implications for America's relative future economic performance. As several authors have pointed out, many children in the United States today are failing to learn even the rudiments of the "3 R's." These children come from groups that comprise an increasing fraction of the labor force. However, it is impossible to gauge precisely the effect this will have on the economy. We are sailing into unchartered waters. No industrial economy has ever before experienced a significant decline in literacy rates among its workforce. There may be legitimate room to doubt the conclusions of those recent studies that indicate that there will be an enormous need in the future for workers who have received highly technical educations. There may even be grounds for suspecting that on-the-job training will serve as an adequate substitute for formal schooling in this respect. But it is an entirely different matter to be sanguine in the face of the great wave of illiterate or barely literate job entrants that seems in the offing.

Anthony P. O'Brien
Robert J. Thornton
Volume Editors

THE AMERICAN SYSTEM OF EDUCATION:
A STATUS REPORT—CONFLICTING EXPECTATIONS

Raymond Bell

In Education, the Facts Don't Mean a Damn
—An unidentified Member of Parliament

INTRODUCTION

The purpose of this volume is to focus on the economic consequences of the problems facing American education, that is, the costs of allowing the quality of American education to continue to erode and the costs of the various policy prescriptions that have been recommended to save this perceived erosion. The volume contains papers written by several distinguished economists and other observers who will focus on the specific aspects of this topic. The purpose of this paper is by way of introduction to paint the backcloth against which these discussions will take place. It will give a brief overview of the major developments in education since 1950, examine the current expectations of the various constituencies and, finally, suggest what major changes might occur which could impact on the financing and the economics of American education into the first two or three decades of the next century.

1

AN HISTORICAL OVERVIEW

The debate over the past seven years regarding the quality of American education arose from the release of the Gardiner Report, *A Nation At Risk: The Imperative for Educational Reform*. The debate reached its height almost exactly a year ago at the educational "summit" in Virginia. It is not a new debate. One might argue that it began in the late nineteenth century with the debate over who should train teachers—professors at liberal arts colleges or professors in schools of education. Prior to the Eisenhower administration, however, there had been no real central governmental effort, nor any business or industrial effort, to attempt to influence what was to be taught in schools or how it related to the national interest. Generally, schools were perceived as serving the purposes of the local community, and there was no overwhelming interest nor any real analysis regarding what those purposes might be.

It was the part that science and mathematics had played in the outcome of the Second World War and was to play in the Cold War that linked academic accomplishment with national survival. These roles were epitomized in the Manhattan Project and personified by such figures as J. Robert Oppenheimer and Edward Teller (atomic bomb) and Wernher von Braun (space). The result of this recognition was to greatly enhance the influence of academe upon educational policy. Myron Atkin notes that even in the late 1940s, "University professors had long been lamenting the quality of pre-college education … saying for fifty years that students were arriving at the University with an education that was insufficient, inaccurate, or unimportant".[1] From this growing influence of the professoriate emerged the movement to reform national science and mathematics curricula. In the mid-1950s we see Max Beberman's University of Illinois Committee on School Mathematics (UICSM) addressing the revision of secondary school math courses with support from the Carnegie Foundation while Jerrod Zacharias' group from Harvard and MIT formed the Physical Science Study Committee (PSSC) to examine the physics curriculum with help from the then recently formed National Science Foundation (NSF). The tone of both the professional and popular press was that UICSM and PSSC were reforming curricula that were criminally deficient, taught by incompetent teachers in schools that were woefully mismanaged (Atkin 1980).

These efforts were only intensified by the events of October 4, 1957, when Sputnik I was launched by the Soviet Union. The burden of addressing this crisis was now thrust into the arms of the federal government. Congress responded by passing the National Defense Education Act (1958) which required that elementary and secondary schools attend to the curricular deficiencies in not only science and mathematics but also foreign languages. In order to implement these remedial actions, appropriations to NSF were increased to provide funding for teacher training and materials development in mathematics and the sciences. It is clear that, although this was an historic change in the role of government *vis-à-vis* public education, there was little objection or even discussion. Schools were accepted by all constituencies as being an instrument of national policy. One might argue that David Gardiner's choice for the title and the message of his Committee's report a quarter of a century later had its origins in the acceptance of this principle.

Then, as now, little attention was paid to the question of how change is actually brought about in schools. It was generally assumed that all administrators and teachers could and would change immediately what they taught and how they taught it, and if authorities "outside" the schools developed new and better programs or systems that they would quickly be accepted into the schools. Nor was there any recognition of all the other complex social and economic input variables which affect both the process within, and the outcomes of, schools. It was left almost solely to James Conant to point out the practical problems of trying to bring about change on such a scale. The hundreds of heavily subsidized workshops held during the summers of the decade of the 1960s for science and math teachers appear to have had little measurable effect on gross performance outcomes in the succeeding twenty years. The importance of examining this period is to draw the obvious parallels between the current debate on, and attitudes toward, the problems facing education. Then, as now, the credibility of schools and teachers was called into question. Schools were acknowledged as instruments of national policy, and increased educational performance was seen as necessary to the national security (Ravitch 1983).

If the years during the Eisenhower administration were devoted to addressing the educational needs of the community for *external* reasons, the Kennedy and Johnson years saw the educational needs become more deserving of care for *domestic social* reasons. With the exception of the continuing interest in space exploration, particularly the Apollo project, the educational focus became primarily concerned with overcoming those conditions of poverty and racial segregation which restricted educational opportunities. Stereotypical of this change in educational priorities was the passage of the Elementary and Secondary Act (1965), Title I of which created compensatory education programs to cope with the acknowledged weaknesses of schools in the economically and racially segregated inner cities. This was the period which saw the creation of Job Corps, Teacher Corps, and Head Start.

By this time we can see the emergence of the two major areas of national concern in education: the continuing recognition that the national interest would require effective science and mathematical education and the realization that educational opportunities must be increased for those disadvantaged groups in society. Both generally reflect the national consensus. The Nixon years, however, were to shatter the confidence that had characterized the preceding decades. The economy experienced a downturn and the increasing conflict surrounding the nation's involvement in an unpopular war in Vietnam and widespread student unrest spilled over into the seventies. This decade became a period of national self-doubt, and resulted in a particularly harsh examination of all aspects of national policy, including educational policy. The duality of expectations in education—protection of national interests and resolution of domestic social problems—remained, but with a growing divergence of purpose and a diminishing focus and confidence. This is evidenced by the growth of special interest groups eager to have their needs equitably addressed in the educational context. By far the most notable of these was the Pennsylvania Association of Retarded Persons (PARC) which, as a result of the PARC Decision, were able to have Congress pass PL 94-142, the Education of All Handicapped Children Act (1976). For the first time the federal government was able to influence the specific educational plan for a specific child in a specific classroom, overriding any sense of professional autonomy or of state regulations or prerogative.

By the end of the decade of the seventies, school districts were becoming more reliant on federal and state funding, and also more accountable as federal and state actions began to exert greater influence and control over what was taught. Such programs as vocational education, drug and alcohol abuse, gifted education, bilingual education, and the history of ethnic groups were introduced by federal and/or state mandate. It would appear that even by the beginning of the Reagan administration the duality of purpose had become splintered into one of conflicting expectation.

Regardless of the examination brought about by the various commissions and reports, the decade of the eighties was to continue to intensify the conflicting—and rising—expectations of what was expected of schools. The problems of crime, violence, youth suicide, sexually transmitted diseases (especially AIDS), homelessness, runaways, teen pregnancy, malnutrition and child care have been implicitly added to the educational agenda. It has been the growing questioning of the effectiveness of schools in their function of preparing students for the world of work, however, that has captured the attention of the corporate world, and has dominated the political agenda and the media. The performance of American students in the traditional "3 R's," and in the areas of science, language, geography, history, and higher level thinking skills has been deemed unacceptable, particularly in comparison to students in those countries with whom America competes in world markets. In that sense, therefore, America's national interests and her economic security are threatened. The arguments heard in the fifties had returned and are echoed in *A Nation At Risk*.

... The educational foundations of our society are presently being eroded by a rising rate of mediocrity that threatens our very future as a nation and a people. What was unimaginable a generation ago has begun to occur ... others are matching and surpassing our educational attainments.... If an unfriendly power had attempted to impose on America the mediocre educational performance that exists today, we might well have viewed it as an act of war (p. 1).

The Gardiner Report, which catalogued a long list of "indicators of risk," was followed by sweeping proposals for school reform. Of special note were those from the National Commission for Excellence in Teacher Education (National Commission for Excellence in Teacher Education 1985), the Carnegie Forum on Education and the Economy Report on Teaching (Carnegie Forum on Education and the Economy 1986). These reports with recommendations to improve both the quality of the curricula and of teaching were given much attention. The reforms adopted have had mixed results, however.

The recommendations of these reports regarding minimal competency testing and the adoption of more difficult curricula have been followed by many states and by professional organizations. The results, at least thus far, appear to be disappointing. There has been no increase in high school or college graduation rates; in fact for some minority groups, graduation rates actually decreased (*Chronicle of Higher Education* 1990a). The trend in SAT scores remains flat at best. The latest "Report Card" published by the U.S. Department of Education is not encouraging (*Chronicle of Higher Education* 1990b).

In the area of standards and expectations, recommendations to standardize and increase the reliability of measures of attainment have run into problems. National examinations for all high school and elementary students, perceived by some to infringe on states and local rights, appear to be impractical and expensive to administer. The attempt to raise admission requirements of four-year colleges has been frustrated by the demographic situation, with many colleges actually reducing admission requirements in order to make a freshman class.

Changes in the time a student spends in school and more efficient use of that time have also been the subject of several recommendations. Here, too, there has been little change in the 180-day agrarian calendar currently followed by the schools because of the increased costs for salaries and air-conditioning which such a change would require.

Perhaps the major impact of the various reports has been upon the teaching profession, whose status has been raised considerably. Within three years of *A Nation At Risk*, 30 states had introduced some kind of minimal quality control, and several states began to encourage or require a post-baccalaureate training program or a Master's degree for teachers. The economic status of teachers, particularly in the Northeast, has increased significantly with minimum starting salaries in the $20,000-22,000 range.

The publication of the nation's educational goals by the White House as an outcome of the Educational Summit at Charlottesville in October, 1989, appears to have been met with controlled apathy, however (The White House 1990). Granted, it is somewhat difficult to assess the outcome or impact of a list of worthy aspirations. But there have been no real initiatives at the national level following the Summit as the country appears to be preoccupied with events first in Eastern Europe and more recently the Middle East, and with the fiscal impact of the budget deficit and the savings and loan bail out. One senses that even the vague educational goals set for the year 2000 will be difficult to meet.

CONFLICTING EXPECTATIONS

The preceding section presented an historic context of what is argued to be the current dilemma of conflicting expectations. Those expectations are frustrating education and may, in fact, be polarizing schools and school people from the political and corporate world. On the one hand schools are expected to prepare students to enter the world of work with all the skills that they might need, and it is in the nation's vital economic interests that they do so. That the schools are not meeting this expectation—or at least appear not to— threatens national security. On the other hand, schools and teachers have been given, or society has abdicated to them, the task of addressing the domestic ills of society which the family or the community have for various reasons been unable to address. The result, it is suggested, is that schools and teachers have difficulty meeting these expectations, because they have no clear mandate. They do not know what to prepare themselves to do; they lack resources and time to meet both challenges; they cannot demonstrate success in much of what they are about. Meeting the realities of the classroom, of the playground, of the home and the street often precludes meeting the expectations of the boardroom, the personnel office, and the State Houses and the White House.

The reports on educational performance referred to above have been seized upon to explain the lack of American industrial competitiveness in the past decade. We have heard that young Americans leave school without the necessary skills to staff "state of the world" manufacturing and assembly plants. The media have led us to believe that the dropout rate is increasing. We are told that students in the United States perform less well than those in other advanced technological societies. These are, of course, matters of concern, even if we allow for such things as the influence of growth in the number of students taking SATs on the mean scores, as well as the cultural and systemic differences between countries where many leave school at sixteen or younger and where highly selective tracking systems are utilized.

With regard to the dropout rate, it should be noted that in fact overall rates have remained fairly flat and for some ethnic groups have showed improvements over the past two decades (Digest of Educational Statistics

1989). This suggests that it is not the dropout rate that is causing problems, although it is always a cause for concern, but rather the greater negative consequences for those who drop out and the fact that dropout patterns are becoming localized. The difficulty for both the dropout and for the high school graduate with little or no technical skills is that employers are no longer recruiting people with this level of educational attainment.

The conflict of expectations in education as it impacts most on such things as jobs, income, and skill levels is probably best exemplified by one datum. Of the 20 million new workers to be added to the American workforce in the last two decades of this century, 82 percent will be a combination of immigrant, nonwhite, and female.[2] Many of these have passed, or are passing, through schools as "at-risk" students. This suggests that, if we are to fulfill the expectation of keeping the nation economically secure, we must address the social problems they face so that we might also educate them to a sufficiently high level to competently fill positions in mid-to high-level technology. It follows, then, that the educational agenda has to be wider than that necessary just to accommodate the narrow view of U.S. competitiveness. The broader needs of society, *including* the needs of national economic security, might best be served if we can reduce youth poverty and its related problems. We may not fair well on comparative tests of academic achievement, but we do much worse in infant mortality rates, ranking 18th in the world behind such countries as Japan, Hong Kong, Singapore, East Germany and our traditional European competitors (Hodgkinson 1989). The academic deficiencies of this segment of our population demand our attention if both the social and national security issues are to be resolved. Steps should be taken to enlarge preschool educational and Head Start programs, to target areas of unusually high dropout rates, and to increase graduation rates from high school AND college, especially poor and minority children of high ability. There is considerable anecdotal support for the need to coordinate programs for students who are at risk from several causes, and who are involved with multiple systems, simultaneously. It is not uncommon for schools to be dealing with students who are failing academically, are on drugs, are either pregnant or fathers-to-be, are delinquent, or are living in dysfunctional homes. Moreover it is often the case that all the agencies involved are ignorant of the involvement of the other agencies.

The results of the conflict of expectations and the seven years of school reform have been far from encouraging. We have had no increase in academic performance nor in high school or college graduation rates; yet we have increased pressures on the "bottom third" of students by establishing minimal competencies (*New York Times* 1990). There has been no reduction of youth poverty, and we have increased the economic and racial marginalization, especially of Hispanics. As an outgrowth of the Gardiner Report, 40 states have adopted higher academic standards in their schools; yet none of them increased their equity funding to provide the resources to actually attain those standards (Hodgkinson 1989). As Milton Goldberg, Director of Research at the U.S. Office of Educational Research and Improvement suggests, "Notwithstanding the considerable attention we have given education in the last couple of year [sic], we don't see the kind of improvements we need .... Few children are receiving the education they need for the 2lst century" (*New York Times* 1990). It is suggested once more that the reason this is not occurring is the conflicting and contradictory expectations being placed on the education system by all of its multiple constituencies.

We should not assume, however, that the United States is alone in this predicament. France has, in 1989-1990, appropriated some $10 billion for improvements to its educational system in the next three to five years, especially in the teaching of science and mathematics. The newly unified Germany has acknowledged need for similar expenditures. In Britain only 35 percent of 16-18 year olds are in school compared to 79 percent in America, 77 percent in Japan, 66 percent in France and 76 percent in Sweden. In his presidential address to the British Association for the Advancement of Science in September 1990, Sir Claus Moser suggested that his country is in danger of becoming one of the least educated of advanced nations. He expressed fear that "the situation is so serious that it is hard to address the subject with the calm and patience expected .... What is needed is a partnership between the worlds of employment and education" (*Manchester Guardian Weekly* 1990). This sounds remarkably familiar and, dare one say it, somewhat reassuring!

THE FUTURE

It need hardly be stated that any prediction of future trends in education must be made with extreme caution. It is difficult to believe, however, that the continuing pressure on schools will not result in radical changes. The fact that the major pressure groups—political, business, parental—appear to agree that it is in the national good for real reform to take place will probably ensure some change. From the perspective of those concerned with the national interest, one obvious place for this to take place is in the area of curricula. Areas widely believed to still be in need of attention are those articulated in *A Nation At Risk*: math, science and higher level thinking skills. Gordon Cawelti, Director of the Association for Supervision and Curriculum Development, also has suggested increased emphasis on global interrelationship and interpersonal skills (Cawelti 1989). These changes in curricula may well be driven by a national system of assessment similar to the one proposed by President Bush's new Educational Policy Advisory Committee and referred to earlier. The trend to increase state and even national control of curricula content by means of system-wide assessments will probably continue. This, of course, creates problems for teachers. For example, there is considerable temptation to ignore input variables in such systems and judge teacher performance on the sole basis of student test scores. In Britain we have seen strong reservations from parents and teachers when such a national assessment system was instituted in the 1988 Reform Bill. There are, it is argued, strong temptations to teach the test with the test then driving the curriculum, resulting in convergent thinking students and reduced teacher initiative and creativity. While this argument may have some validity, the process of moving toward eventual curricular reform, a more centralized system of assessment and thus more control and accountability is probably ineluctable given the growing concern about national competitiveness. This does not, however, mean that curricular reform and centralized assessment will actually bring about the desired increase in performance which the external constituencies seek. We have seen earlier that attempts at reform in the fifties appeared to have few demonstrable effects. As Conant argued then, schools and teachers are hard to change; and as John E. Chubb and Moe argue today, the entrenched educational establishment is not easily moved (Chubb and Moe 1990). As Blaug suggested in his Adams lecture at London University entitled "Where Are We Now In the Economics of Education?", no amount of economic modeling will actually bring about changes in how teachers perform or how schools are organized (Blaug 1983).

It would appear, however, that there is much more hope in successfully predicting changes—even radical changes—in the school calendar. Teachers appear to be willing to exchange substantial pay raises for increases in the length of the school day and the school year. This is also a fairly easy way to demonstrate a willingness to become more "competitive" with those nations whose school day and/or year are longer, consequently falling in line with doing what is in the nation's best interests. There is some hope, too, that the anachronistic agrarian calendar will also be changed, bringing a much better balance to the school year. There are several powerful arguments for this. First of all the regression in learning which takes place over the long summer break will be prevented. The strain on teachers and students brought about by long, uninterrupted marking periods will be ended. The perennial public relations problem of the teachers' nine-month year for a twelve month salary will be put to rest. The physical plant, largely unused over the summer months, will be better utilized. Perhaps most importantly, however, the educational system will gain more time to do all the things expected of it more effectively.

These changes in the school calendar and the length of the school day will, it is argued, be also necessitated by another major development in the next century. The school, given the informal "social" role of solving community problems and addressing children's pastoral needs, will seek to formalize this responsibility. If the schools are to deal with the problems identified by Hodgkinson and discussed previously, then we might expect the school to assume a much more aggressive role as it seeks to improve the educational performance of the increasing number of minority and impoverished children. This would appear to mean that programs in early childhood education would be expanded at all levels. Head Start would address the need of all eligible participants. It would be natural, therefore, for schools to assume day care responsibilities in order that the issues of service delivery can be addressed, coordinated and controlled. Schools would, perforce, open earlier and close later. Evening study schools/classes and expanded community education opportunities will probably be considered. Not only will this demonstrate a broader commitment to communities, it will be an additional rationale for increasing educational expenditures, especially in teachers' salaries.

The issue of financing education and the problems of poor schools vs. rich schools will be addressed in specific detail in other papers so I will not go into detailed discussion of the vast inequalities which exist in Pennsylvania and other states. Suffice it to say that reforming school curricula may be impossible without addressing basic reform in the way in which schools are financed. The issue of teachers' salaries deserves some comment here, however. Recent salary increases appear to have had a positive effect on teacher morale, and although based only on early anecdotal evidence, on the quality of students entering teacher preparation programs. There is a danger of increased hostility to such pay increases by taxpayers, however. The professional organizations have used one negotiated contract as a fulcrum to leverage up others in the same area. Such tactics may cause action by state legislature to preempt this method, and also to gain more control over school financing, by introducing state-wide, state-negotiated pay scales. While such legislation is controversial, it may be quite popular with taxpayers if not with school board members.

If the most recent round of contract settlements has pleased teachers, increased morale, and begun to attract better prepared teachers, then this augurs well for the future. The conditions of the profession will also be improved if the predicted calendar changes come about. A broader social role will also enhance career choices for teachers—long a source of frustration. These advances will have to be offset by a substantial change in the perceived "lack of accountability" on the part of the profession. It is conceivable that state and local education associations will be forced into policing their own ranks, weeding out the few incompetent teachers and decertifying them. For those who would find this difficult to accept, it is suggested that they examine the history of the legal and medical professions. They were forced to police their own ranks as a part of their development toward professional credibility. They don't do it as often as we may like, but they now are seen to do it often enough for the process to be accepted by their own members and respected by society.

While there will be other areas which will undergo radical changes in the early decades of the next century and while there are always uncertainties in predicting any future developments, I believe that the critical areas for reform are the ones presented here.

SUMMARY

In looking backward over the past forty years this paper has tried to develop the thesis that there are two major expectations for public schools which have emerged. One is the formal expectation that American children will have the academic skills to continue to keep the nation in a leadership position. This leadership role may vary with time and perception, but it is irrevocably tied to national security. Its current manifestation is that, as a leader in the international world of manufacturing and commerce, we are no longer "competitive." The second, less formal, expectation is that American schools will solve the "social" problems plaguing its communities. These problems are complex, serious and varied, and are beyond the teachers' traditional role and preparation. These include, but are not limited to, problems associated with poverty, disease, hunger and malnutrition, economic and racial segregation, crime, discipline, sexual habits, and behavioral values—those who are "at risk." These two expectations have, I believe, come into conflict, polarizing the various constituencies, confusing goals, limiting vision and time, restricting or deflecting resources, and consequently calling the credibility of the schools into question. The areas of reform which seem to emerge have been explored, and they reflect the notion that *both* expectations need to be addressed in a more focused, deliberate way. Choices need to be made, and resources allocated. In a real sense this is a major test of national will. How willing are politicians to address the resource questions implied in the solutions? How seriously does the public view the educational needs of this country? Are educators, particularly those in leadership positions in administration and in the professional organizations, really willing to change? Many of the following papers in this volume will focus on what the present situation and the future reforms will cost in economic terms. You will hear many proposals and see several economic models. It is urged that these be placed in the context of the school, the teachers, the administrators, and the children who spend their days in school, and in the communities from which they come. This context can then be extended outward to the nation and to the global village. There is a great need for some sense of understanding on what education is about, on where we are heading, and on what our *real* goals are. With this in mind, I urge you heed the old sailor's warning that "No wind is favorable to a helmsman without a port," and I close with St. Augustine's prayer: "Oh to see the reality of things behind the tyranny of words."

NOTES

1. For an excellent synthesis of the develop;ment of governmental involvement in public education see Atkin (1980), which was given as the Adams lecture at the University of London. The author notes his heavy reliance on this seminal analysis.

2. See Harold L. Hodgkinson's discussion of *Workforce 2000* done by the Hudson Institute (1988) in *The Same Client*. Hodgkinson gives an excellent analysis of the demographics of education and related services in this work.

REFERENCES

Atkin, J.M. 1980. *The Government in the Classroom*. London: Heinmann.

Blaug, M. 1983. *Where Are We Now in the Economics of Education?* London: University of London Institute of Education.

Carnegie Forum on Education and the Economy. 1986. *A Nation Prepared: Teachers for the 21st Century*. New York: Carnegie Corporation.

Cawelti, G. 1989. *How will Schools be Different in the 21st Century?* Washington, DC: Association for Supervision and Curriculum Development.

Chronicle of Higher Education. 1990a. September 27.

Chronicle of Higher Education. 1990b. October 8.

Chubb, J.E. and T. M. Moe. 1990. *Politics, Markets and America's Schools*. Washington, DC: The Brookings Institution.

Hodgkinson, H.L. 1989. *The Same Client*. Washington, DC: Center for Demographic Policy.

Manchester Guardian Weekly. 1990. September 2.

National Commission on Excellence in Education. 1983. *A Nation at Risk*. Washington, DC.

New York Times. 1990. September 2.

Ravitch, D. 1983. *The Troubled Crusade: American Education, 1945-1980*. New York: Basic Books.

The White House. 1990. *National Education Goals*. Washington, DC: Office of the Press Secretary.

U.S. Department of Education, Digest of Educational Statistics. 1989. National Center for Educational Statistics.

THE ECONOMIC CONSEQUENCES OF UNDEREDUCATION

Henry M. Levin

INTRODUCTION

The decade of the eighties has witnessed a plethora of reports that recommend national educational reforms. These have been issued by distinguished national commissions, while others have been published by business groups or those interested in a particular subject.[1] All of these reports have two things in common. First, they decry the present state of American education. They suggest that we are not educating enough students well enough. Second, they suggest that the consequences will extend to the economy and society itself because an undereducated student population will eventually become an undereducated workforce. They show particular concern with the ability of the U.S. economy to compete internationally without bringing our educational rigor up to international educational standards (McKnight et al. 1987; Mullis, Owen, and Phillips 1990).

This paper brings both of these preoccupations together into a single theme, the costs to the economy of undereducation. In addressing this topic we must bear in mind that there is no universally accepted definition of undereducation; nor is there any precise way to ascertain the costs to the economy. That is, this is not a simple accounting exercise. We lack the definitions, measures, and ability to connect education of a given quality with economic productivity at a later time. What we do have are methods of approximating these relations and their consequences. It is possible to suggest some preliminary standards and to use existing evidence to obtain some notion of the magnitude of the costs as well as the payoff to educational improvement.

The next section of the paper begins with some of the definitional and conceptual issues. The following section proceeds to several studies which give some idea of the economic and social costs of undereducation and the payoffs to investments in the undereducated. The final section considers some of the policy implications.

EDUCATION AND THE WORKPLACE

Clearly there is no single or simple definition of undereducation. In some societies, even an eighth grade education is considered to be a high level; in others it would not qualify one for most employment. Clearly, the meaning of the term *undereducation* is embedded in the criteria that one uses to determine what is an adequate education. A person with a Bachelor's degree in biology may be overeducated for a clerical position, but undereducated for a position as a research scientist.

Table 1 shows the educational requirements for occupational positions that are projected by the U.S. Bureau of Labor Statistics (BLS) for the years 1986 and 2000. We should keep in mind that although the BLS uses a very sophisticated method based upon an input-output matrix for the U.S. economy with adjustments for technological trends, these projections are always subject to some error because economic influences cannot be perfectly foreseen. For example, the pattern of economic prosperity based upon the persistently high federal budget deficits of the latter-eighties stimulated more job growth for more educated persons than had been anticipated (Bishop and Carter 1990). But occupational shifts arising from the more recent economic stagnation of the early nineties and reductions in the federal deficit seem to be having the opposite effects. Moreover, the employment implications of unanticipated military mobilization in the Persian Gulf and changes in foreign trade are not taken account of in earlier projections. Yet, evaluations of the past performance of the BLS projections show relatively high validity for predicting the overall educational composition of jobs (Rumberger and Levin 1985).

What is most obvious from this Table is the very wide dispersion of educational attainments associated with jobs in the U.S. economy. That is, there are jobs for persons with a wide range of educational levels. Moreover, while occupations with higher than average levels of education are projected to grow at faster rates than those with lower levels of education, the average level of education associated with jobs in the year 2000 is expected to be only slightly higher than those in 1986. The reason for this is that educational upgrading mainly is reflected in new jobs rather than existing ones, and job growth in the 1986-2000 period is expected to account for only about 16 percent of all jobs

Table 1. Employment and Required Education of Jobs in the United States by Occupation Group; 1986 and Projected to 2000 (Numbers in Thousands)

Occupational Group	Employment Number	Required Education in Years (Percentage Distribution)				
		0-11	12	13-15	16	17+
Existing Jobs, 1986						
Managerial	10,583	5	27	23	29	16
Professional	13,538	2	9	16	29	44
Technicians & related support	3,726	3	32	37	19	8
Sales	12,606	16	40	23	16	5
Administrative support	19,851	8	54	27	9	2
Private household	981	61	30	7	1	1
Protective service	2,055	13	43	31	10	3
Other service	14,500	35	44	17	3	1
Farming, forestry, fishing	3,556	41	41	11	5	2
Precision production, craft, repair	13,924	23	53	18	5	1
Machine operators, assemblers, inspectors	7,665	33	50	12	3	1
Transportation, material handling	4,789	20	48	29	1	2
Handlers, helpers, laborers	4,273	41	45	12	2	0
Total	111,623	18	40	21	12	9
Projected Jobs, 2000						
Managerial	13,616	5	26	24	29	16
Professional	17,191	2	9	17	29	43
Technicians & related support	5,151	3	32	37	19	9
Sales	16,334	16	40	23	16	5
Administrative support	22,109	8	54	27	9	2
Private household	955	60	31	7	1	1
Protective service	2,700	14	43	31	10	2
Other service	19,262	35	44	17	3	1
Farming, forestry, fishing	3,393	41	40	12	5	2
Precision production, craft, repair	15,590	23	53	18	5	1
Machine operators, assemblers, inspectors	6,913	33	50	12	3	1
Transportation, material handling	5,289	20	48	29	1	2
Handlers, helpers, laborers	4,522	40	45	12	2	1
Total	133,030	17	39	21	13	10

Sources: Silvestri and Lukasiewicz, 1987, Table 3; Tabulations based on the March 1986 Current Population Survey, U.S. Bureau of the Census.

in the latter year. Given this background, we can proceed to attempting to answer the question of what is the meaning of undereducation for the economy.

Undereducation and the Workplace

There are two possible meanings of undereducation for the workplace, a qualitative one and a quantitative one. Undereducation in a qualitative sense implies that workers have the appropriate level of educational credentials, but the quality of that education is either lacking or inappropriate to workplace needs. For example, if a job normally requires high school graduates, but recent high school graduates are said to be lacking in the required work skills, we would .call that undereducation in some sense. Such workers can be undereducated because work requirements have changed and they are not yet reflected in what schools are producing; or they can be undereducated because educational standards have fallen relative to some previous period.

Undereducation in a quantitative sense implies that workers do not have the required level or quantity of education for available jobs. In this case, employers face shortages of persons with what they consider to be appropriate levels or types of credentials for the jobs that are available. For example, if there are large numbers of job openings for college graduates, but not enough graduates to fill them, we might think of undereducation as a quantitative problem.

From an economic perspective, either type of undereducation is viewed as a short-run phenomenon. Both the theory of human capital and empirical studies suggest that when there are shortages of educated persons, remuneration will rise. This rise in remuneration, in turn, will stimulate a rise in educational investment, with students selecting those educational credentials that have the highest rates of return and moving away from those that have lower returns because of relative surpluses of job candidates.

At the same time, employers will substitute labor-saving capital for relatively scarce and costly labor skills, one of the inducements for automation. They can raise pay levels to attract back into the labor force retirees or women in households with the appropriate talents; or, they can shift some of their production to countries where such educated labor is more abundant. Both supply and demand adjustments for educated workers can alleviate apparent shortages of educated persons that might occur in the short run, so-called "spot" shortages. And, empirical research suggests that the market for educated labor is, in fact, responsive (Freeman 1971; Willis and Rosen 1979).

But, if this is the case, why should we worry about undereducation? There are at least three reasons. First, the short run may be so long that substantial disruptions occur. For example, educational institutions may be slow to understand new labor force needs. Employers may have little direct communication with school authorities, and rigidities in the educational system may necessitate a slow adjustment to new realities. Further, the gestation period between student decisions and the emergence of large numbers of highly trained workers may be long enough that it takes many years before the educational system responds.

Second, the lack of appropriately trained labor in particular industries may lead to permanent losses of those industries. Without the maintenance of infrastructure of those industries, it may be too costly to start up again when adequate numbers of educated workers become available. Thus, permanent damage can be done if shortages are expected to last even a few years and employers are unable to substitute capital for labor.

Finally, the supply and demand adjustments in the market for educational labor may not work as effectively as we would like. For example, there are cultural and historical reasons that some social groups have not attained levels of education that are consistent with the market incentives for investing in education. Although rates of return to blacks and hispanics for college attendance and completion have been comparable to those for whites in recent years and are considerably higher than historic rates of return, college enrollments of blacks and hispanics are considerably below those of whites (Murphy and Welch 1989; Smith and Welch 1989). Further, as blacks and hispanics and other immigrant groups constitute a larger and larger proportion of both school populations and the entry level labor force, this lack of educational responsiveness of minorities to market incentives can reduce the responsiveness of the entire labor market (Pallas, Natriello, and McDill 1989).

Qualitative Standards

Qualitative standards for measuring undereducation can be set according to the types of education that individuals possess relative to the needs of the economy as well as according to their levels of measured achievement as reflected in test scores. Achievement test scores have become particularly prominent as indicators of educational quality in recent years, perhaps because of the importance attributed to the well-publicized drop in scores on college entrance examinations (Koretz 1986). Indeed, we will suggest that it is an important criterion for considering undereducation among at-risk populations who are least likely to complete high school.

But, several decades of research have shown very little relation between test scores and earnings for the general population. Typically, even a very large difference in test scores for workers of the same educational level and race is associated with a very small difference in earnings. For example, a rise from the 50th to the 84 percentile is typically associated with only a 3-4 percent gain in earnings or less.[2] Researchers who assume that the productivity implications are greater than this argue that profit-maximizing employers are ignorant of the true relation between productivity and test scores, and they use studies by industrial psychologists to buttress their claims (Bishop 1989). However, a recent study of the available evidence by a committee of the National Research Council concluded that a disinterested appraisal of the research on the predictive validity of test scores shows a very modest connection between test scores and productivity (Hartigan and Wigdor 1989). Indeed, an overall summary of the potential economic gains from using test scores for employment selection suggests that the economic claims of advocates are highly exaggerated (Levin 1989).

Alternatively, there are a variety of other educational characteristics of workers that are important in predicting productivity, if workers meet minimal thresholds on achievement. For example, the Toyota automobile plant in Georgetown, Kentucky devotes about 26 hours to testing and interviewing its job applicants. But, less than 3 hours is devoted to cognitive testing to make sure that workers meet threshold levels, and about 23 hours is devoted to the other selection criteria, including evidence of work commitment and the ability of the worker to engage productively in work teams. Brown, Reich, and Stern report on a very successful, multi-national electronics firm that set minimal test scores for hiring that are equivalent to a seventh grade level in reading and fifth grade in mathematics (Brown, Reich, and Stern 1990). Further, they report that the test score performances of employees did not correlate with "team skills" and "work habits," two important ingredients of productivity in that firm.

The same authors found that employment criteria at a very productive Japanese automobile assembly plant in the United States did not require high school graduation, but relied primarily on previous work experience. Workers took a 30 minute mechanical aptitude test and a 20 minute basic math test out of an overall assessment that takes three half-days. That assessment includes simulations of teamwork and performing jobs similar to those on the assembly line. Candidates are scored on team orientation, interpersonal skills, and task orientation in teamwork and on efficiency and quality in production. Scores on simulations are used by the company to assess worker trainability and future productivity. These results also comport well with a study of five firms specializing in high technology products in which workers needed to meet only relatively low threshold criteria in mathematics and reading skills (Levin, Rumberger, and Finnan 1990).

Berlin and Sum (1988) found that among a nationally representative sample of youth who were 18-22 years old in 1979, who were no longer enrolled in school and who had twelve years or less of schooling, annual earnings between 1979 and 1981 were about $5,100 (p. 41). Using a multivariate analysis that controlled for demographic characteristics of the individuals and local labor market conditions, an additional grade-equivalent of basic skills as measured by test scores was associated with about $185 in additional annual earnings, about 3.6 percent (p. 41). But, an additional grade level completed was associated with $715 in additional earnings, about 14 percent; and a high school diploma was associated with an additional $927, or 18 percent (p. 41). Roughly speaking, completing the last year of high school was associated with an increase in annual earnings of ten times as much as an additional grade equivalent of test score gain.

Quantitative Standards

The most common quantitative standard for assessing undereducation is the educational attainment of the population. There is probably universal agreement that the minimum level of education that is needed for the modern workplace is high school graduation. There are a variety of reasons for setting high school graduation as the minimum standard for education for the twenty-first century. First, trainability of workers is enhanced by attaining at least this minimum, and continuing changes in technology and work organization will require workers who can be readily retrained (Carnevele and Gainer 1990; Committee for Economic Development 1990). Second, high school completion is required for eligibility to enter most segments of post-secondary education. If students are to have the option of pursuing post-secondary education, they will need to be high school graduates. This option is especially important given the widening gap between the earnings of high school and college graduates and, therefore, the payoff to having the option to pursue a college degree (Murphy and Welch 1989). Finally, if all students obtain high school diplomas, enrollments in colleges and universities will rise by virtue of more persons taking advantaged of their eligibility to attend institutions of higher education. This means that the potential for alleviating any emergent shortage of persons with post-secondary credentials would also be enhanced by the production of more high school graduates.

Although the overall evidence on test scores and earnings does not support the view that increases in test scores on the average are closely related to earnings, the evidence is stronger for the lowest achievers. Several authors suggest that there are probably minimum levels of academic achievement—perhaps fairly low ones—that are necessary for full economic participation (see, e.g., Brown, Reich, and Stern, 1990; Rumberger and Levin 1989). Among 19-23 year olds in 1981 who were in the bottom fifth on the Armed Forces Qualification Test (AFQT) of basic skills, some 40 percent were jobless, 53 percent were public assistance recipients, 59 percent were unwed parents, and 37 percent had been arrested in the previous year (Berlin and Sum 1988, p. 29).

For the remainder of this paper, we will use education below high school completion as the main criterion for assessing undereducation. That is, persons with less than high school completion will be viewed as lacking sufficient education to fully participate in the nation's economy. However there are two reasons for continued concern about low student achievement—the qualitative standard—as reflected in test scores. First, as indicated above, persons in the lowest test score groups seem to experience particular difficulty in becoming integrated into the economic and social mainstream. And, second, test scores are important predictors of educational success. Even if test scores do not seem to have as powerful an impact on earnings as years of schooling completed, the probability of completing high school and other levels of education is, itself, highly related to a student's academic test scores (Jencks et al. 1972, 1979). Among a national sample of 19-23 year olds in 1981, over half of those with test scores in the bottom fifth of the population had failed to graduate from high school, compared with only about fourteen percent in the general population in that age range (Berlin and Sum 1988, p. 29).

Table 2. Years of School Completed by Persons 25 Years Old and Over
by Sex, Race and Ethnicity, and Age in the U.S.: 1985

(percent distribution)

	Years of Schooling Completed				
	<12	12	13-15	16	17+
Men					
25 years old & over	25.5	34.8	16.6	12.5	10.6
25 to 29 years old	14.2	41.6	21.1	15.4	7.7
Women					
25 years old & over	26.5	41.3	16.2	10.0	6.0
25 to 29 years old	13.5	43.2	22.0	15.6	5.7
White					
25 years old & over	24.5	39.0	16.5	11.5	8.5
25 to 29 years old	13.1	42.3	21.4	16.1	7.1
Black					
25 years old & over	40.2	33.9	14.8	6.9	4.2
25 to 29 years old	19.4	46.2	22.9	8.8	2.7
Hispanic					
25 years old & over*	52.1	28.4	11.0	4.8	3.7
25 to 29 years old	39.1	34.0	15.9	7.6	3.4
Total					
29 years & over	26.1	38.2	16.3	11.2	8.2
25 to 29 years old	13.8	42.4	21.6	15.5	6.7

Note: * Hispanics may be of any race.
Source: U.S. Bureau of the Census, Current Population Reports, Series P-20, No. 415, Educational Attainment
in the United States: March 1982 to 1985 (Washington, D.C.: U.S. Government Printing Office, 1987),
Table 1.

WHO IS UNDEREDUCATED?

On the basis of this discussion of undereducation, we can proceed to an assessment of the magnitude of the undereducation challenge. If we use the failure to complete high school as the primary criterion for delineating undereducation, we can estimate the number of persons who are affected as well as their characteristics. Subsequently, we can assess the profitability of social investments to increase the educational attainments of this group in terms of their costs and benefits to society.

High School Dropouts

Table 2 shows the distribution of education achievement among persons 25 years and older in 1985 according to the U.S. Bureau of the Census. It is important to note that Census definitions and measures of dropouts differ substantially from those provided by the education departments of state governments (Rumberger 1987). Somewhat over a quarter of the population did not complete high school. However, among those from 25-29 years old, the proportion was about 14 percent. Somewhat more ominous is the fact that hispanics and blacks had far higher dropout rates than whites. While only about 13 percent of whites in the 25-29 year old age group had failed to complete high school, some 19 percent of blacks and almost 40 percent of hispanics had not completed high school. Both among minorities and whites, persons from families of low socioeconomic status have considerably higher dropout rates than those from more advantaged backgrounds (Rumberger 1983). Similar patterns exist for academic achievement where those from low socioeconomic backgrounds and of minority status show considerably lower test scores than their white and non-disadvantaged counterparts (Mullis, Owen, and Phillips forthcoming; Smith and O'Day 1990).

Students At Risk of Undereducation

The heavy incidence of minorities who have not completed high school is particularly ominous because it is these very populations that represent a substantial and increasing portion of school enrollments. From 1970 to 1980, U. S. public school enrollments from the pre-primary level to twelfth grade declined from about 46 million to 41 million students (National Center for Educational Statistics 1984). During the same time period, minority enrollments rose from about 9.5 million to about 11 million, or from about 21 to 27 percent of the total (Pallas, Natriello, and McDill 1989). By the year 2020, it is expected that minority children will represent almost half of all children 17 and under, a figure that has already been reached in California and Texas. Minority students comprise three-quarters or more of the enrollments of many of the largest cities of the nation including New York, Chicago, Los Angeles, Philadelphia, Miami (Dade County), and Detroit (McNett 1983).

Minority enrollments have been increasing at a more rapid pace than the general population because of a considerably higher birth rate and because of immigration—both legal and undocumented—that is unprecedented in recent decades. Both factors create rapid growth, particularly among school-age populations. Immigrant and other minority populations tend to be young and of child-bearing age in contrast to an older non-minority population.

When poverty is used as an indicator for "at-risk" populations, a similar pattern emerges. Between 1969 and 1979 the proportion of children in poverty stayed at about 16 percent; but it rose precipitously to 22 percent by 1983 and is projected to reach 27 percent of the 0-17 year olds by 2020 (Koretz and Ventresca 1984). This is a rise from about 15 million to over 20 million children in poverty. Between 1984 and 2020 the number of children who are not living with both parents is expected to rise by 30 percent from 16 million to over 21 million (Pallas, Natriello, and McDill 1989). This is especially foreboding, given that the real incomes of single mothers with children fell in absolute terms by 13 percent between 1970 and 1986 (Congressional Budget Office 1988).

Trends for other indicators of children at-risk have been moving in the same direction. For example, Pallas, Natriello, and McDill project that the number of children raised in families where the mother has not completed high school will rise by 56 percent to over 21 million by 2020 (1989). Of particular importance are the low educational attainments of immigrants who are drawn from rural regions of some of the poorest countries in the world. For example, of the largest single group of immigrants into California—Mexicans—only about 28 percent had more than an eighth-grade education in the early eighties (Muller 1985).

Not only are the numbers of at-risk students increasing, but there is evidence that their degree of disadvantage is increasing too. In the fall of 1972 about 46 percent of hispanic high school graduates participated in post-secondary education immediately following graduation (National Center for Education Statistics 1984). By the fall of 1980 that proportion had fallen to 40 percent, despite the widespread loosening of admissions standards during this period (p. 160). While the participation rate in higher education of hispanics from middle socioeconomic backgrounds fell by about 10 percent, the rate for Hispanics of lower socioeconomic background fell by 22 percent (p. 160). This is even more surprising, given that the high school drop-out rate for hispanics rose over that period, meaning that one would normally expect the high school "survivors" to be better-qualified. This drastic change in participation over such a short period may have been occasioned by poorer academic preparation and thus lower eligibility for post-secondary education or less adequate financial resources, both factors associated with increasing disadvantage.

In summary, the evidence suggests that the proportion of at-risk students is high and increasing rapidly. Estimates derived from the various demographic analyses suggest that upwards of 30 percent of students in kindergarten through 12th grade are educationally disadvantaged or at-risk (Levin 1986). When achievement is used as a criterion, it appears that the number of educationally at-risk students may be as high as 40 percent (Kennedy, Jung, and Orland 1986).

GENERAL ECONOMIC IMPLICATIONS

From the perspective of educational investments, it would appear that these at-risk students represent the highest priority. Before proceeding to an analysis of the profitability to society of those investments, it is worth reviewing the economic implications of rising numbers of at-risk students in three areas: (1) quality of the entry level labor force; (2) the cost and quality of higher education; and (3) the cost of government services.

Quality of Entry Level Labor Force

One consequence of the present educational status of at-risk students will be a serious deterioration in the quality of the labor force. As long as persons from such backgrounds were just a small minority of the population, they could be absorbed by low-skill jobs or relegated to the status of unemployment without direct consequences for the economy. High drop-out rates, low test scores, and poor academic performance of a group that will become a larger and larger portion of the school population mean that a larger portion of the future labor force will be undereducated for available jobs. Here we refer not only to managerial, professional, and technical jobs, but to even the lower-level service jobs that are increasingly important in the U.S. economy (Levin and Rumberger 1987). Clerical workers, cashiers, and salesclerks all need basic skills in oral and written communications, the acquisition of which is hardly guaranteed in the schooling of the disadvantaged (National Academy of Sciences 1984). A U. S. government study in 1976 found that while 13 percent of all 17 year olds were classified as functionally illiterate, the percentages of illiterates among hispanics and blacks were 56 and 44 respectively (National Assessment of Educational Progress 1976). These and other test score results (Mullis, Owen, and Phillips forthcoming; Smith and O'Day 1990) suggest that many at-risk students are not acquiring the foundation that will enable them to either work productively in available jobs or to benefit from employer training that will increase productivity and provide job mobility.

As at-risk populations become an increasing and even dominant share of the labor force, their inadequate educational preparation will be visited on the competitive positions of the industries and states in which they work and on our national economic status. Employers will suffer in terms of lagging productivity, higher training costs, and competitive disadvantages that will result in lost sales and profits. This problem will be especially severe for those states with the largest growth in the disadvantaged population such as California and Texas, where minorities already represent the majority of all students. It will also be most serious in those industries that will be dependent upon this population for their labor needs. As a result, the state and federal governments will suffer a declining tax base and a concomitant loss of tax revenues which could be used to fund improvements in education and other services.

Cost and Quality of Higher Education

The implications for higher education are also severe. Even with high drop-out rates, an increasing proportion of high school graduates will come from disadvantaged backgrounds. Without earlier educational interventions, these students will leave high school with serious learning deficits which will prevent many of them from benefiting from current levels of instruction in colleges and universities.

High school graduation entitles the at-risk student to pursue post-secondary study in community colleges and many of the state universities. Even if increasing numbers of disadvantaged students gain college entry, their low achievement means that a high proportion of them will experience academic failure and leave without a degree. Among the group that entered college in 1972, only 13 percent of the hispanics, 16 percent of the native Americans, and 24 percent of the blacks completed a bachelor's degree by 1976 in comparison with 34 percent of whites (Garibaldi 1986). Although, ultimate completion rates were higher for all groups, differences remained, and it took longer—on average—for minority students to complete their degrees.

One obvious response is to provide massive remedial functions to assist educationally disadvantaged students to reach levels where they can benefit from conventional instruction. According to a recent survey by the U.S. Department of Education, in the early eighties one in every four freshmen was already enrolled in a remedial mathematics course and one in every six in remedial reading (Abraham 1988). A similar study for 15 southern states in 1986 found that about 36 percent of freshmen in the public institutions of higher education in those states were taking at least one remedial course in reading, writing, or mathematics (Abraham 1988).

High levels of college failures and dropouts and massive remedial interventions are costly consequences to both students and institutions. Large numbers of failures mean wasted time for students and wasted resources for colleges, not to mention the psychological costs to students of not being able to "make it." Substantial remedial activities require additional faculty, and student programs will take longer with a greater cost in tuition and lost earnings during the extended training period that will be required. Also, as a college or university takes on remedial functions, it is likely to approve some of these courses for degree credit with the effect of watering down the overall curriculum and level of standards.

Cost of Public Services

A final consequence of failing to address the challenge of at-risk students will be rising costs of public services as more and more citizens must rely upon public assistance and as undereducated teens and adults pursue illegal activities to fill idle time and obtain income. Many of the disadvantaged will continue to have difficulty finding regular jobs as adults, so their families will need to depend upon the availability of public assistance to survive. When one applies a teenage unemployment rate of 40 percent or so to a larger and larger group of school dropouts, there are likely to be increasing numbers of undereducated youth taking their activities to the streets rather than to the workplace.

Among the national sample of 19-23 year olds in 1981, 72 percent of the jobless, 79 percent of those on public assistance, and 68 percent of those arrested in the previous year had scored below the average on the AFQT measure of basic skills (Berlin and Sum 1988, p. 29). A study of black women in their mid-thirties in 1982 found that each additional year of schooling was associated with a reduction of about 7 percent in the probability of receiving public assistance (Owens 1990). Moreover, participation in public assistance seems to be coming even more education-dependent over time, with education having twice as large an impact on the relation in 1982 as in 1967 (Owens 1990). Among 18-23 year old males in 1981, those with a high school diploma had a 94 percent lower probability of arrest; and among girls 18-21 the high school graduates had a 54 percent lower probability of having an out-of-wedlock baby (Berlin and Sum 1988, p. 42).

A projection of these outcomes on an expanding at-risk population will not only make the United States a less desirable place to live, but will increase the costs of police services and the criminal justice system. At the same time, the potential decline in economic activity created by an under-prepared workforce will erode tax revenues. This situation will place additional pressures on the middle class to pay higher taxes for welfare and the system of criminal justice at the same time that the economy is flagging. As such it will exacerbate the political conflict between the haves and have-nots as taxpayers resist raising taxes in the light of a faltering economy and mounting pressures for higher expenditures.

Summary of General Economic Implications

To fail to address the present and future educational deficits of the educationally disadvantaged will be to incur high social costs in terms of reduced economic productivity and productivity in higher education as well as rising costs of public services. Not only is education linked to public assistance and criminal justice, it is also linked to health status and a variety of other important social outcomes (Haveman and Wolfe 1984). In fact, when all of the identifiable outcomes associated with education are taken into account, it has been estimated that education has twice as high a return as when only its effect on income is ascertained (Haveman and Wolfe 1984).

BENEFIT-COST STUDIES
OF EDUCATIONAL INVESTMENT

To know that there are economic and social benefits from investing in undereducated populations is not an adequate criterion for investment. Although there are likely to be considerable benefits for such investments, there are also likely to be considerable costs. From an economic perspective we need to know if the benefits exceed the costs and if they exceed them by magnitudes that are equal to or greater than alternative social investments. In this section, we will review the results of benefit-cost studies of educational investments among those populations suffering from undereducation.

Programs for Reducing High School Dropouts

A number of economic studies have addressed the costs and benefits of reducing high school dropouts. In a classic study on the subject, Weisbrod compared the impact of a St. Louis program designed to reduce dropouts among "dropout-prone" high school students with the situation of a control group of similar students who did not have such a program (Weisbrod 1965). The dropout prevention program was associated with a high school completion rate that was about 7 percent higher than that of the control group. Weisbrod estimated the cost for each of the additional graduates and contrasted it with the estimated income benefits of high school graduation for these students. He found that the costs of the program exceeded its benefits.

There are at least two reasons for believing that more recent analyses of more recent programs would show stronger benefits. Weisbrod used 1959 Census data to estimate the additional incomes of the graduates. For reasons of discrimination and other factors, the earnings of women and minorities were a much smaller portion of white male earnings some 30 years ago than they are today. Since the dropout-prone group included considerable numbers of females and minorities, the benefits were probably understated considerably relative to what would be obtained with more recent data. Further, the earnings advantages of high school graduates relative to dropouts has increased. Finally, the program that Weisbrod evaluated was initiated some 30 years ago when dropout prevention was in its infancy.

In contrast, a more recent study of dropout prevention found large net benefits (Stern et al. 1989). This evaluation was based upon the success in reducing dropouts among 11 academies created in public high schools in California. These academies were special programs or schools within the larger high school setting that provided both vocational training for careers in which students stood a good chance of placement as well as academic training. Students were given special attention from their teachers and representatives of local employers. When students were matched with a similar group of students in the regular school programs, it was estimated that the academies had saved 29 persons who would have been expected to drop out.

The marginal costs of the academy program beyond the costs of the regular school program for all 327 students were compared to benefits in terms of the additional earnings of the 29 persons who were "saved" from dropping out. The overall benefits of the program were found to exceed overall costs by considerable amounts, the specifics depending on which assumptions were used regarding benefits. However, the results also show that for some of the academies net benefits were positive and for others net benefits were negative; that is costs exceeded benefits. This suggests that a more refined evaluation of individual programs would be useful to understand which were the most promising in terms of a benefit-cost analysis.

In contrast to studies of a single dropout program, Levin undertook a national study on the economic consequences of high school dropouts (Levin 1972). This study calculated the additional lifetime earnings and tax revenues that would have been generated if the entire cohort of 25 to 34 year old males in 1970 had graduated from high school. It was assumed that even if existing dropouts had graduated they would *not* have done as well as those who had actually graduated from high school. Thus, additional earnings of dropouts who would be induced to graduate were assumed to be only 75 percent of those of conventional high school graduates. But, it was also assumed that a portion of the induced graduates would continue into higher education with additional earnings from that source as well.

The total loss of lifetime earnings for this group as a result of failure to complete at least high school was estimated at about $237 billion. The additional cost for achieving this result was comprised of two parts: first, there was the cost of the additional years of schooling undertaken by members of the group; second, there was the cost of the additional expenditures to prevent dropping out. It was assumed that it would have been necessary to increase annual schooling expenditures on those at-risk of dropping out by 50 percent a year for all of their elementary and secondary schooling to keep them in school until completion of high school. On this basis it was estimated that the total costs of achieving at least high school graduation for all members of the cohort was about $40 billion, producing a benefit of six dollars for each dollar of cost. The additional lifetime earnings would have generated about $71 billion in government revenue or about $1.75 in tax revenues for each $1.00 in cost. The study also estimated that inadequate education was contributing about $6 billion a year to the costs of welfare and crime in 1970.

This analysis was replicated more recently for that cohort of Texas ninth graders in 1982-1983 who were projected to drop out before their anticipated graduation in 1986 (Robledo et al. 1986). The authors estimated the benefits of a dropout prevention program as those attributable to savings for public assistance, training and adult education, crime and incarceration, unemployment insurance and placement, and higher earnings associated with the additional high school graduates. Such benefits were calculated at $17.5 billion, and the costs to eliminate dropouts for this cohort were estimated at slightly less than $2 billion—or a ratio of $9 in benefits for each $1 of costs. Estimates of additional tax revenues were 2.5 times greater than costs to the taxpayer.

Catterall did a similar type of analysis for persons who dropped out of the Los Angeles high school class of 1985 (Catterall 1987). He found that because of high school dropouts, the Los Angeles class of 1985 was projected to generate over $3 billion *less* in lifetime economic activity than if all of its members had graduated. In contrast, Catterall suggested that the cost of investing successfully in dropout reduction would be a mere fraction of this amount. Further, he found that Los Angeles was addressing the dropout problem with specific programs that were spending the equivalent of only about $50 per dropout, or less than one-half of one percent of school spending, even though 40 percent of its students were not graduating.

Pre-School and Higher Education

There is evidence that even preschool investments in at-risk populations can reduce dropping out as well as provide other types of benefits. Barnett undertook a cost-benefit analysis of the Perry Preschool Project in Ypsilanti, Michigan (Barnett 1985). The Perry Preschool approach is one that has been studied for two decades, and it has been used as a model for hundreds of preschools for disadvantaged students across the country including the national Head Start program. Students who had been enrolled in the preschool project were followed until age 19. It was found that relative to a matched control group, enrollees in the project experienced better school achievement, educational placement, educational attainment, and employment. Monetary values for the benefits were calculated on the basis of the apparent effect of these advantages on the value of childcare during the programs; reduced school expenditures for remediation, special services, and grade repetition; reduced costs of crime, delinquency, and welfare; and higher earnings and employment.

It was found that the benefits exceeded the costs by a large margin under a wide range of assumptions. The one year program showed benefits of seven dollars for every dollar of costs, a benefit-cost ratio of about 7:1, and the two year program showed a benefit-cost ratio of about 3.6:1 (Berrueta-Clement et al. 1984). About 80 percent of the net benefits were received by taxpayers in the form of higher tax contributions and lower expenditures on education, crime, and welfare, and by potential crime victims in the form of lower costs for property losses and injuries.

A study of benefits and costs for financial aid to stimulate participation in higher education for low income students has also indicated high benefits relative to costs for government investment (St. John and Masten 1990). This study compared tax revenues generated by the additional income produced by the higher levels of college participation among low income students with the costs of financial aid that induced these higher enrollments. The net present value of additional tax revenues was four times as great as the cost of the aid program for students in the high school class of 1980. That is, from the perspective of the federal treasury, such programs had a benefit-cost ratio of 4:1.

These particular studies suggest that investments in at-risk students yield high returns to society. Such social investments are highly worthwhile in that their benefits exceed costs and that the margin by which they exceed costs is competitive with or superior to that of other highly productive investments. Of greatest importance is that higher tax revenues and reductions in the costs of social services more than compensate for the investments. In fact, in the case of the early childhood intervention program established by the Perry Preschool, most of the net benefits accrued to taxpayers (Barnett 1985).

Summary of Benefit-Cost Results

These benefit-cost results suggest that investments in the education of students who are at-risk of undereducation are likely to have high payoffs to society. While each study can be questioned because of imperfect information and the need to make assumptions on both the cost and benefit sides of the equation, the overall pattern among studies is remarkably consistent. This interpretation is buttressed by a recent study that found that increased investment in schooling quality among states was consistently associated with higher earnings of the adults who were schooled in those states, holding constant other influences (Card and Krueger 1990).

Estimated benefits for educational interventions tend to be about three to six times as high as estimated costs for at-risk students. Even these tend to be understated because most of the studies tend to be limited to the effects of educational investments on productivity and earnings and do not capture the pecuniary effects of reductions in resource allocation to publicly-supported costs of health, public assistance, and criminal justice. While it is not possible to place an overall economic cost on undereducation in the United States, it is clear that the cost is substantial and that the economic imperative for addressing it is supported by the benefit-cost results.

FUTURE RESEARCH

What is clear is that we need to develop overall models that link education to a large range of outcomes including earnings, health status, participation in the systems of public assistance and criminal justice, reductions in training costs, and so on. These can be constructed from statistical estimates based on some of the large data sets such as the National Longitudinal Survey of the U.S. Department of Labor, the Panel Study on Income Dynamics of the University of Michigan, and the High School Class of 1972 of the U.S. Department of Education. These statistical models can be used to simulate impacts of changes in educational attainments on social and economic outcomes.

Second, particular educational interventions need to be identified for raising educational attainments. These interventions must be evaluated in order to ascertain their impacts on raising educational achievement. Thus, the wide range of educational interventions for at-risk students and others should be reviewed using rigorous evaluation methodologies in order to ascertain their specific promise for raising educational attainments for those groups.

Finally, these results need to be placed in a benefit-cost framework for comparing the attractiveness of different investments. That is, we need to know the resource requirements of the alternative interventions to estimate their costs. We also need to link their educational results to the statistical models that can predict the impact of those results on the various economic and social outcomes. These economic and social outcomes need to be converted into monetary measures of benefits in order to compare with costs of the interventions.

In this way, we can inform social policy by simulating particular educational interventions through the model in order to determine their costs and benefits. I and my colleagues are just beginning to construct this type of study. We are hoping that we can provide information in the future that will allow systematic comparisons of educational investment policies according to comprehensive benefit-cost assessments.

NOTES

1. As examples, see Carnegie Forum on Education and the Economy, (1986); Committee for Economic Development (1987); National Commission on Educational Excellence (1983); and National Science Board (1983).

2. See a summary of some of the evidence in Bishop (1989, pp. 1-84).

REFERENCES

Abraham, A.A. 1988. "Remedial Education in College: How Widespread is It?" *Issues in Higher Education* 24.

Barnett, S.W. 1985. "Benefit-Cost Analysis of the Perry Preschool Program and its Long-Term Effects." *Educational Evaluation and Policy Analysis* 3, 333-342.

Berlin, G. and A. Sum. 1988. Toward a More Perfect Union: Basic Skills, Poor Families and Our Economic Future, Occasional paper 3. New York: Ford Foundation.

Berrueta-Clement, J. 1984. *Changed Lives: The Effects of the Perry Preschool Program on Youths Through Age 19.* Ypsilanti, MI: High/Scope Press.

Bishop, J. 1989. "Incentives for Learning: Why American High School Students Compare so Poorly to Their Couterparts Overseas." Pp. 1-84 in *Commission on Workforce Quality and Labor Market Efficiency, Investing in People.* Washington, DC: U.S. Department of Labor.

Bishop, J. and S. Carter. 1990. "The Deskilling Debate: The Role of BLS Projections." Paper prepared for presentation at the Conference on Changing Occupational Skill Requirements: Gathering and Assessing the Evidence. Providence, RI: Brown University.

Brown, C., M. Reich, and D. Stern. 1990. "Skills and Security in Evolving Employment Systems: Observations from Case Studies." Paper prepared for presentation at the Conference on Changing Occupational Skill Requirements: Gathering and Assessing the Evidence. Providence, RI: Brown University.

Carnegie Forum on Education and the Economy. 1986. *A Nation Prepared: Teachers for the 21st Century*. New York: Carnegie Corporation.

Carnevale, A.P., and L. Gainer. 1990. *The Learning Enterprise*. Washington, DC: American Society for Training and Development/U.S. Department of Labor.

Catterall, J.S. 1987. "On the Social Costs of Dropping Out of School." *The High School Journal* (October/November):19-30.

Committee for Economic Development. 1987. *Children in Need: Investment Strategies for the Educationally Disadvantaged*. New York: CED.

————. 1990. *An America that Works: The Life-Cycle Approach to a Competitive Work Force*. New York:CED.

Congressional Budget Office. 1988. *Trends in Family Income: 1970-1986*. Washington, DC: U.S. Government Printing Office.

Freeman, R.B. 1971. *The Market for College-Trained Manpower*. Cambridge, MA: Harvard University Press.

Garibaldi, A. 1986. "Sustaining Black Educational Progress: Challenges for the 1990's. *Journal of Negro Education* 55(3): 390.

Hartigan, J.A. and A.K. Wigdor, eds. 1989. *Fairness in Employment Testing: Validity Generalization, Minority Issues, and the General Aptitude Test Battery*. Washington, DC: National Academy Press.

Haveman, R. and R. Wolfe. 1984. "Schooling and Economic Well-Being: The Role of Nonmarket Effects." *The Journal of Human Resources* 19(3): 377-407.

Jencks, C. and S. Bartlett. 1979. *Who Gets Ahead?* New York: Basic Books.

Kennedy, M.M., R.K. Jung, and M.E. Orland. 1986. *Poverty, Achievment, and the Distribution of Compensatory Education Services*. Washington, DC: Office of Educational Research and Improvement, U.S. Department of Education.

Koretz, D. 1986. *Trends in Educational Achievment*. Washington, DC: U.S. Congressional Budget Office.

Koretz, D. and M. Ventresca. 1984. *Poverty Among Children*. Washington, DC: Congressional Budget Office.

Levin, H.M. 1986. *Educational Reform for Disadvantaged Children: An Emerging Crisis*. West Haven, CT: NEA Professional Library.

————. 1989. "Ability Testing for Job Selection: Are the Economic Claims Justified?" In *Test Policy and the Politics of Opportunity Allocation: The Workplace and the Law*, edited by B. R. Gifford. Boston: Kluwer Academic Publishers.

Levin, H.M. and R.W. Rumberger. 1987. "Educational Requirements for New Technologies: Visions, Possibilities and Current Realities." *Educational Policy* 3: 333-354.

Levin, H.M., R.W. Rumberger, and C. Finnan. 1990. "Escalating Skill Requirements or New Skill Requirements?" Paper prepared for presentation at the Conference on Changing Occupational Skill Requirements: Gathering and Assessing the Evidence. Providence, RI: Brown University.

McKnight, C.C., F.J. Crosswhite, J.A. Dossey, E. Kifer, J.O. Swafford, K.J. Travers, and T.J. Cooney. 1987. *The Underachieving Curriculum: Assessing U.S. School Mathematics from an International Perspective*. Champaign, IL: Stipes.

McNett, I. 1983. *Demographic Imperatives for Education Policy.* Washington, DC: Congressional Budget Office.

Muller, T. 1985. *The Fourth Wave: California's Newest Immigrants.* Washington, DC: Urban Institute Press.

Mullis, V.S., E.H. Owen, and G.W. Phillips. 1990. *Accelerating Academic Achievement: A Summary of Findings from 20 Years of NAEP.* National Assessment of Educational Progress. Princeton, NJ: Educational Testing Service.

Murphy, K. and F. Welch. 1989. "Wage Premiums for College Graduates: Recent Growth and Possible Explanations." *Educational Researcher* 18(4):17-26.

National Academy of Sciences. 1984. *High Schools and the Changing Workplace.* Washington, DC: National Academy Press.

National Assessment of Educational Progress. 1976. *Functional Literacy and Basic Reading Performance.* Washington, DC: U.S. Office of Education, Department of Health, Education and Welfare.

National Center for Educational Statistics. 1984. *The Condition of Education.* Washington, DC: U.S. Government Printing Office.

National Commission on Educational Excellence. 1983. *A Nation at Risk.* Washington, DC: U.S. Government Printing Office.

National Science Board. 1983. *Commission on Precollege Education in Mathematics, Science, and Technology. Educating Americans for the 21st Century.* Washington, DC: National Science Foundation.

Owens, J.D. 1990. "The Social Benefits of Education: An Intertemporal Analysis." Unpublished Manuscript, Wayne State University.

Pallas, A.M., G. Natriello, and E.L. McDill. 1989. "The Changing Nature of the Disadvantaged Population: Current Dimensions and Future Trends." *Educational Researcher* 5:16-22.

Rumberger, R.W. 1983. "Dropping out of School: The Influences of Race, Sex, and Family Background." *American Educational Research Journal* 20:199-220.

————. 1987. "High School Dropouts: A Review of Issues and Evidence." *Review of Educational Research* 57:101-121.

Rumberger, R.W. and H.M. Levin. 1985. "Forecasting the Impact of New Technologies on the Future Job Market." *Technological Forecasting and Social Change* 27:399-417.

Smith, M.S. and J. O'Day. 1990. "Educational Equality: 1966 and Now." In *Spheres of Justice in American Schools,* edited by D. Verstegen. New York: Harper & Row.

Smith, J.P. and F. Welch. 1989. *Black Economic Progress After Mydal* 27(2):519-564.

Stern, D., C. Dayton, I.W. Paik, and A. Weisberg. 1989. "Benefits and Costs of Dropout Prevention in a High School Program Combining Academic and Vocational Education: Third-Year Results from Replications of the California Peninsula Academies." *Educational Evaluation and Policy Analysis* 11(4): 405-416.

Weisbrod, B.A. 1965. "Preventing High School Dropouts." Pp. 117-148 in *Measuring Benefits of Government Investments,* edited by R. Dorfman. Washington, DC: The Brookings Institution.

Willis, R. and S. Rosen. 1979. "Education and Self-Selection." *Journal of Political Economy* 87(5):7-36.

COMMENTS

Dennis Patrick Leyden

Perhaps the biggest problem associated with the study of the economic effects of undereducation is that of definition and measurement. Recognizing this fact, this paper is both a survey of what we know to date about the economic effects of undereducation and a discussion of the issues which must be confronted if we are to construct rational policies for addressing the problems of undereducation. In both tasks, the paper succeeds and is thus a useful introduction to the economic consequences of undereducation and policy formulation. The paper argues that (1) the primary problem lies with those who do not get a high school education, (2) policies ought to focus on those populations with the greatest likelihood of not earning a high school diploma, and (3) cost-benefit analysis provides a rational tool for developing and evaluating policies.

My purpose here is to suggest a complementary perspective which I believe would be useful both in defining what we mean by undereducation and in developing appropriate and politically feasible policies. The problem of measuring the economic consequences of undereducation and suggesting a process for policy formulation is an interesting one for two reasons. First, though often motivated in national terms (e.g., their effect on the nation's international competitiveness), education policies are, and most likely will continue to be, effected for the most part at the state and local level. Second, though the benefits to reducing undereducation are often discussed from the general perspective of society, the political and financial support for such policies must ultimately be borne by individual voters and politicians whose perspectives are typically much narrower. As a result, while the study of undereducation at the national level and in general societal terms is important for determining overall policy strategies, the study of undereducation from the perspective of the trenches is valuable in the search for policies which both work and will be chosen by the voters and politicians who make many of the decisions.[1]

WHO SAYS THERE IS UNDEREDUCATION?

Consider first the issue of defining undereducation. The issue is of considerable importance. Levin is right in saying that there is some ambiguity in whether to define undereducation in qualitative or quantitative terms. Interestingly, it appears that most investigators (perhaps driven by problems of empirical tractability) choose to view it in quantitative terms.

A complementary approach to this definitional issue is to take account of the fact that the existence of undereducation may depend on one's perspective. Three possibilities suggest themselves.[2]

The Merit Good Perspective

In this case, individuals do not choose the level of education which is in their narrow self-interests because they have mistaken beliefs about benefits and costs. Clearly, this is undereducation both from the perspective of the individual (though he does not know it) as well as from the perspective of society. Though the problem may be either qualitative or quantitative in nature, I suspect it is more likely to be viewed in quantitative terms. Mandatory attendance policies are an example of attempts to redress this form of undereducation. Interestingly, mandatory attendance and performance policies are once again being considered to help solve the problems of undereducation. North Carolina, for example, is considering raising to 18 the minimum age at which a student can drop out.

The Externality Perspective

Here, the level of education which individuals get may be individually rational but is insufficient from society's perspective because of the positive externalities generated. The problem may be qualitative or quantitative in nature. Because the externalities from education are widespread and diffuse, solutions to this form of undereducation will typically require state-wide, if not nation-wide, coordination.

The Government Failure Perspective

Finally, individuals may be unable to get the level of education they believe to be optimal because of failures in the delivery system. This results in undereducation from society's perspective as well as from the individual's perspective. This problem is most likely a qualitative one and therefore requires policies which address curricular and structural issues. Arguments for policies in which public schools would compete for students come from a belief that current school structures have failed qualitatively.

All three perspectives are implicit in the paper although most of the focus seems to be on the merit good and externality perspectives. I would argue, however, that recognition of the government failure perspective suggests additional policy options not readily apparent when viewed from the other two perspectives.

WHO IS UNDEREDUCATED?

Who is undereducated, then, depends on the perspective taken. The paper argues rightly, I believe, that the most serious problem lies with those at the bottom, who never graduate from high school, and justifies this argument with essentially merit good arguments (e.g., increased lifetime earnings) and externality arguments (e.g., reductions in crime).

However, it may also be that there are others who, though achieving and perhaps exceeding minimum standards, are nonetheless also undereducated. Though harder to measure and less important than the problems of those who fail to reach minimum standards, this also represents a possible cost to society. Moreover, it is likely that this group will have more political clout than those at the very bottom. Hence, it is this group which in large part will affect the choice of policies. To the extent this is true, only policies which are perceived to be in the interest of this group are likely to find broad support.

BENEFITS AND COSTS

The paper goes much of the way toward incorporating the arguments above in its advocacy of cost-benefit analysis. The studies cited generally approach the problem at the state or local level and calculate cost and benefits in terms likely to be valued by policymakers and their constituents. As the paper argues, further empirical work in this areas would go a long way to identifying effective and acceptable policies.

Two notes of caution, however, are warranted. First, arguments that highlight the benefits which appear to accrue only to those for whom the program is directly intended (and here I am thinking of increased earnings capacity) are less likely to be persuasive than arguments that highlight the increased tax revenues or decreased expenditures derived from such income. Secondly, high discount rates are probably appropriate when measuring future increased tax revenues and expenditure savings. Especially at this time in our history with budget crises at the national, state, and local levels, I suspect voters are suspicious of promises of future tax and expenditure benefits.[3]

CONCLUSIONS

Where does this leave us? Henry Levin's paper is valuable both for its documentation of the economic costs of undereducation as well as for its suggestions on how to better understand and rectify the problem. My comments have been directed for the most part to calling for recognition that undereducation is often in the eyes of the beholder and that to be effective policies must be politically feasible.

That there is a problem of undereducation seems clear from where we sit. However, what also seems clear is that many do not perceive the problem to be sufficiently important to warrant extraordinary means. Clearly, then, if policies are to be effective, they must persuade a political majority that their lives can be made better if the problem is addressed. Although I have no policy prescriptions, I suspect this is possible with the right mix of programs aimed both at the core problem and at those in the middle, and justified in terms likely to hit home with the average citizen. Clearly, however, a research agenda along the lines advocated by this paper is needed to discover what those policies are.

NOTES

1.   One example of the importance of incorporating such a perspective exists in the analysis of redistributive intergovernmental grant policies. In the presence of tax limitation referenda, voters may choose to impose a restriction in order to reduce the degree of redistribution. See Leyden (1988).

2.   A general introduction to the notions of merit goods, externalities, and government failure can be found in the early chapters of Stiglitz (1988).

3.   The argument for high discount rates is based on an interest in discovering which policies are politically feasible. The seeming contradiction between this argument and the standard one that a low discount rate ought to be used is based on a difference of perspective. The standard argument is based on an interest in determining what is socially effecient and ignores issues of political feasibility. For an introduction to the standard argument see Gramlich (1990).

REFERENCES

Gramlich, E.M. 1990. *A Guide to Benefit-Cost Analysis,* Second Edition. Englewood Cliffs, NJ: Prentice Hall.
Leyden, D.P. 1988. "Intergovernmental Grants and Successful Tax Limitation Referenda." *Public Choice* 57, 144-154.
Stiglitz, J.E. 1988. *Economics of Public Sector,* Second Edition. New York: W.W. Norton.

WHAT'S WRONG WITH AMERICAN SECONDARY SCHOOLS?
CAN STATE GOVERNMENTS FIX IT?

John H. Bishop

Ninety-three percent of 17 year-olds do not have "the capacity to apply mathematical operations in a variety of problem settings" (National Assessment of Educational Progress 1988).

Twenty-five percent of the Canadian 18 year-olds studying chemistry know as much chemistry as the top 1 percent of American high school graduates taking their second year of chemistry, most of whom are in Advanced Placement classes (IAEEA 1988).

In October of 1985, 1986, 1987 and 1988, 28 percent of the previous June's noncollege-bound white high school graduates had no job. Fifty-five percent of the black graduates had no job (U.S. Bureau of Labor Statistics 1988).

The high school graduates of 1980 knew about 1.25 grade level equivalents less math, science, history and English than the graduates of 1967. This decline in the academic achievement lowered the nation's productivity by $86 billion in 1987 and will lower it by more than $200 billion annually in the year 2010 (Bishop 1989).

The real wage of young male high school graduates fell 20 percent between 1979 and 1988 (Kosters 1989).

The poor performance of American students is sometimes blamed on the nation's "diversity." Many affluent parents apparently believe that their children are doing acceptably by international standards. This is not the case. In Stevenson, Lee and Stigler's study of 5th grade math achievement, the best of the 20 classrooms sampled in Minneapolis was outstripped by every single classroom studied in Sendai, Japan and by 19 of the 20 classrooms studiec in Taipeh, Taiwan (Stevenson, Lee, and Stigler 1986). The nation's top higl school students rank far behind much less elite samples of students in othei countries. In mathematics the gap between Japanese and Finnish high schoo seniors and their white American counterparts is about twice the size of the two to three grade level equivalent gap between blacks and whites in the Unitec States (IAEEA 1986). The learning deficit is pervasive.

LOW EFFORT: THE PROXIMATE CAUSE OF THE LEARNING DEFICIT

This poor record of achievement is caused by the limited amount of time, money and, above all, psychic energy devoted to academic learning in American high schools. Students, parents and the public are all responsible.

Student Effort

Learning is not a passive act; it requires the time and active involvement of the learner. In a classroom with 1 teacher and 18 students, there are 18 learning hours spent to every 1 hour of teaching time. Student time is, therefore, the critical resource, and how intensely that time is used affects learning significantly.

Studies of time allocation using the reliable time diary method have found that the average number of hours per week in school is 25.2 hours for primary school pupils, 28.7 hours for junior high students and 26.2 hours for senior high students. The comparable numbers for Japan are 38.2 hours for primary school, 46.6 hours for junior high school and 41.5 hours for senior high school (Juster and Strafford 1990). In addition, school years are longer in both Japan and Europe.

Studies show that American students actively engage in a learning activity for only about half the time they are scheduled to be in school. A study of schools in Chicago found that public schools with high-achieving students averaged about 75 percent of class time for actual instruction; for schools with low achieving students, the average was 51 percent of class time (Frederick 1977). American students average nearly 20 absences a year; Japanese students only 3 a year (Berlin and Sum 1988). Overall, Frederick, Walberg and Rasher estimated 46.5 percent of the potential learning time is lost due to absence, lateness, and inattention (Frederick, Walberg, and Rasher 1979).

In the High School and Beyond Survey, students reported spending an average of 3.5 hours per week on homework (National Opinion Research Corporation 1982). Time diaries yield similar estimates: 3.2 hours for junior high school and 3.8 hours for senior high school. Time diaries for Japanese

Table 1. Time Use By Students

	T.V.		Reading Time
	Students	All Adults	Students
United States	19.6	15.9	1.4
Austria	6.3	10.6	4.9
Canada	10.9	13.3	1.5
Finland	9.0	9.0	6.0
Netherlands	10.6	13.4	4.3
Norway	5.9	7.2	4.3
Switzerland	7.7	9.0	4.8

Source: Data on weekly hours devoted to each activity is from Organization of Economic Cooperation and Development, *Living Conditions in OECD Countries,* Tables 17.2, 18.1, 18.3 and 18.4.

students reveal that they spend 16.2 hours per week studying in junior high school and 19 hours a week studying in senior high school (Juster and Strafford 1990). With the sole exception of Sweden, students in other countries report spending a good deal more time on homework than Americans (Robitaille and Garden 1989). When homework is added to engaged time at school, the total time devoted to study, instruction, and practice in the United States is only 18-20 hours per week—between 15 and 20 percent of the student's waking hours during the school year. By way of comparison, the typical senior spends nearly 20 hours per week in a part-time job (NORC 1983) and 19.6 hours per week watching television. Thus, TV occupies as much time as learning. In Table 1 we can see that secondary school students in other industrialized nations watch much less television: 55 percent less in Finland, 70 percent less in Norway and 44 percent less in Canada (Organization of Economic Cooperation and Development (1986). In other countries high school students watch less TV than adults; in the United States they watch more. Reading takes up 6 hours of a Finnish student's non-school time per week, 4.8 hours of a Swiss or an Austrian student's time but only 1.4 hours of an American student's time.

Even more important than the time devoted to learning is the intensity of the student's involvement in the process. At the completion of his study of American high schools, Sizer (1984) characterized students as "all too often docile, compliant, and without initiative" (p. 54). Goodlad (1983) described "a general picture of considerable passivity among students" (p. 113). The high school teachers surveyed by Goodlad ranked "lack of student interest" as the most important problem in education.

The student's lack of interest makes it difficult for teachers to be demanding. Sizer's (1984) description of Ms. Shiffe's biology class illustrates what sometimes happens:

She wanted the students to know these names. They did not want to know them and were not going to learn them. Apparently no outside threat—flunking, for example—affected the students. Shiffe did her thing, the students chattered on, even in the presence of a visitor....Their common front of uninterest probably made examinations moot. Shiffe could not flunk them all, and, if their performance was uniformly shoddy, she would have to pass them all. Her desperation was as obvious as the students' cruelty toward her (pp. 157-158).

Some teachers are able to overcome the obstacles and induce their student to undertake tough learning tasks. But for most, the student's lassitude i demoralizing. Teachers are assigned responsibility for setting high standard but they are not given any of the tools that might be effective for inducin student observance of the academic goals of the classroom. They finally mus rely on the force of their own personalities. All too often teachers compromis academic demands because the bulk of the class sees no need to accept ther as reasonable and legitimate.

Nevertheless, American students do not appear to realize how poor thei performance is. Even though American 13 year-olds were one-fourth as likel as Korean students to "understand measurement and geometry concepts an [to be able to] solve more complex problems," Americans were three time more likely to agree with the statement "I am good at mathematics" (Lapoint et al. 1989).

Proposed reforms of secondary education include stricter graduatio requirements, more homework, increases in the amount and difficulty of cours material, greater emphasis on the basics (English, math, science, social scienc computer science), and improvements in the quality of teaching through highe salaries, career ladders, and competency tests for teachers. Although desirable these reforms are limited in that they emphasize changes in the content an quality of what is offered by schools and require the student to work harde These reforms have ignored the problem of *motivating* students to tak rigorous courses and to study harder. New York State, for example, tried t increase the rigor of high school curricula by upgrading the requirements fc the Regents diploma, but the result has been a substantial drop in the number of students getting the Regents diploma; and an increase in the number o students receiving local diplomas.

Parental Effort

The second major reason for the low levels of achievement by America students is parental apathy. High school teachers rank "lack of parenta interest" as the second most important problem in education (Goodlad 1983) An NSF-funded survey of 2,222 parents of 10th graders found that 25 percen thought their child should take only 1 or 2 science classes in high schoc (Longitudinal Survey of American Youth 1988). When 2829 high schoc sophomores were asked whether "my parents...think that math (science) is a very important subject," 40 percent said no with respect to mathematics and 57 percent said no with respect to science (Longitudinal Survey of American Youth 1988). Only 30 percent of 10th graders reported their parents "want me to learn about computers" (Longitudinal Survey of American Youth 1988).

Despite the poor performance of Minneapolis 5th graders in mathematics, their mothers were much more pleased with the performance of their local schools than the Taiwanese and Japanese mothers. When asked "How good a job would you say _____ 's school is doing this year educating _____ ", 91 percent of American mothers responded "excellent" or "good" while only 42 percent of Taiwanese and 39 percent of Japanese parents were this positive (Stevenson, Lee, and Stigler 1986). Table 2 presents data from this study. Despite the small size of Japanese and Taiwanese homes, 95-98 percent of the fifth graders in these two countries had a desk of their own specifically for studying, while only 63 percent of the Minneapolis children had a desk. Mathematics workbooks had been purchased for their children by 56-58 percent of Taiwanese and Japanese parents but by only 28 percent of American parents. Science workbooks had been purchased by 51 percent of Taiwanese parents, 29 percent of Japanese parents, but by only 1 percent of American parents (Stevenson, Lee, and Stigler 1986). This is not because they love their children any less; they have different priorities such as teaching responsibility and work habits by requiring that they do chores around the house. Clearly, American parents hold their children and their schools to lower academic standards than Japanese and Taiwanese parents.

If American parents were truly dissatisfied with the academic standards of their local public schools, they would send their children to private schools offering an enriched and rigorous curriculum as many parents do in Australia,

Table 2. Learning Is A Low Priority Of Parents

	Minneapolis	Sendai Japan	Taipeh Taiwan
Mothers Attended College	58%	22%	15%
5th Grader Has Study Desk	63	98	95
Parents Purchased Workbook For Additional Homework			
Mathematics	28	58	56
Science	1	29	51
5th Grader Assigned Chores	95	76	28
Parents Believing Their School is Doing an "Excellent or Good Job"	91	39	42

Source: Stevenson, Lee, and Stigler, "Mathematics Achievement of Chinese, Japanese and American Children," *Science,* February 1986.

and tutoring after school would be as common as it is in Japan. Japanese families allocate 10 percent of the family's after-tax income to educational expenses; American families only 2 percent. Most parents who send their children to private day schools appear to be attracted by their stricter discipline and religious education, not by more rigorous academics and better qualified teachers. At the great majority of private day schools, students do not learn at an appreciably faster rate than public school students (Cain and Goldberger 1983).

Public Effort: Educational Expenditure—a Deceptive Indicator

According to a study by Mishel and Rasell, the ratio of per pupil expenditure in kindergarten through 12th grade to per capita GNP is lower in the United States than in 10 of 11 other advanced Western nations (Mischel and Rasell 1990). This statistic suggests that education receives lower priority in the United States than other nations. People who disagree with this implication point to another statistic, per pupil expenditure deflated by a cost of living index on which the United States ranks second among the same group of 12 nations (U.S. Department of Education 1990). This second form of comparison is not very useful, however, because the costs of recruiting competent teachers are much higher in the United States than abroad. Labor compensation accounts for 90 percent of education costs and, clearly, the wage that must be paid to recruit qualified teachers is substantially higher in countries with higher standards of living. A wage index for other college graduates in the society would probably be a reasonable proxy for this cost but such data are not generally available. Deflation by GNP per worker or per capita GNP is the next best thing and comes substantially closer to the ideal than deflation by the cost of living. The result, however, is by no means a perfect index.

Even with the correct deflator, expenditure per pupil remains a deceptive indicator of a nation's investment in education because different countries budget school costs differently and assign public schools different functions. Mishel and Rasell's study included the costs of preschool education in their expenditure figure. Preschool education is funded through public education budgets in many European countries but not in the United States. This inflates European expenditure per pupil figures relative to those in the United States. On the other hand, costs of transportation are generally not included in school budgets in Japan and Europe where students, even 1st graders, use the public transportation system to go to school. In many European countries after-school sports are sponsored and organized by local government, not the school. This removes the capital costs of extensive school-based sports facilities and the salaries of coaches and maintenance personnel from the school budget.

Vocational education is more expensive than traditional academic courses. The fact that the United States, Sweden, and France have their schools provide

Table 3.   Relative Salaries by College Major

	U.S. Adults 1984	U.S. Prev. Yr. Grads. 1985	Australia Prev. Yr. Grads.	
			1979	1989
Education	100	100	100	100
Humanities	106	101	86	92
Physical Science	205	127	97	102
Engineering	228	175	102	110
Economics	224	—	91	100
Business (BA)	216	136	—	—
(MBA)	317	—	—	—

Source: Census, Current Population Report, CPR, P70, No. 13; Digest of Educ. Statistics 1987; Graduate Careers Council of Australia, "Graduate Starting Salaries 1989."

occupational training to large numbers of 16-18 year-olds raises costs per student relative to the costs in Germany, Switzerland and Austria where employers are responsible for most of these costs. In 1980, German employers invested an average of $6000 per year in the training of each apprentice they took on as part of the dual system of vocational training (Noll et al. 1984). American schools perform functions such as after-school sports, after-school day care, hot lunches, and driver education that other countries often assign to other institutions. When data are carefully adjusted for all of these factors and deflated by a cost of education index reflecting compensation levels in alternative college level occupations, American spending per pupil is likely to be lower than in many European nations.

The primary reason for low real expenditure on education in the United States is the low levels of teacher compensation. When college graduate earnings are compared, education majors come out at the very bottom. In 1967, males with undergraduate degrees in engineering earned 67 percent more and those with bachelors degrees in business administration earned 36 percent more than males with education degrees (U.S. Bureau of the Census 1967). Despite recent increases in teacher salaries the earnings gap between teachers and other college graduates has grown even larger. Data on relative salaries are presented in the first column of Table 3. In 1984, physical science majors earned 105 percent more, engineers earned 128 percent more, economics majors 124 percent more and business majors 116 percent more than education majors. Social science majors earned 35 percent more and liberal arts, humanities and English majors earned 6-8 percent more than education majors. An MBA was worth 88 percent more, a Masters in Engineering 70 percent more and a law degree 114 percent more than a Masters or Ph.D. in Education (U.S. Bureau of the Census 1984).

It is not an immutable law of nature that teachers should be paid substantially less than other occupations. Australian university graduates with education degrees start at the same salary as graduates in economics/business, 8 percent ahead of those who majored in humanities and only 2 percent below those who majored in physical science. Graduating engineers are paid only 10 percent more than education majors in Australia; they are paid 75 percent more in the United States. No wonder it is so difficult to attract the best and brightest into the teaching profession. The SAT test scores of entering freshman expressing an interest in majoring in education are lower than for any other major. No wonder it is particularly difficult to recruit science and mathematics teachers.

Comparisons with other industrialized societies tell the same story. Since many countries fund pensions and medical insurance through mandated social security taxes, it is essential to include both voluntary and compulsory contributions for these purposes in the calculation of teacher compensation. Estimates of total compensation per teacher deflated for cost of living differences between countries are presented in the first column of Table 4. In 1982-1984, total compensation was 24 percent higher in Canada and Sweden, 6-7 percent higher in Germany and Holland, 20 percent higher in Belgium and 28 percent higher in France than in the United States (Barro and Suter 1988).[1] Despite lower overall standards of living, these six countries paid their teachers more than we did. Compensation was 37 percent lower in the United Kingdom, 40 percent lower in Italy and 26 percent lower in Japan. Relative to output per hour worked, however, Japan paid its teachers 25 percent more than we did. The relative compensation of teachers was thus lower in only two countries, Britain and Italy.

The question that tends to be raised by statistics such as these is "Why do American voters choose to pay teachers so little?" Why do voters not demand higher standards of academic achievement at local high schools? Why do school boards allocate scarce education dollars to interscholastic athletics and the band rather than better mathematics teachers and science laboratories? It is to questions such as these that we now turn.

Voter Apathy Regarding Academic Achievement

One of the unique characteristics of the American education system is that all the really important decisions—budget allocations, hiring selections, salary levels, homework assignments, teaching strategies, grading standards, course offerings, pupil assignments to courses and programs, disciplinary policies, and so forth—are made by classroom teachers and school administrators who are responding to local political pressures. Federal and state officials are far removed from the classroom, and the instruments available to them for inducing improvements in quality and standards are limited. They do not have effective control of the standards and expectations that prevail in the classroom. They do not control the allocation of school funds between academics and athletics.

Table 4.   Relative Teacher Compensation

	Teacher Compensation* 1982-84	GDP Per Hour Worked** 1977-81	Ratio Teacher Index/ GDP/hr
United States	100	100	1.0
Belgium	120	94	1.28
Canada	124	88	1.41
France	128	95	1.35
Germany	107	95	1.13
Italy	60	68	.88
Japan	74	59	1.25
Netherlands	106	97	1.09
Sweden	124	79	1.57
United Kingdom	63	78	.81

Notes: * Total compensation including compulsory health & pension contributions deflated by cost of living. (Index with US = 100) Source: UNESCO.

** Total domestic output divided by total hours worked deflated by cost of living. (Index with US = 100) Source: Angus Maddison.

State aid can be increased, but econometric studies suggest that increases in state aid reduce local property tax collections by a significant amount (Carroll 1982). Only about 50 cents of every dollar of non-categorical state aid to local school districts appears to be spent on education. For categorical programs like Title I of the Elementary and Secondary Education Act, the increase in local education spending is larger, but some leakage appears to be inevitable.

School boards are the primary mechanism by which the voters exercise authority over local schools. In most parts of the country only bond issues need go to the voters for approval. The board determines the budget and sets the property tax rates necessary to fund that budget. Parents are typically a minority of voting age adults in the community, but only about 10 percent of the non-parents in a community typically vote in school board elections. Parents are more likely to vote in school board elections, so they have effective control of the school board in many communities. In all other communities, they could easily gain control of the board if they voted in concert. Parents pay less than a third of school taxes in most communities, so voting for school board members who promise to support increased educational spending and higher standards is, for them, a low cost way of improving the school attended by their child. Why hasn't this potential power been exercised to raise academic standards and teacher salaries? Why are less than a third of parents voting in most school board elections? Why do so many parents vote against increases in school taxes? When additional money is available, why is so much of it spent on upgrading the sports program, band and vocational education?

If, as indicated above, the parents of a community are satisfied with academic outcomes which leave their children years behind students of other nations in mathematics and science, federal and state efforts to raise standards will have no lasting effect.

THE ABSENCE OF REWARDS FOR EXCELLENCE: THE ROOT CAUSE OF THE LEARNING DEFICIT

The fundamental cause of the low effort level of American students, parents, and voters in school elections is the absence of good signals of effort and learning in high school and a consequent lack of rewards for effort and learning. In the United States the only signals of learning that generate substantial rewards are diplomas and years of schooling. In most advanced countries mastery of the curriculum taught in high school is assessed by essay examinations which are set and graded at the national or regional level. Grades on these exams signal the student's achievement to colleges and employers and influence the jobs that graduates get and the universities and programs to which they are admitted. How well the graduating seniors do on these exams influences the reputation of the school and in some countries the number of students applying for admission to the school. In the United States, by contrast, students take aptitude tests that are not intended to assess the learning that has occurred in most of the classes taken in high school. The primary signals of academic achievement are grades and rank in class—criteria which assess achievement relative to other students in the school or classroom, not relative to an external standard.

Consequently, *the students who do not aspire to attend selective colleges benefit very little from working hard while in high school, and parents have little incentive to vote the tax increases necessary to upgrade the academic quality of local schools.* This is a consequence of nine phenomena:

1.   Because their student bodies are so diverse, American high schools offer an incredible variety of courses at vastly different levels of rigor. Most students choose courses that have the reputation of being fun and not requiring much work to get a good grade. The rigor of the courses taken is not efficiently signaled to colleges and employers, so taking rigorous courses is seldom rewarded. Teachers know this and adjust their style of teaching and their homework assignments with an eye to maintaining enrollment levels. Course selection is subject to a Gresham's law in which easy electives drive out rigorous courses.

2.   The peer group actively discourages academic effort. No adolescent wants to be considered a "nerd, brain, geek, grade grubber or brown noser"; yet that is what happens to students who study hard and are seen to study hard. Peers

have a personal interest in persuading each other not to study, because the school's signals of achievement assess performance relative to fellow students through grades and class rank not relative to an external standard.[2]

3. Setting higher academic standards or hiring better teachers does not on average improve the signals of academic performance—rank in class, GPA and SAT scores—that selective colleges use for making admission decisions and a few employers use to make hiring decisions. Higher standards for graduation are not likely to be supported by the parents of children not planning to go to college, because they would put at risk what is most important, the diploma. Higher standards do not benefit students as a group, so parents as a group have little incentive to lobby strongly for higher teacher salaries, higher standards and higher school taxes.

4. There is no effective way of holding most high school and middle school teachers individually accountable for the learning of their students. Unionization is not the critical barrier, for unionized European and Japanese secondary school teachers and most American primary school teachers feel accountable for the learning of their students. The lack of accountability in the United States stems from: (1) the rarity of high stakes examinations assessing student achievement in particular subjects relative to an external standard, and (2) the fact that most secondary school students receive instruction in English, mathematics, history, and science from many different teachers. The exceptions to this norm are the coaches of the athletic teams, the band conductor, teachers of advanced placement classes, and vocational teachers (who are often evaluated for their success in placing students in good jobs). In Europe, students who are preparing to take a particular exam at the end of their secondary education typically remain together in one class and are taught by the same teacher in successive years. In Japanese junior high schools, a team of teachers, each responsible for a different subject, teach all the 7th graders one year, the 8th graders the next year, and the 9th graders the third year. Examinations taken during 9th grade determine admission to competitive high schools so teachers feel great pressure to assure that their students do well on these examinations.

5. In most American communities, students and parents cannot choose which local public high school to attend. In Europe and Japan, by contrast, the family can, within the constraints of competitive admissions policies, often select which secondary school a student attends. Barriers to attending a school other than the closest one are lower in these countries because public transportation is available, opportunities to participate in sports and music are often organized by the community not the school, and centralized funding of schools means that money follows the student even when a non-public school is selected. The centralization of funding and the free choice of schools result in stronger competitive pressure on schools to excel and smaller quality differentials between schools of the same type than in the United States.

6. In most American communities, studying hard in primary school and middle school does not lead to opportunities to attend a better or more rigorous high school. In Japan and most European countries, by contrast, some upper secondary schools offer more rigorous educational programs than others and there is stiff competition for admission to many of these schools. The consequence of this system is that students there put a good deal more effort into their studies in lower secondary school than in the United States.

7. Most American colleges and universities do not set rigorous standards for admission. High school students know that taking undemanding high school courses and "goofing off" in these courses will not prevent them from going to college.

8. Where admission to college does depend on high school performance, it is not based on an absolute or external standard of achievement in high school subjects. Rather, it is based, in part, on aptitude tests which do not assess the high school curriculum, as well as on measures of student performance such as class rank and grade point averages, which are defined relative to classmates' performances.

9. The labor market fails to reward effort and achievement in high school. Analysis of the Youth Cohort of the National Longitudinal Survey indicates that *during the first 18 years after leaving high school, greater competence in science, language arts and mathematical reasoning lowers wages and increases the unemployment of young men. For young women, verbal and scientific competencies have no effect on wage rates, and a one grade level increase in mathematical reasoning competence raises wage rates by only one-half of one percent* (Bishop 1986). As a result, students who plan to look for a job immediately after high school see very little connection between how much they learn and their future success in the labor market. Less than a quarter of 10th graders believe that geometry, trigonometry, biology, chemistry, and physics are needed to qualify for their first choice occupation (Longitudinal Survey of American Youth 1988).

Although the economic benefits of higher achievement to the employee are quite modest and do not appear until long after graduation, the benefits to the employer (and, therefore, to national production) are immediately realized in higher productivity. Over the last 80 years, industrial psychologists have conducted hundreds of studies, involving hundreds of thousands of workers, on the relationship between productivity in particular jobs and various predictors of that productivity. They have found that competence in reading, mathematics, science and problem solving are strongly related to productivity in almost all of the civilian and military jobs studied (Hunter, Crosson, and Friedman 1985).

Despite their significantly higher productivity, *young workers who have achieved in high school have not been receiving appreciably higher wage rates after high school.* Apparently, when a non-college-bound student works hard in school and improves his or her competence in language arts, science and mathematical reasoning, the youth's employer reaps much of the benefit.[3]

Employers believe that school performance is a good predictor of job performance. Studies of how employers rate job applicant resumes which contain information on grades in high school have found that employers give substantially higher ratings to job applicants with high grade point averages (Hollenbeck and Smith 1984). However, they have great difficulty getting information on school performance. If a student or graduate has given written permission for a transcript to be sent to an employer, the Federal Education Rights and Privacy Act obligates the school to respond. Many high schools are not, however, responding to such requests. In Columbus Ohio, for example, *Nationwide Insurance sent over 1,200 requests for transcripts signed by job applicants to high schools in 1982 and received only 93 responses.*

An additional barrier to the use of high school transcripts in selecting new employees is that when high schools do respond, it takes a great deal of time. In most high schools, the system for responding to transcript requests has been designed to meet the needs of college-bound students rather than the students who seek jobs immediately after graduating. The result is that a 1987 survey of a stratified random sample of small-and medium-sized employers who were members of the National Federation of Independent Business (NFIB) found that transcripts had been obtained prior to the selection decision for only 14.2 percent of the high school graduates hired.[4] Only 15 percent of the employers had asked high school graduates to report their grade point average. The absence of questions about grades on most job application forms reflects the low reliability of self-reported data, the difficulties of verifying it, and the fear of EEOC (Equal Employment Opportunity Commission) challenges to such questions.

Hiring on the basis of recommendations by high school teachers is also uncommon. In the NFIB survey, when a high school graduate was hired, the new hire had been referred or recommended by vocational teachers in only 5.2 percent of the cases and referred by someone else in the high school in only 2.7 percent. Tests are available for measuring competency in reading, writing, mathematics, science, and problem solving; but, after the 1971 Griggs decision, almost all firms were forced to stop employment testing by EEOC guidelines which made it prohibitively costly to demonstrate test validity.[5] The 1987 NFIB survey found that basic skills tests had been given in only 2.9 percent of the hiring decisions studied. Other countries handle the signaling of high school accomplishments to colleges and to prospective employers very differently.

Incentives to Learn in Other Nations

The tendency not to reward effort and learning in high school appears to be a peculiarly American phenomenon. Marks in school are the major determinant of who gets the most preferred apprenticeships in Germany. In Europe and Japan, educational systems administer achievement exams which are closely tied to the curriculum. While the Japanese use a multiple choice exam, all other nations use examinations in which students write essays and show their work for mathematics problems. Generally, regional or national boards set the exams and oversee the blind grading of the exams by committees of teachers. These are not minimum competency exams. In many subjects the student may choose to take the exams at two different levels of difficulty. Excellence is recognized as well as competence (Noah and Eckstein 1988).

Performance on these exams is the primary determinant of admission to a university and to particular fields of study, such as medicine and law. Good grades on the toughest exams—physics, chemistry, advanced mathematics—carry particularly heavy weight. Exam grades are included in resumes and are asked for on job applications (see Exhibits 1 and 2).

In Japan, clerical, service, and blue collar jobs at the best firms are available only to those who are recommended by their high school. The most prestigious firms have long-term arrangements with particular high schools to which they delegate the responsibility of selecting new hires for the firm. The criteria by which the high school is to make its selection are, by mutual agreement, grades and exam results. In addition, most employers administer their own battery of selection tests prior to hiring. The number of graduates that a high school is able to place in this way depends on its reputation and the company's past experience with graduates from the school. Schools know that they must be forthright in their recommendations because if they fail just once to make an honest recommendation, the relationship will be lost and their students will no longer be able to get jobs at that firm (Rosenbaum and Kariya 1989). This system has the consequences one might expect. Rosenbaum's (1990) study of the high-school-to-work transition in Japan finds that good grades, no discipline problems, and participation in extracurricular activities all have significant positive effects on obtaining jobs at large firms and entering a white collar occupation. In the United States, by contrast, the job outcomes of males are not improved by good grades, few absences from school, a lack of discipline problems or participation in extracurricular activities. For female high school graduates, obtaining a white collar job is associated with high grades, but it is also positively associated with being a discipline problem in school.

Parents in Europe and Japan know that a child's future depends critically on how much is learned in secondary school. In many countries the options for upper secondary schooling depend primarily on the child's performance in lower secondary school, not on where the parents can afford to live, as in the United States. Since the quality and reputation of the high school are so important, the competitive pressure often reaches down into lower secondary school. National exams are the yardstick, so achievement tends to be measured

Exhibit 1. Resume from Republic of Ireland, including Intermediate and Final National Examination Grades

CURRICULUM VITAE

NAME:

ADDRESS:

DATE OF BIRTH: AGE:

NATIONALITY:

TELEPHONE NO.:

EDUCATIONAL DETAILS

Primary School

Post Primary

Secretarial Course

Office Procedures Course

EXAMINATIONS

	Intermediate Certificate		1985
SUBJECTS	English	B - L.C.	
	Irish	C - L.C.	
	Maths	B - L.C.	
	Science	C	
	Geography	C	
	History	C	
	Home Economics	D	
	Leaving Certificate		1987
SUBJECTS	English	D - L.C.	
	Irish	C - L.C.	
	Maths	C - L.C.	
	Biology	C - H.C.	
	Geography	C - L.C.	
	French	D - L.C.	
	Home Economics	B - L.C.	

relative to everyone else's in the nation and not just relative to the child's classmates. As a result, parents in most other Western nations demand more and get more from their local schools than we do and are, nevertheless, more dissatisfied with their schools than American parents.

Japanese teenagers work extremely hard in high school, but once they enter college, many stop working. For students in non-technical fields a country club atmosphere prevails. The reason for the change in behavior is that when employers hire graduates with non-technical majors, they base their selections on the reputation of the university and a long series of interviews and not on teacher recommendations or other measures of academic achievement at the

Exhibit 2. British Job Application Requiring Grades
as well as Course Information

APPLICATION FOR APPOINTMENT

Appointment applied for.. Distribution Projects Manager (B+Q) Ref.No. ....

PERSONAL DETAILS: (block capitals)

Surname.......................... Title...Mr..... Forenames ..Mervyn John..........

Address...

.... Postal Code..................... Tel.No.Home............... Work ....

Marital Status ....M..............Children/Dependants (with ages).1 x 4yrs., 1 x 1yr....

Age......33.....Date of Birth..5-8-55.... Nationality..British.. Place of Birth.............

State of health .... OK .... Height....6'....Weight 13st 12lbs

Any disabilities/recurrent medical problems? .....None..................... Regd.disabled ....—...

Driving Licenses...........Car.................... Car Owner ....✓.... Company Car............—...

Endorsements, convictions, accidents, etc. ......None.................................

Leisure activities and offices held in clubs and societies.....Cycling/Walking...........

EDUCATION:

Secondary Education

From	To	School	Exams Taken (inc. grades)	Other achievements
1966	1972	Barnstaple Grammar	'O' Level: Eng. Lang. (2), Maths (3), French (3), Geog.(3), Statistics (3), Chemistry(3), Addl. Maths (6), Hist. (6), Physics (6) 'A' Level: Chem. (E) Physics (E), Maths (0)	Middle Sch. Games Captain

Further Education

From	To	College/Univ.	Course & results (inc.class/grades)	Other achievements
1972	1973	Univ. of Bradford	Applied Chemistry - left after 1 year - domestic reasons	

Other training and qualifications (inc. in-company and external courses, etc.)

From	To	Establishment	Training/Qualifications
1979		Farnley College, Leeds	Cert. of Prof. Competence (transport ofs.)
1983	1984	Bradford College	Inst. of Industrial Management Cert.
1984	1989	In-Company	Numerous Management Classes

Membership of professional bodies

Date	Association/Institute	Grade of membership	Offices held

university. Students in engineering and other technical programs work much harder than their liberal arts counterparts largely because job opportunities depend entirely on the recommendation of their major professor. Studying hard is not a national character trait; it is a response to the way Japanese society rewards academic achievement.

American students, in contrast, work much harder in college than in high school. This change is due, in part, to the fact that academic achievement in college has important effects on labor market success. When higher level jobs requiring a bachelors or associates degree are being filled, employers pay more attention to grades and teacher recommendations than when they hire high school graduates. The NFIB survey found that when college graduates were hired, 26 percent of the employers had reviewed the college transcript before making the selection, 7.8 percent had obtained a recommendation from a major professor and 6.3 percent had obtained a recommendation from a professor outside of the graduate's major or from the college's placement office.

STATE POLICY RESPONSES

The key to motivating students to learn is recognizing and rewarding learning effort and achievement. Some students are attracted to serious study by an intrinsic fascination with the subject. They must pay, however, a heavy price in the scorn of their peers and lost free time. Society offers them little reward for their effort. Most students are not motivated to study by a love of the subject. Sixty-two percent of 10th graders agree with the statement, "I don't like to do any more school work than I have to" (Longitudinal Survey of American Youth 1988, QAA37N). As a result, far too few high school students put serious time and energy into learning and society suffers. If this situation is to be turned around, the peer pressure against studying must be greatly reduced and rewards for learning must be increased. The full diversity of types and levels of accomplishment needs to be signaled so that everyone—no matter how advanced or far behind—faces a reward for greater time and energy devoted to learning. Learning accomplishments need to be described on an absolute scale so that improvements in the quality and rigor of the teaching and greater effort by all students in a school makes everybody better off. Colleges need to be induced to select students on the basis of externally validated achievements, not by "aptitude" test scores or rank in class.

Increasing numbers of employers need workers who are competent in mathematics, science, technology, and communication. If these employers know who is well educated in these fields, they will provide the rewards needed to motivate study. Ninety-two percent of 10th graders say they "often think about what type of job I will be doing after I finish school" (Longitudinal Survey of American Youth 1988, QAA13C). If the labor market were to begin rewarding learning in school, high school students would respond by studying harder, and local voters would be willing to pay higher taxes so as to have better local schools. The Secretary of Labor's Commission on Workforce Quality and Labor Market Efficiency (1989) advocates such a change:

> The business community should...show through their hiring and promotion decisions that academic achievements will be rewarded.
>
> High-school students who excel in science and mathematics should be rewarded with business internships or grants for further study (pp. 9, 11).

Some might respond to this strategy for achieving excellence by stating a preference for intrinsic over extrinsic motivation of learning. This, however, is a false dichotomy. Nowhere else in our society do we expect people to devote thousands of hours to a difficult task while receiving *only* intrinsic rewards. Public recognition of achievement and the symbolic and material rewards received by achievers are important generators of intrinsic motivation. They are, in fact, one of the central ways a culture symbolically transmits and promotes its values.[6]

Recommendations for policy initiatives by state governments have been grouped into four categories:

1. Better signals of learning accomplishment,
2. Inducing students to pursue a more rigorous curriculum,
3. Creating new opportunities for learning in schools,
4. Generating additional recognition and rewards for learning.

Better Signals of Learning Accomplishment

Without a better system of signaling student accomplishments in high school to parents, colleges, employers, and the public, it is unlikely that there will be sustained improvements in the academic achievement of American high school students. The National Commission on the Skills of the American Workforce (1990) recently provided a description of what a national system of performance measurement might look like:

The Foundation Skills

A new educational performance standard should be set for all students, to be met by age 16. This standard should be established nationally and benchmarked to the highest in the world.

All of our students should meet a national standard of educational excellence by age 16, or soon thereafter, which will equal or exceed the highest similar standard in the world for students of that age. A student passing a series of performance based assessments that incorporate the standard should be awarded a Certificate of Initial Mastery.

In order to adequately prepare our young people for working life, we must first see that they acquire the educational skills necessary to become effective players in a highly productive society. The establishment of a system of national standards and assessment would ensure that every student leaves compulsory school with a demonstrated ability to read, write, compute and perform at world-class levels in general school subjects (mathematics, physical and natural sciences, technology, history, geography, politics, economics and English). Students should also have exhibited a capacity to learn, think, work effectively alone and in groups and solve problems. Among other things, the Certificate of Initial Mastery would certify labor market readiness, and a mastery of the basic skills necessary for high productivity employment. The same Certificate would also be required for entry into all subsequent forms of education, including college preparatory and certified professional and technical programs.

The assessment system would establish objective standards for students and educators, motivate students and give employers an objective means to assess the capabilities of job applicants. The Certificate of Initial Mastery would not indicate the completion of student's formal education. Rather, for the vast majority of students, this achievement would serve as a foundation for more advanced forms of education or training.

A Cumulative Assessment System

The assessment system should allow students to collect credentials over a period of years, perhaps beginning as early as entrance into the middle school. This kind of cumulative assessment has several advantages over a single series of examinations:

- It would help to organize and motivate students over an extended period of time. Rather than preparing for a far-off examination (the form and demands of which a 12-year-old can only dimly imagine), students could begin early to collect specific certifications.
- It would provide multiple opportunities for success rather than a single high-stake moment of possible failure. Cumulating certificates would greatly enhance the opportunity for the undereducated and unmotivated to achieve high educational standards. All could earn credentials at their own pace, as the criteria for any specific credential would not vary, regardless of the student's age.
- It would allow students who are not performing well in the mainstream education system to earn their credentials under other institutional auspices.

An Independent Examining Organization

To set the assessment standards and certification procedures, we recommend the establishment of an independent national examining organization that broadly represents educators, employers and the citizenry at large. The organization should be authorized to convene working commissions in a variety of knowledge and skill areas to help train judges, set and assess standards and conduct examinations. The organization should be independent of schools and school systems and protected from political pressures (pp. 69-70).

Instituting Statewide Achievement Examinations

Until a national system of performance assessment is established, states should implement such systems on their own. Statewide tests of competency and knowledge that are keyed to the courses students are taking (e.g., New York State's Regents Examinations and California's Golden State

Examinations) should be made a graduation requirement. Students should have to complete a series of these exams before being awarded grants or subsidized loans and before being admitted to public colleges. Results on these exams should replace SAT and ACT test scores in the admission and selection process and determine the award of state merit based scholarships. Students should be given a credential certifying performance on these exams and employers should be encouraged to factor examination results into their hiring decisions.

An exam system such as this maximizes incentives to study. All employers would have access to information on the academic achievements of job candidates, not just the employers who choose to give employment tests. The connection between effort in school, performance on the exams and job placement would become clearly visible to all.

This approach to signaling academic achievement has a number of advantages. By retaining control of exam content, educators and the public influence the kinds of academic achievement that are rewarded by the labor market. Societal decisions regarding the curriculum (e.g., all students should read Shakespeare's plays and understand the Constitution) tend to be reinforced by employer hiring decisions. Tests developed solely for employee selection purposes would probably place less emphasis on Shakespeare and the Constitution. Because it is centralized and students take the exam only once or twice, job applicants do not have to take a different exam at each firm they apply to, and the quality and comprehensiveness of the test can be much greater. There is no need for multiple versions of the same test and it is much easier to keep the test secure.

Shifting emphasis away from teacher assessment to external assessment also has important pedagogical benefits. It transforms the relationship between teachers and students into a more cooperative one in which they work jointly to prepare the students for the external assessment.

Develop Better Assessment Mechanisms

As student recognition and rewards come increasingly to depend on the results of school assessments of competency, it becomes more and more important that we improve methods of assessing academic achievement. Linking assessment to curriculum also implies a need for a greater diversity of assessment mechanisms. However, the need for multiple versions of the assessment instrument and for fairness to minorities make test development very expensive. The federal government should underwrite state consortia and other organizations that seek to develop alternatives to currently available tests and assessment mechanisms. Priority needs to go to developing methods of assessing higher order thinking skills and hands on performance through simulations, portfolios of the student's work, and demonstrations of skills conducted in front of judges. High cost has been the primary barrier to the use of these richer forms of assessment. Consequently, consideration should be given to subsidizing these more costly assessment mechanisms.

Achievement Exams and College Admission

There should occur either a complete transformation of SAT and ACT Tests or a substitution of Advanced Placement and national or state sponsored achievement exams for purposes of awarding state scholarships and selection for competitive colleges. While national examinations are necessary, the Scholastic Aptitude Test is not the kind of test that is helpful. The SAT suffers from two very serious limitations: the limited range of the achievements that are evaluated and its multiple choice format. The test was designed to be curriculum free. To the extent that it evaluates the students' understanding of material taught in schools, the material it covers is vocabulary and mathematics. Most of the college preparatory subjects studied in high school—science, social studies, technology, art, music, computers, trigonometry and statistics—are completely absent from the test. As a result, it fails to generate incentives to take the more demanding courses or to study hard. The new version of the ACT test is a definite improvement, for it tests science and social science knowledge and attempts to measure problem solving in science. The newly revised SAT is not a major improvement over the old test. Both tests suffer from the common problems that arise from their multiple-choice format. National and provincial exams in Europe are predominantly essay and extended-answer examinations. The absence of essays on the SAT and ACT tests contributes to the poor writing skills of American students. The tests advertise themselves as ability tests, but are in fact achievement tests measuring a very limited range of achievements. Jencks and Crouse (1982) have recommended that either the SAT evaluate a much broader range of achievements or be dropped in favor of Advanced Placement examinations. Knowledge and understanding of literature, history, technology, science, and higher order thinking skills should all be assessed. These exams should not be limited to a multiple choice format and essays should be required where appropriate. Foreign language exams, for example, should test conversational skills as well as reading and writing. Students taking science courses should be expected to conduct experiments and demonstrate the use of lab equipment.

It is not clear if there is a federal role in engineering necessary changes in the selection methods of colleges and universities. Major revisions of tests like the SAT and ACT are quite expensive. Possibly the federal government could induce the testing organizations to undertake the effort by offering to subsidize development costs.

Certifying Competencies and Releasing Student Records

> Schools should develop easily understood transcripts which at the request of students are
> readily available to employers. These transcripts should contain documentable measures
> of achievement in a variety of fields as well as attendance records. State governments should
> provide assistance to facilitate the standardization of transcripts so that they will be more
> easily understood (Commission on Workforce Quality and Labor Market Efficiency 1989,
> p. 12).

Schools should provide graduates with certificates or diplomas that certify the students' knowledge and competencies, rather than just their attendance. Competency should be defined by an absolute standard in the way Scout merit badges are. Different types and levels of competency need to be certified. Minimum competency tests for receiving a high school diploma do not satisfy the need for better signals of achievement in high school. Some students arrive in high school so far behind, and the consequences of not getting a diploma are so severe, that as a result we have not been willing to set the minimum competency standard very high. Once they satisfy the minimum, many students stop putting effort into their academic courses. What is needed is a more informative credential which signals the full range of student achievements (e.g., statewide achievement exam scores, competency check lists).

One of the saddest consequences of the lack of signals of achievement in high school is that employers with good jobs offering training and job security are unwilling to take the risk of hiring a recent high school graduate. They prefer to hire workers with many years of work experience. One important reason for this policy is that the applicant's work record serves as a signal of competence and reliability that helps the employer identify who is most qualified. In the United States recent high school graduates have no such record and information on high school performance is not available, so the entire graduating class appears to employers as one undifferentiated mass of unskilled and undisciplined workers. A common employer view of 18 year-olds was expressed by a supervisor at New York Life Insurance who commented on television, **"When kids come out of high school, they think the world owes them a living"** (Public Broadcasting System 1989). Surely this generalization does not apply to every graduate, but the students who are disciplined and academically well prepared currently have no way of signaling this fact to employers.

Schools can help students get good jobs by developing an equitable and efficient policy for releasing student records. School officials have the dual responsibility of protecting the student's right to privacy and helping them find good, suitable jobs. The student and his or her parents should receive copies (encased in plastic) of transcripts and other records that might be released so that they may make them available to anyone they choose. Schools might also develop a sheet explaining to parents and students their rights, as well as the pros and cons of disclosing information.

According to the Federal Education Rights and Privacy Act, all that a student/graduate must do to have school records sent to a prospective employer is sign a form specifying the purpose of disclosure, which records are to be released, and who is to receive the records. The waiver and record request forms used by employers contain this information, so when such a request is received, the school is obliged to respond. Requiring that graduates fill out a school devised form—as one high school I visited did—results in the employer not getting the transcript requested and the graduate not getting the job. There are probably millions of high school graduates who do not realize that they failed to get a job they were hoping for because their high school did not send the transcript that was requested. Schools can best serve students by handling all inquiries expeditiously and without charge.

Credential Data Bank and Employee Locator Service

It may, however, be unrealistic to expect 22,902 high schools to develop efficient systems of maintaining student records and responding quickly to requests for transcripts. An alternative approach would be to centralize the record keeping and dissemination function in a trusted third party organization. This organization would be easy to regulate and thus everyone could be assured that privacy mandates are being observed. The student would determine which competencies are to be assessed and what types of information are to be included in his or her competency portfolio. Competency assessments would be offered for a variety of scientific, mathematical and technological subjects and for language, writing, business, and occupational skills. Tests with many alternate forms (or which are administered by computer using a large test item bank) would be used so that students could retake the test a month later if desired. Only the highest score would remain in the system. Students would be encouraged to include descriptions of their extracurricular activities, their jobs and any other accomplishments they feel are relevant, and to submit samples of their work such as a research paper, art work, or pictures of a project made in metal shop. Files could be updated after leaving high school.

Students would have three different ways of transmitting their competency profiles to potential employers. First, they would receive certified copies of their portfolio which they could carry to job interviews or mail to employers. Second, they would be able to call a 900 number and request that their portfolio be sent to specific employers. Third, they could ask to put themselves in an employee locator data bank similar to the student locator services operated by the Educational Testing Service. A student seeking a summer or post-graduation job would specify the type of work sought and dates of availability. Employers seeking workers could ask for a printout of the portfolios of all the individuals living near a particular establishment who have expressed interest in that type of job and who pass the employer's competency screens. Student locator services have been heavily used by colleges seeking to recruit minority students and an employee locator service would almost certainly be used in the same way. This will significantly increase the rewards for hard study because the employee locator service is likely to result in a bidding war for the qualified minority students whose portfolios are in the system.

The National Alliance of Business, the American Business Conference, the Educational Testing Service and the California Department of Education are currently involved in developing systems like the one just described. Pilot programs are underway in Hillsborough County, Florida; Orange County, California; Fort Worth, Texas; and New Jersey. It is doubtful that a federally sponsored credential data bank would have the credibility with business that is essential for success. With respect to the credential data bank, the best role for the federal government is probably verbal and limited financial support for a private initiative. Federal funding of the research and development necessary to develop the high quality assessments that might be used by this system would be desirable. A federally sponsored system of subject matter exams taken at the end of high school would speed the development of a credential data bank and would be desirable for other reasons. Current plans, however, envision constructing the credential data bank, state by state and city by city.

Inducing Students to Pursue a More Rigorous Curriculum

The analysis of the causes of the American apathy regarding teaching and learning has important implications for the curriculum. Many of the weaknesses of math and science curricula—the constant review and repetition of old material, the slow pace and minimal expectations—are adaptations to the low level of effort most students are willing to devote to these subjects. When considering proposed revisions of the curriculum, **one must remember that motivating students to take tough courses and to study hard must be a central concern.**

This problem would remain even if parents and students were allowed to choose their school. Even though American high schools differ greatly in standards and quality, employers do not appear to be using high school reputation as a signal when making hiring selections (Hollenbeck and Smith 1984). About 200 competitive colleges do take high school quality into account when evaluating a student's GPA, but most colleges do not. In such an environment it is not clear what will impel parents to send their children to a school that promises a rigorous academic program involving a great deal of homework rather than to a school with a reputation for excellence in football or hockey.

A second constraint that must be recognized is the great diversity of the learning goals and capabilities of high school students. On the NAEP mathematics scale, 15 percent of 13 year-olds have better mathematics skills than the average 17 year old student, and 7 percent of 13 year-olds score below the average 9 year old (National Assessment of Education Progress 1988). On the NAEP reading scale, 16.5 percent of 13 year-olds have better reading skills than the average 17 year old student, and 9 percent of 13 year-olds score below the average 9 year old (National Assessment of Education Progress 1986). **Consequently, once they have completed their Certificate of Initial Mastery, it is neither feasible nor desirable for all senior high school students to pursue the same curriculum.** While some nations have a common curriculum with no tracking in elementary school and lower secondary schools, no advanced country has been foolish enough to force all senior high students to take the same courses. Some students will want to pursue subjects like mathematics and science in greater depth and rigor than others. Some students will want to concentrate on technology, not pure science. **Some courses will be easier than others, and students will inevitably be able to choose between rigorous and less demanding courses.**

State requirements that students take more math and science courses to graduate will have little effect on learning if students meet the requirement by taking undemanding courses. Holding background characteristics and the rigor of the math and science courses constant, an additional three courses in math and science during high school increased the gain in math competency between 10th and 12th grade by only .19 of a grade level equivalent, and *reduced* science gains by .09 of a grade level equivalent and English and social studies gains by .17-.18 of a grade level equivalent. Holding constant background characteristics and the total number of courses taken in other specific fields, taking five college preparatory math and science courses—chemistry, physics, algebra II, trigonometry and calculus—increased the gain on math and science tests by .75 of a grade level equivalent and increased the gain in English and social studies by .34-.44 of a grade level equivalent (Bishop 1985). These data clearly imply that learning rates are determined by the rigor, not the number, of courses taken in a subject.

Another strategy that can have only very limited effects is requiring passage of a multiple choice minimum competency exam before graduation. There is a danger that many students will stop putting effort into their courses, once they satisfy the minimum.

How then do we convince students to study hard? How do we induce them to select courses that require a lot of work just to be an average achiever in the class? The answer is by: **(1) developing rigorous courses that teach students concepts and material that they will use after leaving high school, (2) convincing students that the material being taught is useful by presenting it as solutions** to practical real world problems, (3) defining accomplishment in a way that students who work hard will perceive themselves as successful, and then (4) recognizing and rewarding accomplishment.

Usefulness is an absolutely central criterion for selecting the topics to be included in a curriculum for three reasons. First, the social benefits of learning derive from the use of the knowledge and skills, not from the fact they are in someone's repertoire. Second, skills and knowledge that are not used deteriorate rapidly. In one set of studies, students tested 2 years after taking a course had forgotten 1/2 of the college psychology and zoology, 1/3 of the high school chemistry, and 3/4 of the college botany that had been learned (Pressey and Robinson 1944). Skills and knowledge that are used are remembered. Consequently, if learning is to produce long term benefits, the competencies developed must continue to be used after the final exam (either in college, the labor market or somewhere else). Finally, usefulness is essential because students are not going to put energy into learning things they perceive to be useless. Furthermore, the labor market is not in the long run going to reward skills and competencies that have no use. Indeed, selecting workers on the basis of competencies that are not useful in the company's jobs is in most circumstances a violation of Title VII of the Civil Rights Act.

Differentiating the Curriculum

By 10th grade most students have a pretty good idea of what kinds of jobs they want after finishing their education. Ninety-seven percent can select a particular occupation they expect to be doing at age 40 and 77 percent agree with the statement: "I am quite certain about what kinds of jobs I would enjoy doing when I am older" (Longitudinal Survey of American Youth 1988, QAA13C, QAA22A). Students who are planning careers in science and engineering need to be able to take college preparatory biology, chemistry and physics courses that prepare them for the core courses they will face in college. The students not planning on scientific careers, however, quite often fail to see how these courses will be useful to them. As noted earlier, less than a quarter of 10th graders believe that geometry, trigonometry, biology, chemistry, and physics are needed to qualify for their first choice occupation (Longitudinal Survey of American Youth 1988, QBA24B, QBA25D).

One approach to this problem, of course, is to point out to students how the material in standard college prep courses is useful in non-scientific jobs and everyday life. Presumably, teachers already try to do this. Another approach is to modify the standard curriculum. That is the approach of the new math and science curriculums proposed by the National Council of Teachers of Mathematics (1989) and the American Association for the Advancement of Science (1989). This makes sense in the first 8 or 9 years of schooling. There is, however, no standard curriculum in 10th, 11th and 12th grade; and it is not realistic to propose that everyone take the same courses. At these grade levels the most effective way to motivate students to take demanding courses and to study hard is to tailor courses to the student's career interest and to insure that prospective employers are aware that the student took challenging rigorous courses.

Teaching Science and Math by Infusing it into Technology Courses

Analyses of labor market success of young men and of job performance in the military indicate that young people who expect to have jobs in which they use or maintain complicated pieces of equipment should receive a thorough technology education (Hunter et al. 1990). Computer classes are one example of the kinds of courses needed. High school sophomores described their computer classes as "very useful" for their careers 53 percent of the time and as of "no use" only 6 percent of the time (Longitudinal Survey of American Youth 1988, QAACOMF).

The *Principles of Technology* (PT) course developed by a consortium of vocational education agencies in 47 states and Canadian provinces in association with the Agency for Instructional Technology and the Center for Occupational Research and Development is another example of a course that meets this need very well. This two-year applied physics course is both academically rigorous and practical. Each six-day subunit deals with the unit's major technical principle (e.g., resistance) as it applies to one of the four energy systems—mechanical (both rotational and linear), fluid, electrical, and thermal. A subunit usually consists of two days of lectures and discussion, a math skills lab, two days of hands-on physics application labs, and a subunit review. This approach appears to be quite effective at teaching basic physics. When students enrolled in regular physics and Principles of Technology courses were tested on basic physics concepts at the beginning and end of their junior and senior year in high school, the PT students started out behind the regular physics students but obtained an average score of 81 at completion as compared to an average of 66 for those completing a physics course (Perry 1989). Another study by Roper (1989) obtained similar results. Comparable courses have been developed for other fields of technology. This is an area of study that needs much more attention than it has been getting from educational reformers and curriculum developers.

Massively Expand Advanced Placement Courses

The Advanced Placement program is a cooperative educational endeavor which offers course descriptions, examinations, and sets of curricular materials in 28 different academic subjects. Students who take these courses and pass the examinations receive college credit for high school work. Unlike the SAT, the ACT and all other standardized aptitude and achievement tests which employ the multiple-choice answer format exclusively, these exams require students to write long essays and to work out complicated science and mathematics problems. Hence they are similar in format to the French Baccalaureate, the English A Level, and other exams taken by European students completing secondary school. They are also of roughly comparable difficulty. Consequently, the number of students taking and passing these exams is a good way of monitoring progress toward the goal of closing performance gaps in mathematics and science.

Expanding the AP program should be a centerpiece of any effort to promote excellence in American high schools. It clearly meets a felt need, for it is growing rapidly. The numbers of students taking AP exams more than doubled between 1983 and 1988. Nevertheless, in 1990 only 8,022 of the 22,902 U.S. high schools participated in the Advanced Placement Program, and only 52 AP exams were taken on average in each participating high school. In the Class of 1990 only 3.8 percent took the AP English Literature and Composition exam, 3.6 percent took the American History exam, 3.0 percent took the AP calculus exam, 1.3 percent took the AP biology exam, .8 percent took the AP chemistry exam and .7 percent took the AP physics exam (College Board 1988/1990).

The nation's 50 governors, President Bush, and Speaker of the House of Representatives Thomas Foley, speaking for the Democratic Party, have all proclaimed the goal of surpassing all other countries in mathematics and science by the year 2000. This is a worthy goal. We should be satisfied with nothing less. But it will not be easy to achieve. In the Second International Science Study, for example, the 24 percent of Norwegian youth who take physics in their 12th year of school were better prepared than the less than one percent of American high school seniors who were taking the second year of an AP physics course. Twenty-five percent of Canadians pursue a rigorous chemistry sequence in high school and perform at the same level as the two percent of American seniors who are taking their second year of chemistry (IAEEA 1988). To achieve the goal of catching up with Canada, Norway, Finland, Germany and France, more than 25 percent of the nation's high school graduates will have to take mathematics and science courses of AP rigor, and the standards of these courses will have to increase. In other words, the number of students taking calculus will have to increase by a factor of 8 and the number of students taking courses in Biology, Chemistry, and Physics of AP rigor will have to increase by a factor of 25.

The nation should set a goal of doubling every two years the number of AP courses taken and AP exams passed. New AP exams should be established in principles of technology, electronics, algebra, geometry and trigonometry, probability and statistics, psychology, and business mathematics so that larger numbers of 10th and 11th graders and students planning to attend 2-year technical colleges may participate in the AP program. Acting in concert, the college presidents of a large group of selective 2-year and 4-year colleges should send a letter to every high school principal in the country (with copies to the school board and local newspaper) urging them to establish AP courses in science, mathematics, and technology. They should also announce that starting in 1998, students seeking admission to their school should have taken and passed at least one AP course in their junior year and be taking more than one AP course their senior year.[6]

Federal and state governments can facilitate the growth of the AP program by underwriting the development of AP exams for new subjects, by financing summer institutes for the teachers of AP courses, by subsidizing the fees charged for taking the exam and by offering AP Excellence Awards to students who achieve passing scores on the exam.

To insure that attending a summer institute is considered a plum, compensation should be generous. In 1988, about 40,000 teachers taught AP courses. Rapid expansion of the program will require a yearly increase of 20,000 in the stock of teachers teaching AP courses; and if 30 percent of the increment to the stock were to experience summer institute training for 6 weeks, the cost would be about $42 million.

The amount of the scholarship award should depend both on the student's score and on the eligibility of the student for Pell grants. If the award schedule for those not eligible for Pell grants was $300 for a 5 (the top score), $200 for a 4 and $100 for a 3, and twice that for students eligible for Pell grants, the average award would probably be $250. In 1990, 326,025 students would have been eligible for an AP excellence award, so the scholarship program would have cost $82 million. If a good deal of publicity were attached to these awards, they would induce a major expansion of the program and stimulate an upgrading of standards throughout middle school and high school.

Statewide Networks of Science, Math, History, Literature and Technology Clubs

At present, only 3.2 percent of high school sophomores are members of a science club, only 2.5 percent are members of a math club, and only 1.6 percent are members of a computer club (Longitudinal Survey of American Youth 1988). Only 19,000 students (less than 0.2 percent of all high school students) participate in the annual Westinghouse Science Talent Search.

Memberships in these clubs and participation in the Westinghouse Science Talent Search should be greatly expanded. The clubs should be stitched together into state and national networks. The student organizations should sponsor interschool competitions, visits to science museums, and science and technology project competitions that would feed into statewide and national competitions, like the Westinghouse Science Talent Search program. The state and national organizations would function in much the same way as the state and national offices of Boy Scouts, Future Farmers of America, and Vocational and Industrial Clubs of America. They would provide training to teachers and student leaders and develop program activity packets to help local science and math teachers devise activities for their clubs. The federal government can help stimulate the formation of national club networks in academic fields by offering to pay travel costs for the first few national conventions and by contributing to national programming costs. The state club organizations could also be conduits for reimbursing local schools for some of the expenses of local club activities. One of the reasons for the very low participation rates in the Westinghouse Talent Search is the paltry size, only $140,000, of its national scholarship budget. State and federal money needs to be pumped into this program to a point where states the size of Maryland are awarding more than $200,000 a year in Science Scholarships.

Creating New Opportunities for Learning in School

Two Hours of Homework a Night for All Secondary School Students

States and school districts should have a policy that all high school students are assigned at least 2 hours of homework on weeknights and 4 hours on weekends. In many American high school classes, homework is not even assigned. Powell (1985) describes one school he visited:

> Students were given class time to read *The Scarlet Letter, The Red Badge of Courage, Huckleberry Finn,* and *The Great Gatsby* because many would not read the books if they were assigned as homework. Parents had complained that such homework was excessive. Pressure from them might even bring the teaching of the books to a halt....[As one teacher put it] "If you can't get them to read at home, you do the next best thing. It has to be done....I'm trying to be optimistic and say we're building up their expectations in school."

It's not just reading that teachers feel they cannot require. A high school history teacher who had previewed PBS's 11 hour series on the Civil War and who had participated in developing teaching materials associated with the series was asked by a reporter whether he was assigning it to his class. The teacher replied that unfortunately he could not because 11 hours was way beyond what most high school students were willing to commit to an assignment.

A careful time budget study conducted in the early 1980s found that American high school students spent an average of only 3.8 hours a week on homework compared to an average of 19.6 hours per week in Japan (Juster and Stafford 1990). If American high schools assigned and American students did a great deal more homework, achievement would be substantially higher. That is the conclusion of Cooper's meta-analysis of the literature on homework. Experimental studies find that when high school students are assigned homework, they score about half a standard deviation higher on the post-test than the control group. The impact of homework on the rate at which middle school students learn is also significant, though somewhat smaller. There is no evidence of diminishing returns as the amount of homework is increased. Non-experimental studies tend to find that the relationship between homework and learning is linear (Cooper 1989).

Turn Schools into All-Day Learning Centers

The length of the school day should be extended from 6 to 7 hours. A full range of remedial and enrichment programs and extracurricular activities and intramural sports should be offered during the extra hour. Students making normal progress might choose whatever alternative they desire. Many students do not have a quiet place to study at home, so the library, the computer lab, and a number of classrooms should remain open and supervised during this period. Extra help would be available for students having difficulty with the core curriculum. Volunteers to provide tutoring and to offer special interest courses could be recruited from the community. Private teachers of music, art, and other subjects might also be allowed to use school facilities during these hours. The benefit of this reform is that: (1) the regular school day would be freed up for more intensive study of the core curriculum, (2) more homework could be assigned and all students would have a quiet place to study, (3) slower students would be given the extra instruction they need, (4) enrichment programs could be expanded, and (5) the phenomenon of the latch key child would be reduced.

Increase the School Year from 180 to 200 Days

Longitudinal studies of learning have found that students appear to forget during the summer a portion (up to 1 to 2 months worth) of the mathematics they learned during the previous school year. Rates of gain in reading ability tend to either decline or slow dramatically during the summer (see Appendix). The learning loss is particularly large for disadvantaged students and for minority students (Heyns 1987). As a result, much of September is devoted to review and practice of the material taught the previous year. In *The Underachieving Curriculum*, the report which presented and analyzed the reasons for poor American performance in the Second International Mathematics Study, McKnight et al. severely criticized the practice of allocating so much time to review of old topics rather than to the presentation of new material. These findings clearly suggest that school attendance is essential if math and reading skills are to improve and that a longer school year would not only increase learning time but also reduce forgetting time. Adding a month to the school year could very well produce a more than proportionate increase in learning.

Studies of the effect of summer school confirm the educational impact of additional instruction time. The best study of this issue used a random assignment control group methodology to evaluate the Summer Training and Employment Program (STEP), a program for disadvantaged youth that combines a part time summer job with about 90 hours of remedial instruction. It found that adding the instruction to the summer job raised academic achievement by .5 grade level equivalents above that of youths receiving only a part time job (Sipe, Grossman, and Millner 1988). The documented success of the STEP intervention has resulted in its replication (with federal support) in 33 different school systems. This evidence indicates that extending the school year would not only raise educational standards generally, it would also help children from educationally and economically disadvantaged backgrounds keep up with their more advantaged peers.

Accelerating the Pace of Instruction

Increasing the time devoted to learning by one-ninth or more has major implications for the curriculum. The learning objectives specified for each year would need to be changed. In subjects which follow a sequence such as mathematics, reading, and spelling, material taught at the beginning of 3rd grade might be moved to the end of 2nd grade, 8th grade topics might be taught in seventh grade, and so forth. In mathematics, for example, algebra might now begin in 7th grade, geometry in 8th or 9th, and probability and statistics (which is necessary for implementing statistical process control) might become a regular part of the high school curriculum. For students headed for college, the final two years would be given over to AP courses. College freshman would arrive much better prepared than they are now. A decision would have to be made whether (a) the bachelors degree should become a three year degree, (b) the number of credits for graduation should be increased, or (c) college courses should be made more rigorous with a corresponding reduction in the number of credits that students can carry per semester.

The Federal Government Role in Instigating a Lengthening of the School Year

A major increase in the length of the school year is unlikely to evolve without federal leadership and funding support. If one state were to try to do it alone, it would confront all sorts of difficulties. Standard textbooks would not fit the new curriculum and the per-pupil costs of curriculum revision would be very high. Graduates would be more productive workers, but one doubts that employers would pay graduates who attended school ten months a year a higher wage than graduates who attended nine months a year. While local public colleges could be expected to adapt, problems would arise when students attend college out-of-state.

The most significant barrier to this reform, however, is the cost. If teachers are to spend 11 percent more time teaching, yearly salaries must be increased by a comparable percentage. Since current public expenditures on elementary and secondary education were $156 billion in 1988 (U.S. Bureau of the Census 1989)—some of which would not have to be increased (e.g., central office staff already have 11 month contracts)—the taxpayer cost would be about $15 billion. This is not really as big a number as one might think. For comparison, between 1985 and 1988 total compensation of employees rose $73 billion in state and local government as a whole and rose $50 billion in the health care industry. Since more than half of the mothers of school children work, the savings in day care costs would be substantial. If one-fifth of the 45 million school children attending school an extra 20 days would have required day care costing $3.00 an hour for 6 hours a day, the savings would be $3.24 billion. If most teachers and students do not work in the summer, the increase in learning time would come primarily out of leisure, not work, time and GNP would increase. If GNP rises, taxes will rise as well, so the change would be partially self-financing.

The long term benefits would be very large. Because a longer school year reduces summer forgetting at the same time it increases learning time, it is quite possible that a more-than-proportionate learning response (on a grade level equivalent scale) would result. Let us, however, make the conservative assumption that the 11 percent increase in learning time increases 12th grade achievement (scaled in grade level equivalents) by 11 percent or 1.33 U.S. grade level equivalents. Student cohorts experiencing the longer school year for 13 years would have their compensation increased by about 5.6 percent or $896 a year.[8]

The productivity effects of test score increases are 50 percent larger than wage rate effects (Bishop 1987). Consequently, increasing the school year by 20 days is estimated to raise the productivity of the average adult by $1248 per year (7.7% of mean compensation). Since a one year age cohort contains 3.7 million people, the benefit is about $ 4.62 billion dollars per year. The yearly real rate of return is 30.7 percent on the taxpayer contribution to the additional learning investment.[9] Only investments in R&D have real rates of social return this high. If the real rate of social discount is 6 percent and the growth of labor productivity is projected at 2 percent per year, the ratio of present discounted benefits to costs is 4.9 to 1.[10] Even if the additional month of school produces only a third or a half month of learning gains, the investment has a higher payoff than most other uses of taxpayer dollars.

Voluntary Summer School

A variety of remedial, enrichment, and special interest short courses should be offered during the rest of the summer. While many of the teachers would

be regular school staff, an education degree and state certification would n
be required. Private teachers of music, art, athletics, and academic subjec
could also offer their own courses at the school. Where appropriate, academi
credit would be given for the summer school courses. The school district woul
provide transportation.

Generating Additional Recognition and Rewards for Learning

A Massive Dose of Mastery Learning

Students who are not learning at the desired rate should be expected t
commit additional time to the task after school and during the summer. A
the beginning of the school year school personnel would meet with the studen
and his or her parents to set goals. Students who are not performing at grad
level in core subjects and who do not make normal progress during the schoc
year should be kept after school for tutoring and remedial instruction an
required to attend summer school. Assessments of progress should be mad
at appropriate points during the school year to inform students of their progres
and to enable those who are participating in remedial programs after schoc
to demonstrate they are now progressing satisfactorily. Course grades an
teacher evaluations would be a central part of the assessment process, but ther
should be an external yardstick as well. The external yardstick might be
competency check list, a mastery test keyed to the textbook, or an exan
specified by the state, the school or collectively by the teachers in that grad
level or department. The assessment tools would be established at the beginnin
of the school year. The reason for the external yardstick is that it helps insur
that students perceive the standard to be absolute rather than relative to other
in the class, and it helps create a communality of interest between teacher an
student. Teachers need to be perceived as helping the student achieve th
student's goals not as judges meting out punishment. Final decisions regardin
who would be required to attend summer school could be made by committee
of teachers, possibly with some administrative representation. Because student
will want to avoid being required to get remedial instruction after school an
during the summer, this will be a powerful incentive for them to devot
themselves to their studies.

Acting as a Source of Informal Contacts

School personnel can be a reference and a source of job contacts for thei
students. Some students may feel that they do not have and cannot develop
good employment contacts. School personnel can help out by building and
maintaining trusting relationships with local employers and then helping to
match employer and student needs. Students from disadvantaged backgrounds

have special need for this kind of help, because their relatives and neighbors typically lack the employment contacts of middle-class families. Many schools provide job placement and referral services for their students and graduates. Three and a half million people found their current job through a referral by a teacher, school or college (Rosenfeld 1975). This function of schools is a lot more important than is generally thought.

Whenever possible, there should be a one-on-one relationship between a specific teacher or administrator and an employer. A study by McKinney et al. (1982) found that *when schools formalize this relationship by creating a placement office, the number of jobs found for vocational students tended to decrease.* The best example of an informal contact system is the one that exists for many vocational students. Vocational teachers often know local employers in related fields; they also know their students well enough to recommend them. This kind of informal system could be expanded to include all students not planning to attend college.

Developing a Job Search Portfolio

Schools should consider providing students with a job search portfolio or competency profile that records all their accomplishments in one place. Students attempting to market themselves to employers will have greater success if all their school achievements are summarized in one compact, standardized document. Compactness and standardization make it easier for employers to use information in their hiring decisions and this facilitates information flow.

The coverage and format of the document are probably best worked out cooperatively by a committee that includes school administrators, employers, and other interested parties. Developing and using such a document might be part of a campaign to enlist commitments from major local employers to hire the school's graduates. Developing the information system cooperatively is a good way to ensure that the finished form will be beneficial to schools, employers, and students.

Students have many talents and skills that can be highlighted in such a document. The job search portfolio should emphasize accomplishments and performance indicators that are most useful in identifying a good match between a job and a youth. Students and parents should receive copies of it, and students should be encouraged to bring copies with them when they apply for jobs. Employers should be encouraged to ask to see the portfolio and keep a copy when a job application is filed.

Honoring Academic Achievement

Schools should strengthen their awards and honors systems for academic and non-academic accomplishments. The medals, trophies, and school letters awarded in interscholastic athletics are a powerful motivator of achievement on the playing field. Academic pursuits need a similar system of reinforcement. Awards and honors systems should be designed so that almost every student can receive at least one award or honor before graduation if he or she makes the effort. Outstanding academic performance (e.g., high grades or high test scores) would not have to be the only way of defining excellence. Awards could be given for significant improvements in academic performance since the previous year or since the beginning of the school year, for public service in or out of school, for perfect attendance records, and for student of the week (criteria could vary weekly). The standard for making an award should be criterion referenced: if greater numbers achieve the standard of excellence, more awards should be given.

A prominent place in the school should be reserved for bulletin boards where pictures of the most recent winners and reasons for their receiving recognition could be posted. Another form of recognition could be displays of student work: art, science, social studies, vocational education projects, and so forth. Periodically, the parents of the most recent award winners and sponsoring teachers should be invited to an evening assembly at which time the principal would award the students the certificate or plaque recognizing their accomplishments.

Award Scholarships on the Basis of Past Academic Achievement as Well as Need

At present, almost all grant aid for attending college is awarded on the basis of financial need. Athletic achievement also results in generous scholarships for attending state universities. Academic achievement does not. A balance needs to be restored. States should either start or expand existing scholarship programs which award grants on the basis of academic achievements assessed by criteria that are external to school such as the Advanced Placement exams, Westinghouse Science Competitions and statewide Vocational-Industrial Club Competitions, New York State Regents Exams or the national examination proposed in Goals 2000. These scholarships should not be awarded on the basis of rank in class or GPA, for this pits students from the same school against each other and results in peer norms which scorn the student who spends his or her time studying. Aptitude test scores should also not be used to make scholarship awards. The purpose of scholarships is to reward effort and accomplishment, not talent or IQ.

League Competitions between Schools in the Academic Arena

Band and athletic programs receive very generous support from the community because the band and the team are viewed as representing the entire high school to neighboring communities and the rest of the state and because their accomplishments are highly visible. A similar spirit of competition between communities needs to be developed in the academic arena. States should establish a system of highly visible competitions for each academic subject and for extracurricular activities like debate, inventions club, Junior Achievement, school newspaper, and the stock market game. As many students as possible should participate. This can be accomplished by arranging separate competitions for each grade, requiring (where possible) the school to field a team that includes all students taking a particular course and having the share of the student body that is on the team be one of the criteria by which schools are judged. As in sports, fair competition can be insured by placing small schools and schools serving disadvantaged populations in a separate league or by establishing a handicapping system.

The competitions should not be a glorified *Trivial Pursuits* game. While cable TV broadcasts of High School Bowl like contests might be a component of the program, most of the points obtained by a school's team should come from assessments of the performance of the entire team on authentic tasks like writing an essay, giving a speech, determining the chemical composition of a compound, working out long mathematics problems, writing a computer program, or fixing a car. As much as possible the tasks should be aligned with the state curriculum for that subject. Teams should consist of entire classrooms of students, and everyone on the team should receive gaudy tee shirts proclaiming membership on the school's team.

Winning schools and departments should receive a silver cup symbolizing their victory and a sum equal to $100 per team member that can be used the following year for materials and travel. A celebration dance for the entire school might be organized and paid for by a special prize fund. Members of teams placing in the top ten percent of their league would be recognized at an evening assembly, receive school sweaters or jackets proclaiming their victory and a $100 scholarship. These competitions could also serve as a basis for individual recognition and scholarships.

EFFECTS OF PROPOSED REFORMS ON UNDER-REPRESENTED MINORITIES

The two blue ribbon commissions that have recommended improvements in the signaling of academic achievement to colleges and employers included substantial representation from the minority community.[11] Nevertheless, the reader may be wondering about the likely impacts of the reform proposals just described on the labor market chances of minority youth. Because minority students receive lower scores on achievement tests, it might appear at first glance that greater emphasis on academic achievement will inevitably reduce their access to good colleges and to good jobs. This is not the case, however, for four reasons.

If academic achievement becomes a more important basis for selecting students and workers, something else becomes less important. The consequences for minorities of greater emphasis on academic achievement depends on the nature of the criterion that becomes de-emphasized. Substituting academic achievement tests for aptitude tests in college admissions *improves minority access* because minority-majority differentials tend to be smaller (in standard deviation units) on achievement tests (e.g., the NAEP reading and math tests) than on aptitude tests (e.g., the SAT). Greater emphasis on academic achievement *improves the access of women* to high level professional, technical, craft, and managerial jobs because it substitutes a criterion on which women do well for criteria—sex stereotyped beliefs about which jobs are appropriate for women—which have excluded women in the past.

For the same reason, greater emphasis on academic achievement when selecting young workers will not reduce minority access to jobs if it substitutes for other criteria which also place minority youth at a serious disadvantage. The current system in which there is almost no use of employment tests and little signaling of high school achievements to the labor market clearly has not generated jobs for minority youth. In October of each year from 1985 to 1988, only 45 percent of the previous spring's black high school graduates not attending college were employed (Bureau of Labor Statistics 1989). One reason why minority youth do poorly in the labor market is that most of the criteria now used to make selections—previous work experience, recommendations from previous employers, having family friends or relatives at the firm, proximity of one's residence to stores which hire youth, performance in interviews, and prejudices and stereotypes—work against them. These criteria will diminish in importance as academic achievement becomes more important. There is no way of knowing whether the net result of these shifts will help or hinder minority youth seeking employment. In some models of the labor market the relative position of minority workers improves when academic achievement is better signaled (Aigner and Cain 1977).

The second way in which minority youth may benefit from improved signaling of school achievements is that it will give recent high school graduates, both black and white, the first real chance to compete for high-wage, high-training content jobs. At present all youth are frozen out of these jobs because primary labor market employers seldom consider job applicants who lack considerable work experience. Experience is considered essential, partly because it contributes to productivity but also because it produces signals of competence and reliability that employers use to identify who is most qualified. Recent high school graduates have no such record, and information on the student's high school performance is not available; so the entire graduating class appears to employers as one undifferentiated mass of unskilled and undisciplined workers. A black personnel director interviewed for a CBS special on the educational reform proudly stated, "We don't hire high school graduates any more, we need **skilled workers**"(CBS, September 6, 1990). Surely this generalization does not apply to every graduate, but those who are disciplined and have skills currently have no way of signaling this fact to employers. State exams, competency portfolios and informative graduation credentials would change this unfair situation and give students a way of demonstrating that the stereotype does not apply to them. Young people from minority backgrounds must overcome even more virulent stereotypes, and they often lack a network of adult contacts who can provide job leads and references. By helping them overcome these barriers to employment, competency portfolios are of particular help to minority youth.

The third way in which these proposals will assist minority students is by encouraging greater numbers of firms to undertake affirmative action recruitment. The creation of a competency portfolio data bank that can be used by employers seeking qualified minority job candidates would greatly reduce the costs and increase the effectiveness of affirmative action programs. Affirmative action has significantly improved minority representation in managerial and professional occupations and has contributed to a substantial increase in the payoff to schooling for blacks (Freeman 1981). One of the reasons why it has been particularly effective in this labor market is that college reputations, transcripts and placement offices provide brokering and pre-screening services which significantly lower the costs of recruiting minority job candidates. The competency portfolio data bank would extend low cost brokering and pre-screening services to the labor market for high school graduates. The creation of such a data bank would almost certainly generate a great deal of competition for the more qualified minority youth in the portfolio bank.

The final and most important way in which these reforms will benefit minority youth is by bringing about improvements in academic achievement and productivity on the job. Student incentives to study hard, parental incentives to demand a better education, and teacher incentives to both give more and expect more from students will all be strengthened. Because of the way affirmative action is likely to interact with a competency profile data bank, the rewards for learning will become particularly strong for minority students. Learning will improve and the gap between minority and majority achievement will diminish. Society has been making considerable progress in closing achievement gaps between minority and majority students. In the early National Assessment of Educational Progress (NAEP) assessments, black high school seniors born between 1952 and 1957 were 6.7 grade level equivalents behind their white counterparts in science proficiency, 4 grade level equivalents behind in mathematics, and 5.3 grade level equivalents behind in reading. The most recent National Assessment data for 1986 reveal that for blacks born in 1969, the gap has been cut to 5.6 grade level equivalents in science, 2.9 grade level equivalents in math, and 2.6 grade level equivalents in reading. Koretz's analysis of data from state testing programs supports the NAEP findings (Koretz et al. 1986). Hispanic students are also closing the achievement gap. These positive trends suggest that despite their limited funding, Head Start, Title I, and other compensatory interventions have had an impact. The schools attended by most minority students are still clearly inferior to those attended by white students, so further reductions in the school quality differentials can be expected to produce further reductions in academic achievement differentials.

The students of James A. Garfield High School's Advanced Placement calculus classes have demonstrated to the nation what minority students from economically disadvantaged backgrounds can accomplish. The Garfield student body is made up predominantly of disadvantaged minorities; yet in 1987 only three high schools in the nation (Alhambra High School in California and Bronx Science and Stuvesant High School in New York City) had a larger number of students taking the AP calculus exam. This high school and its two very talented calculus teachers, Jaime Escalante and Ben Jimenez, are responsible for 17 percent of all Mexican Americans taking the AP calculus exam and 32 percent of all Mexican Americans who pass the more difficult BC form of the test (Matthews 1988). There is no secret about how they did it; they worked extremely hard. Students signed a contract committing themselves to extra homework and extra time in school, and they lived up to the commitment. This success establishes that minority youngsters can be persuaded to study just as hard as the academic track students in Europe and that if they do they will achieve at world class levels. The success at Garfield High is replicable.

POSTLUDE

Institutional arrangements of schools and the labor market have profound effects on the incentives faced by students, teachers, parents, and school administrators. The passivity and inattention of students, the low morale of teachers, the defeat of so many school levies, and low rankings on international measures of achievement are all logical outcomes of institutional arrangements which weaken student incentives to study and parental incentives to fund a high quality education. Only with an effective system of rewards within schools and in the labor market can we hope to overcome the pervasive apathy and achieve excellence.

APPENDIX

The Summer Drop Off in Student Performance

Studies which have administered mathematics tests to students both in the spring and the fall of a calendar year find that mathematics competence declines

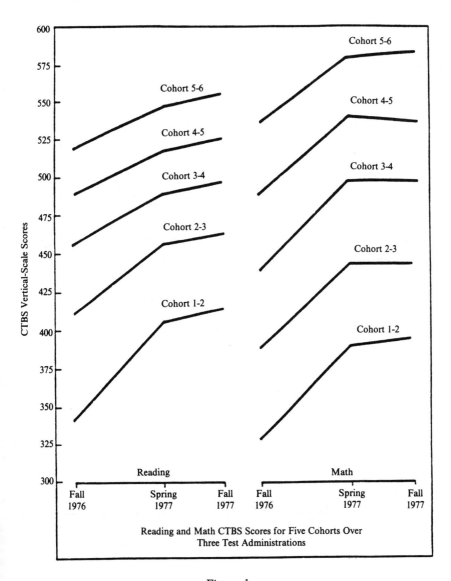

Figure 1

during the summer months (Heyns 1987). Entwisle and Alexander's (1989, Table 1) study of 1st and 2nd graders in Baltimore, for example, found no gain in mathematics skills between the April test administration and the October test administration, even though that period contained two full months of classroom study of arithmetic.

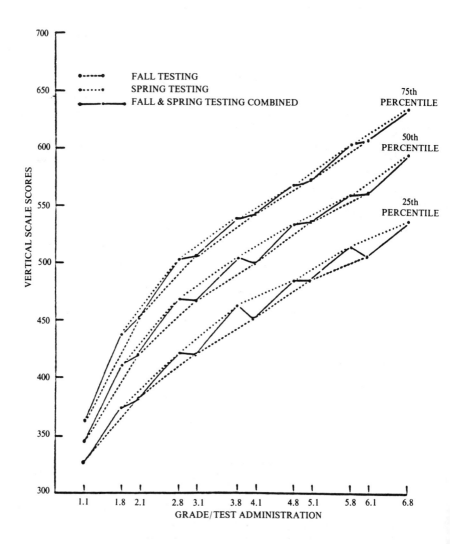

Note: The spring-to-fall differences are always associated with cross-sectional changes in samples and are frequently also associated with differences in test levels. Negative 'growth', when it occurs, may be attributed to sample differences and test-level differences. When raw scores are compared for the same test levels, the differences are either positive or small when negative. Therefore, the ziz-zag nature of the curves above should not be carelessly attributed to 'summer drop-off'.

Source: Hemenway et al. (1978, Figure 1-1, p. 29).

Figure 2. Vertical Scale Scores as a Function of Grade Level by Quartiles for the Debiased CTBS Reading Test

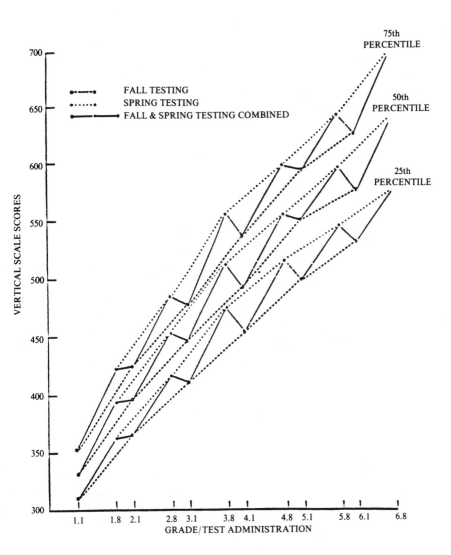

Note: The spring-to-fall differences are always associated with cross-sectional changes in samples and are frequently also associated with differences in test levels. Negative 'growth', when it occurs, may be attributed to sample differences and test-level differences. When raw scores are compared for the same test levels, the differences are either positive or small when negative. Therefore, the ziz-zag nature of the curves above should not be carelessly attributed to 'summer drop-off'.

Source: Hemenway et al. (1978, Figure 1-2, p. 30).

Figure 3. Vertical Scale Scores as a Function of Grade Level by Quartiles for the Debiased CTBS Math Test

In the Sustaining Effects Study, the beginning-of-the-year test was administered during the third week of school and the end-of-year test was administered five weeks before the end of the term. Consequently, the school year testing period was only 7 months long and the 5 month "summer gap" between spring and fall testing contained 2 months of school learning time. As one can see in Figure 1, gains in reading slow considerably during the 5 month summer gap period, and math competence hardly rises at all (Klibanoff and Haggart 1981). If children were learning during the 2 months of classes included in the summer gap period at anything like the rate they learn during the rest of the school year, their reading and math skills must have declined during the summer months. In most classrooms the first few weeks are spent reviewing and practicing skills taught in previous years. Old material can probably be relearned at a more rapid rate than new material is learned, so this is likely to be a period of particularly rapid rise in test scores. The most reasonable assumption is that learning rates during school time are constant. Figures 2 and 3 (taken from Hemenway et al. 1978) present the results of calculating learning trajectories and the 3 month summer drop off under the assumption of constant learning rates during the school year.

Direct evidence on this issue can be found in the evaluation of STEP. In this study the pre-test was administered after the end of school in June and the post-test prior to the beginning of school in the fall. In this study the control group which received no instruction during the summer experienced very large declines in mathematics and substantial declines in reading (Sipe, Grossman, and Milliner 1988).

ACKNOWLEDGMENTS

The research that culminated in the paper was sponsored by the Center for Advanced Human Resource Studies, the National Center on the Educational Quality of the Workforce, the National Center for Research in Vocational Education and the Secretary of Labor's Commission on Workforce Quality and Labor Market Efficiency. I would like to thank Peter Mueser, Richard Murnane and James Rosenbaum for helpful comments on earlier versions of the paper. This paper has not undergone formal review or approval of the faculty of the ILR school. It is intended to make results of Center research available to others interested in human resource management in preliminary form to encourage discussion and suggestions.

NOTES

1. Estimates of average total compensation of teachers in the United States were obtained by multiplying teacher salaries derived from NEA data by the ratio of compensation to wages and salaries in the public education sector, 1.25, from the national income accounts. The data on average compensation in other countries is from UNESCO Statistical Yearbook, 1985 and

1986. Purchasing power parity exchange rates were calculated by Professor Robert Sommers from OECD data. See Barro and Suter (1988).

2.   In game theory language, we have here a repeated game in which players may make side payments using the currency of friendship. Parents and college admissions officers (but not employers) offer prizes to those who do best in the academic game, but if everyone improves together the total amount of prize money does not rise. Some players are offered larger prizes than others. For most players the offered prizes are small by comparison to the costs of hard study and the side payments available from peers. The result is that only a few students (those facing the biggest prizes and the smallest costs of study) choose the non-cooperative solution and the great majority of students choose the cooperative, "let's all take it easy," solution.

3.   After a worker has been at a firm a while, the employer presumably learns more about the individual's capabilities and is able to observe performance on the job. Workers assigned to the same job often produce very different levels of output. (Hunter, Schmidt, and Judiesch 1988). Why, one might ask, are the most productive workers (those with just the right mix of specific competencies) not given large wage increases reflecting their higher productivity? The reason appears to be that workers and employers prefer employment contracts which offer only modest adjustments of relative wages in response to perceived differences in relative productivity. There are a number of good reasons for this preference: the unreliability of the feasible measures of individual productivity (Hashimoto and Yu 1980), risk aversion on the part of workers (Stiglitz 1974), productivity differentials that are specific to the firm (Bishop 1987a), the desire to encourage cooperation among coworkers (Lazear 1989) and union preferences for pay structures which limit the power of supervisors. In addition, compensation for differences in job performance may be non-pecuniary—praise from one's supervisor, more relaxed supervision, or a high rank in the firm's social hierarchy (Frank 1984). A study of how individual wage rates varied with initial job performance found that when people hired for the same or very familiar jobs are compared, someone who is 20 percent more productive than average is typically paid only 1.6 percent more. After a year at a firm, better producers received only a 4 percent higher wage at nonunion firms with about 20 employees, and they had no wage advantage at unionized establishments with more than 100 employees or at nonunion establishments with more than 400 employees (Bishop 1987a). If relative wage rates only partially compensate the most capable workers in a job for their greater productivity, why don't they obtain promotions or switch to better paying firms? To some degree they do, particularly in managerial and professional occupations. This explains why workers who score high on tests and/or get good grades are less likely to be unemployed and more likely to be promoted, and why many years after graduation they eventually obtain higher wage rates (Wise 1975; Bishop 1989). Since, however, worker productivity cannot be measured accurately and cannot be signaled reliably to other employers, this sorting process is slow and only partially effective. Consequently, when men and women under the age of 30 are studied, the wage rate effects of specific competencies may not correspond to their true effects on productivity; and, therefore, direct evidence on productivity effects of specific competencies is required before conslusions may be drawn.

4.   The Survey was of a stratified random sample of the NFIB membership. Larger firms had a significantly higher probability of being selected for the study. The response rate to the mail survey was 20 percent and the number of usable responses was 2014.

5.   EEOC regulations evolved out of the Supreme Court's 1971 *Griggs* vs *Duke Power* decision interpreting Congressional intent in Title VII of the Civil Rights Act. These regulations made the use of employment selection tests measuring competence in reading and mathematics prohibitively expensive. Before such a test could be used, the firm had to conduct a very expensive validity study of the proposed test and alternative tests at their own work sites. Separate studies had to be done for men and women, blacks, hispanics, and whites. Most firms did not have enough workers in each category to do a reliable study. Litigation costs and the potential liability are enormous, so companies became extremely cautious about testing. The result has been to greatly diminish the use of tests for employee selection.

6.   Another possible argument against policies designed to induce employers to reward high school students who study is that poor students will not be considered if an employer learns of this fact. What those who make this argument do not realize is that the policy of providing no information to employers about performance in high school results in no recent graduates (whether good or poor student) getting a job that pays well and offers opportunities for training and promotions. In effect it is being proposed that the interests of the students who do not study and are discipline problems should take precedence over the interests of the students who lived by the schools rules and studied hard. There is nothing unfair about letting high school GPA's influence the allocation of young people to the best jobs. The GPA's are an average which reflects performance on hundreds of tests and the evaluations of over 20 teachers each of which is based on 180 days of interaction. Selection decisions must be made somehow. If measures of performance in school are not available, the hiring selection will be determined by the chemistry of a job interview and idiosyncratic recommendations of a single previous employer. Since many employers will not request the information, providing information on student performance does not prevent the poorer student from getting a job; it only influences the quality of the job that the student is able to get.

7.   This proposal sounds radical but, in fact, is only a modest change from current practice at these selective colleges. A survey of college placement officials conducted by *USA Today* and interviews of officials at Cornell and SUNY Binghamton conducted for this paper found that students were expected to take AP courses if they are offered and grade point averages were adjusted for the difficulty level of the courses taken. High school students and parents are generally unaware of this policy, however, and many have not factored it into their high school course selections. The announcement, therefore, has two effects; it informs students and parents of existing admissions policies and warns that come 1998 those seeking admission to selective colleges will not necessarily be held harmless if a local high school does not offer AP courses. This announcement will generate strong political pressure on principals and school boards to expand their AP program and allow additional students to take AP courses. Students at schools not offering AP might be offered other ways of demonstrating college level proficiency such as an AP independent study option, taking courses during the summer at a local college, or high schools on the afternoon subject matter SAT exams or New York State Regents exams. Exceptions would have to be made for students from under represented minorities, foreign students and in other individual cases but expectations should not become the rule.

8.   A one population standard deviation increase in test scores raises an adult's wage rate by 21 percent. A population standard deviation is equivalent to about 5 grade level equivalents, so the wage effect is 5.6 percent $= (1.33/5)$ x 21 percent. The mean yearly compensation of adults 18 to 65 years old is about \$16,000 when the nonemployed are included in the denominator, so the dollar impact is \$896 $= .056$ x \$16,000.

9.   Our estimate of the productivity benefit of a 1.33 grade level equivalent increase in achievement is very conservative. College graduation raises wages of males by 50 percent or by 12.5 percent per year of college. If one were to assume instead that 13 months of additional time in elementary and secondary school is equivalent to a year in college, the estimated productivity benefit triples to 12.5 percent. In addition the social costs of adding 20 days to the school calendar are probably smaller than \$15 billion, for child care costs will be substantially reduced. Although 16-18 year olds will be earning less during the summer this effect is substantially smaller than the savings in child care costs. It should be noted that student leisure time is significantly reduced and that except for the lost work time of teenagers this is not counted as cost. This is standard operating procedure when doing benefit-cost studies of educational interventions.

10.   The present value of the benefits in year 0 of \$4.62 billion a year starting in year 13 and running to year 60 are \$4.62(25)(.853)(.588) $=$ \$57.94 billion. The present value of costs are (\$15/13)25(1-.588) $=$ \$11.88 billion.

11.   The Commission on Workforce Quality and Labor Market Efficiency included in its membership Constance E. Clayton, Superintendent of Schools of Philadelphia; Jose I. Lozano,

Publisher of *La Opinion*, William J. Wilson, author of The Truly Disadvantaged. The Commission on the Skills of the American Workforce included in its membership Eleanor Holmes Norton, former Chairwomen of the Equal Employment Opportunity Commission; John E. Jacob, President of the National Urban League, Badi Foster, President of Aetna Institute for Corporate Education; Thomas Gonzales, Chancellor of Seattle Community College District VI; Anthony J. Trujillo, Superintendent of Sweetwater Union High School District.

REFERENCES

Aigner, D. and G. Cain. 1977. "Statistical Theories of Discrimination in Labor Markets." *Industrial and Labor Relations Review*, 175-87.

American Association for the Advancement of Science. 1989. *Science for All Americans*. Washington, DC: American Association for the Advancement of Science.

Barro, S. and L. Suter. 1988. "International Comparisons of Teachers' Salaries: An Exploratory Study." National Center for Education Statistics, Table 5.

Beicht, N.I., G. Boll, W. Malcher, and S. Wiederhold-Fritz. 1984. Nettakosten der Betrieblichen Ber Ufsbildung Schriften Berufsbildungsforschung, Band 63. Beuth Verlag GMBH, Berlin.

Berlin, G. and A. Sum. 1988. *Toward a More Perfect Union: Basic Skills, Poor Families, and our Economic Future*. Ford Foundation Project on Social Welfare and the American Future. New York: Ford Foundation.

Bishop, J. 1985. Preparing Youth for Employment. Columbus, OH: The National Center for Research in Vocational Education.

_____. 1987a. "The Recognition and Reward of Employee Performance." *Journal of Labor Economics* 5 (4): S36-S56.

_____. 1987b. "Information Externalities and the Social Payoff to Academic Achievement." Center for Advanced Human Resource Studies Working Paper #87-06, Cornell University. Ithica, New York.

_____. 1989a. "Is the Test Score Decline Responsible for the Productivity Growth Decline?" *American Economic Review* 79 (1).

_____. 1989b. "The Productivity Consequences of What is Learned in High School." *Journal of Curriculum Studies* 22 (2): 101-126.

Bureau of Labor Statistics. 1989. " Nearly Three-Fifths of the High School Graduates of 1988 Enrolled in College." USDL 89-308.

Carroll, S. 1982. "The Search for Equity in School Finance." Pp. 237-266 in *Financing Education: Overcoming Inefficiency and Inequity*, edited by Walter McMahon and Terry Geske, Urbana, IL: University of Illinois Press.

Cain, G. and A. Goldberger. 1983. "Public and Private Schools Revisited." *Sociology of Education* 56, 208-218.

Commission on the Skills of the American Workforce. 1990 . Pp. 69-70 in *America's Choice: High Skills or Low Wages!* Rochester, NY: National Center on Education and the Economy.

Commission on Workforce Quality and Labor Market Efficiency. 1989. *Investing in People: A Strategy to Adress America's Workforce Crisis*. Washington, DC: Department of Labor.

Cooper, H. M. 1989. *Homework*. White Plains, NY: Longman.

Entwisle, D. and K. Alexander. 1989. *Issues of Inequality and Children's Transition to Full-time Schooling*. Baltimore, MD: John Hopkins University.

Frank, R. 1984. "Are Workers Paid Their Marginal Product?" *American Economic Review* 74(4): 549-571.

Frederick, W., H. Walberg, and S. Rasher. 1979. "Time, Teacher Comments, and Achievement in Urban High Schools." *Journal of Educational Research* 73(2): 63-65.

Freeman, R. 1981. "Black Economic Progress after 1964: Who has Gained and Why." In *Studies in Labor Markets,* edited by Sherwin Rosen. Chicago, IL: University of Chicago Press.

College Board. 1988. *AP Yearbook.* New York: College Entrance Examination Board.

Goodlad, J. 1983. *A Place Called School.* New York: McGraw-Hill.

Grossman, S. and Millner. 1988. *Summer Training and Education Program: Report on the 1987 Experience.*

Hashimoto, M., and B. Yu. 1980. "Specific Capital, Employment and Wage Rigidity." *Bell Journal of Economics* 2, 536-549.

Hemenway, J.A., M. Wang, C.E. Kenoyer, R. Hoepfner, M.B. Bear, and G. Smith. 1978. The Measures and Variables of the Sustaining Effects Study, Technical Report #9. Santa Monica, CA: Systems Development Corporation.

Heyns, B. 1986. "Summer Programs and Compensatory Education: The Future of an Idea." Prepared for the Office of Educational Research and Improvement, Chapter One Study Team, Conference on the Effects of Alternative Designs in Compensatory Education Washington, DC. New York University.

————. 1987. Schooling and Cognitive Development: Is There a Season for Learning." *Child Development* 58 (5):1151-1160.

Hollenbeck, K., and B. Smith. 1984. *The Influence of Applicants' Education and Skills on Employability Assessments by Employers.* Columbus, OH: The Ohio State University.

Hunter, J.E., J.J. Crosson, and D.H. Friedman. 1985. *The Validity of the Armed Services Vocational Aptitude Battery (ASVAB) For Civilian and Military Job Performance.* Washington, DC: Department of Defence.

Hunter, J.E., F. Schmidt, and M.K. Judiesch. 1988. *Individual Differences in Output as a Function of Job Complexity.* University of Iowa: Department of Industrial Relations and Human Resources.

International Association for the Evaluation of Educational Achievement. 1988a. *Science Achievement in Seventeen Nations.* New York: Pergamon Press.

International Association for the Evaluation of Educational Achievement. 1988b. *The Underachieving Curriculum, Assessing U.S. School Mathematics from an International Perspective.* Champaign, IL: Stipes Publishing Company.

Jencks, C. and J. Crouse. 1982. "Aptitude vs. Achievement: Should We Replace the SAT?" *The Public Interest.*

Juster, T. and F. Strafford. 1990. *The Allocation of Time: Empirical Findings, Behavioral Models and Problems of Measurement.* Ann Arbor, MI: Survey Research Center, Institute for Social Research.

Kliobanoff, L., and S. Haggart. 1981. *Summer Growth and the Effectiveness of Summer School.* Report No. 8 from the Study of Sustaining Effects of Compensatory Education on Basic Skills, RMC Research Corporation.

Koretz, D., N. Mead, and G. Phillips. 1986. *Trends in Educational Achievement.* Washington: Congressional Budget Office.

Kosters, M. 1989a. "Wages and Demographics." Paper presented at Wages in the 1980's, November 3, conference sponsored by the American Enterprise Institute.

Lapointe, A. 1989. *A World of Differences.* Princeton, NJ: Educational Testing Service.

Lazear, E.P. 1989. "Pay Equality and Industrial Politics."

Lee, S., and Stigler. "Mathematics Achievement of Chinese, Japanese & American Children."

Longitudinal Survey of American Youth. 1988. *Data File User's Manual.* Dekalb, IL: Public Opinion Laboratory.

Matthews, J. 1988. *Escalante: The Best Teacher in America.* New York: Henry Holt.

McKinney, F., S. Franchhak, I. Halasz, I. Morrison, and P. Fornash. 1982. *Factors Relatiing to the Job Placement of Former Secondary Vocational Educational Students.* Columbus, OH: The National Center for Research in Vocational Education, The Ohio State University.

Mischel, L. and M.E. Rasell. 1990. "Does the U.S. Spend More on Education?" *Testimony before the House Committee on Education and Labor.* Washington, DC: Economic Policy Institute.

National Assessment of Educational Progress, 1986. *The Reading Report Card.* Princeton, NJ: Educational Testing Service.

————. 1988a. *The Mathematics Report Card.* Princeton, NJ: Educational Testing Service.

————. 1990. *Accelerating Achievement.* Princeton, NJ: Educational Testing Service.

National Council of Teachers of Mathematics. 1989. *Curriculum Evaluation Standards for School Mathematics.* Washington, DC: National Council of Teachers of Mathematics.

Noah, H.J. and M.A. Eckstein. 1988. "Tradeoffs in Examination Policies: An International Perspective." Paper presented at the annual meeting of the British Comparative and International Education Society, University of Bristol.

Organization for Economic Cooperation and Development. 1986. "Living Conditions in OECD Countries: A Compendium of Social Indicators." Social Policy Studies 3. Paris France: Organization for Economic Co-Operation and Development.

Perry, N. J. 1989. "The New Improved Vocational School." *Fortune* 127-138.

Powell, A., E. Farrar, and D. Cohen. 1985. *The Shopping Mall High School.* New York: Houghton Mifflin.

Pressey, S. and F. Robinson. 1944. *Psychology and New Education.* New York: Harper and Brothers Publication.

Public Broadcasting System. 1989. "Learning in America."

Robitaille, D.F. and R.A. Garden. 1989. *The IEA Study of Mathematics II: Contexts and Outcomes of School Mathematics.* New York: Pergamon Press.

Roper, J. 1989. "Technology Creates a New Physics Student." *The Physics Teacher* 26-28.

Rosenfeld, C. 1975. "Job Seeking Methods Used by American Workers." *Monthly Labor Review* 98 (8): 39-42.

Rosenbaum, J. 1990. *Do School Achievements Affect the Early Jobs of High School Graduates? Results from the High School and Beyond Surveys in the US and Japan.* Evanston, IL: Northwestern University.

Rosenbaum, J.E. and T. Kariya. 1989. "From High School to Work: Market and Institutional Mechanisms in Japan." *American Journal of Sociology* 94 (6): 1334-1365.

Sipe, C., J. Grossman, and J. Milliner. 1988. *Summer Training and Education Program: Report on the 1987 Experience.* Philadelphia, PA: Public/Private Ventures.

Sizer, T.R. 1984. *Horace's Compromise: The Dilemma of the American High School.* Boston: Houghton Mifflin.

Stevenson, H., S.Y. Lee, and J.W. Stigler. 1986. "Mathematics Achievement of Chinese,Japanese & American Children." *Science* 231, 693-699.

Stiglitz, J. 1974. "Risk Sharing and Incentives in Sharecropping." *Review of Economic Studies* 61, 2.

Tsang, M.C. and H. Levin. "The Impact of Intergovernmental Grants on Educational Expenditure." *Review of Educational Research* 53 (3): 329-367.

U.S. Bureau of the Census. 1989. *Statistical Abstract.* Washington, DC: US Government Printing Office.

U.S. Bureau of the Census. 1967. *Characteristics of Men with College Degrees: Current Population Reports, Population Characteristics,* Series P20, No. 201, p. 23.

U.S. Bureau of the Census. 1984. *Current Population Reports, Series P-70, No. 11, What's It Worth? Educational Background and Economic Status.* Washington, DC: U.S. Government Printing Office.

U.S. Bureau of Labor Statistics. 1989. *Nearly Three-fifths of the High School Graduates of 1988 Enrolled in College.* USDL.

U.S. Department of Education. 1990. *Digest of Educational Statistics.*

Williams, E. 1982. "Current Use of Tests for Employment." *Ability Testing: Uses, Consequences, and Controversies,* Part 11: Documentation Section.

Wise, D.A. 1975. "Academic Achievement and Job Performance." *The American Economic Review* 65 (3): 350-366.

COMMENTS

George P. White

FOCUSING EDUCATIONAL REFORM

In "What's Wrong with American Secondary Schools: Can State Governments Fix It?" John Bishop clearly demonstrates that American students are ill-prepared to function successfully in a global society. He outlines what he believes to be the root causes of this sad state of affairs. His list includes: the lack of effort on the part of students, parents and the community; the absence of tangible rewards for excellence; and the lack of an effective and efficient method of assessing what students have learned and what they can do.

For each of the identified problem areas Bishop proposes a detailed set of solutions. He suggests that more homework be assigned; better assessment systems be developed; employers demonstrate a clearer linkage between success in school and higher wages; more courses be developed that integrate learning across disciplines; and advanced placement courses be required for admittance to college. Viewed collectively these and the other suggestions proposed present the beginnings of a well-developed plan for school reform.

I have no quarrel with Bishop's assertion that American education is not meeting the needs of our global society; the data he provides makes this fact very clear. Nor do I quarrel with his proposed outline of solutions. What concerns me, however, is that he has failed to address the key cause of these problems—the governance of education in this country. In order to have a major impact under our current system of education, Bishop's reform plan, or the countless other plans that have been proposed, must occur simultaneously in over 16,000 individual school districts. Each of these districts has its own governance board consisting of from five to nine lay community leaders, its own educational agenda, and its own political problems. These districts are organized in a loosely-coupled fashion under the direction of 50 state education bureaucracies—again with their own agenda, structure, and political realities. This system of organization creates a fragmentation of purpose, a lack of clear vision, and a diffusion of leadership resulting in the semi-organized anarchy of our educational program.

What is needed in order for *real* educational reform to be implemented is a unified nationalized educational policy. It must be a policy that establishes a clear sense of purpose for education in the United States. It must also be a policy that outlines the critical competencies to be learned by all students and develops a national assessment system to measure results. First steps in the development of this policy have already begun with the establishment of a set of national educational goals set down by the fifty state governors at the 1989 Education Summit. Further steps must be taken, however, in order to insure that community representatives, business and industry leaders, and local, state, and national educational specialists are involved in the process of developing a clear mission statement which outlines specific goals to be achieved. This task can be accomplished through a series of town meetings and regional forums which will serve to broaden the awareness of the educational problems we face and provide ample opportunity for citizen participation.

Once the mission statement and goals have been established, federal resources should be targeted to developing a nationalized core curriculum which *all* students would be expected to master. In addition, resources would be directed to developing a comprehensive multifaceted program to determine what students have learned and what they can do. Currently each school district chooses which standardized test it will use. In most cases these tests show little correlation with the written or taught curriculum presented in the district. Under a nationalized policy student assessment would be content-specific, would occur on a yearly cycle, and could require each student to develop a portfolio of his/her work products similar to those that art students now maintain. Because the system would be consistent across the country, employers would be able to use the results to determine the skills and competencies of prospective employees in specific areas and then use this information for employment and salary decisions, as proposed by Bishop.

The national policy should focus only on outcomes and be production oriented. The local education agency (school or school district) should have the responsibility to determine the process to be used in order to meet the outcome standards. The school would have maximum flexibility under this restructured schema to identify and develop the necessary programs and support systems in order to insure that all students meet the established standards. Federal and state resources would be targeted to systems demonstrating the greatest need. In addition, a state or federal takeover option should be developed in order to address the needs of those systems having students who continually fail to achieve the core competencies.

This shifting of responsibility for the governance of education will take time, hard work, and, above all, visionary leadership. However, without this fundamental change and other equally drastic changes, the proposals put forth by Bishop and other school reform specialists will not have the intended impact of reestablishing the United States as an educational leader. Continuing the current system is the same as putting new wine in old bottles: the look may change but the taste remains the same.

COLLECTIVE BARGAINING AMIDST EDUCATION REFORM

Samuel B. Bacharach, David Lipsky,
and Joseph Shedd

INTRODUCTION

It is increasingly clear that the prospects for educational reform in America and the future of collective bargaining in public education are closely intertwined and becoming more so. The authors of this paper attempt to provide a framework for understanding both sets of developments and their interrelationships. Tracing the evolution of the current reform movement, then discussing the origins of the present system of bargaining in public education, we argue that reformers and bargainers alike are beginning to grapple with the same realities: new issues and new kinds of power that are inherent in the changing labor and product markets, work processes and management systems of public education itself.

As we will note, the present system of collective bargaining in public education was patterned largely after the top-down management ideology that was ascendant in education when teacher unions first won recognition. The basic dilemma for school managers and teacher unions alike is that there has never been anything but an imperfect match between that management ideology and the basic work processes and public expectations in most school systems. Frustration with this dilemma is one of the factors that has prompted teacher unions to abandon the reactive approach that industrial unions have typically followed and prompted them to join, as active participants, the debate over how school systems should be managed.[1]

WAVES OF REFORM

When Terrell Bell came to Washington in 1981 to become Ronald Reagan's first Secretary of Education, he expected to stay just long enough to fulfill one of President Reagan's campaign pledges: the dismantling of the Department of Education. But complaints were mounting about the quality of education in this country, and these complaints captured Secretary Bell's full attention. In short order Bell formulated a proposal to establish a National Commission on Excellence in Education, obtained the President's support for his proposal, and proceeded to appoint the members of the commission.

The result of the commission's work, of course, was the now famous report, *A Nation at Risk,* published in April, 1983. In the most frequently quoted passage in the report, the commission said, "The educational foundations of our society are presently being eroded by a rising tide of mediocrity.... If an unfriendly foreign power had attempted to impose on America the mediocre educational performance that exists today, we might well have viewed it as an act of war" (National Commission on Excellence in Education 1983). The commission documented many signs of mediocre performance, such as declining scores on standardized tests, persistently high dropout rates, and a growing level of functional illiteracy.

On the basis of its findings, the commission then made many recommendations: reforming curricula (more English, math, and science), lengthening the school day (to seven hours) and the school year (to at least 200 days), relying more on standardized tests, improving student discipline policies, and raising college admissions standards. Its recommendations on teachers' pay proved to be especially controversial. It advocated not only substantially increasing teacher salaries, but abandoning the traditional teacher salary schedule in favor of a system of merit pay, and developing career ladders and master teacher plans.

The publication of *A Nation at Risk* inaugurated what has been called the "first wave" of the education reform movement. Its initial theme was a return to traditional values in the classroom. In part it was a reaction to the reforms of the 1960s. Then, reform efforts had stressed values such as relevance, equity, and choice. Reformers of that period wanted to use the schools to promote equal opportunity and social welfare. But in the 1980s, new concerns—with economic competitiveness and worker productivity—caught the attention of education reformers. *A Nation at Risk* focused reform efforts on making standards tougher and more uniform, testing teachers and students, and paying teachers according to merit. In the 1980s, we began to stress sound training in the "three Rs" rather than "relevance," excellence rather than equity, and selectivity rather than equal access. Our concerns with the competitiveness and productivity of the economy overwhelmed our concerns with equal opportunity and social welfare.

The first wave of education reform in the 1980s was thus a movement that emphasized conservative values. When William Bennett succeeded Bell as Secretary of Education, the conservative reformers found a new and effective spokesperson, who added a new theme to the debate. Bennett insisted that the country was already spending enough money on public education—over $300 billion. He maintained that we ought to be able to improve the quality of education in this country without spending an extra dime. The key, in Bennett's view, was accountability. Accountability became the central theme sounded by the Reagan administration and its conservative allies (see Olson 1987, pp. 1, 16).

But conservatives have not been the only ones calling for reform. The education reform movement of the last decade was—and is—a complex and multidimensional movement characterized by different, sometimes conflicting, values and themes. What has been characterized as a "second wave" of reform was launched by the 1986 publication of *A Nation Prepared: Teachers for the 21st Century* by the Carnegie Forum on Education and the Economy (1986). The principal theme enunciated by the Carnegie report was the need to transform teaching "from an occupation into a profession." To achieve this objective, *A Nation Prepared* offered numerous recommendations: abolish the bachelor's degree in education and require future teachers to major in one of the traditional disciplines, create a new Master's degree in teaching based on internships and residencies, restructure teaching staffs by creating new teaching positions (lead teachers, managing teachers), provide teachers with more support staff (paraprofessionals, interns, residents, people on loan from corporations, volunteers, etc.) and increase the pay of top teachers by 50 to 100 percent.

A Nation Prepared held that the members of the new category of "lead teachers" should be chosen from experienced and highly regarded teachers in a school. These lead teachers would continue to teach but would also undertake a variety of other tasks such as the supervision of new teachers and the design of new curricula. Lead teachers and managing teachers, in the view of the Carnegie report, should manage the academic side of the schools while principals would have the scope of their responsibilities sharply reduced.

A Nation Prepared also called for the creation of a National Certification Board, which was to be charged with setting standards for the profession as well as preparing and administering a national certifying exam for teachers comparable to the bar exam for lawyers. The Carnegie report recommended that a majority of the proposed board's members be drawn from the nation's outstanding teachers. Subsequently, in May 1987, the Carnegie Foundation did create the National Teacher Certification Board, headed by former Governor James B. Hunt, Jr. of North Carolina. A majority of the members of the board are teachers.

From the outset of these reform debates, the nation's teacher unions have played an important and increasingly proactive role. The National Education Association, with over two million members, and the American Federation of Teachers, with roughly three-quarters of a million, were initially cast in the role of opposing reform (although the AFT managed to deflect most of the criticism onto its larger rival.) The NEA was already poised to challenge the Reagan Administration's efforts to eliminate the new Department of Education, created during the Carter administration with strong NEA support (and over AFT objections). When *A Nation at Risk* was then published, the President focused on its merit pay recommendations and their anticipated contribution to ridding the nation's schools of incompetent teachers. In a commencement address at Seton Hall University, delivered in May 1983, he declared, "Teachers should be paid and promoted on the basis of merit.... Hard earned tax dollars should encourage the best. They have no business rewarding incompetence and mediocrity" (Reagan 1983). The President's focus on incompetent teachers—and Secretary Bennett's subsequent argument that significant reforms could be accomplished without new expenditures—provoked a strong reaction from the National Education Association and, to a lesser degree, from the American Federation of Teachers.

But the leaders of both unions were astute enough to recognize that dissatisfaction with the quality of public education offered them opportunities to win new public support for education and more influence for their organizations and their members, provided that the terms of the debate could be redefined. It is not surprising, then, that the NEA's president, Mary Hatwood Futrell, and the AFT's Albert Shanker were both active members of the Carnegie Task Force that initiated the "second wave" of reform. Shanker warmly endorsed the recommendations contained in *A Nation Prepared*, saying, "This report deserves full support. It promises to turn teaching into a full profession, make major structural changes in schools, and take giant steps in the improvement of learning" (Shanker 1986). Futrell endorsed many of the report's ideas "wholeheartedly," but expressed reservations about others. She applauded its call for higher teacher salaries and greater teacher involvement in educational decision-making, but had "deep reservations about some of the report's conclusions and recommendations because they are inconsistent with what my many years of experience in the classroom and as an NEA leader tell me will help students learn." She expressed particular concern about the lead teacher concept because "it suggests that some teachers are more equal than others" and "it is not adequately differentiated from the flawed merit pay and job ladder plans" (Futrell 1986).

Despite Futrell's lukewarm support, the Carnegie report was viewed by many as strongly pro-teacher. Some critics have complained that principals, superintendents, and school board members have played only a limited role in the Carnegie reform efforts. Others have gone farther and have charged that implementation of the Carnegie recommendations would be tantamount to turning over control of the schools to the teachers. And in the view of some critics, this meant ceding control of the schools to the teacher unions. In 1987, for example, Gabler (1987), President of the American Association of School Administrators, labelled the new certification board "an attempted takeover of American schools by the teacher unions." At the same time, the National School Boards Association appeared prepared to challenge the NEA and AFT directly for the control of the schools. In April 1987, the NSBA set up a task force to study "alternatives to collective bargaining in public education." Thomas Shannon, President of the NSBA, said, "Collective bargaining is a massive stumbling block to change. You can't have collegial relations in an adversarial setting." He suggested that the NSBA might be prepared to try to phase out collective bargaining in education (Mitgang 1990).

But employers, too, have taken different positions with respect to the roles of collective bargaining and teacher unions in educational reform. While the national leaders of different unions and associations spar with one another, many state and local leaders have proceeded to forge new arrangements, using state legislation and local collective bargaining agreements to redefine the roles that teachers play, both individually and collectively, in the management of school systems. Collective bargaining is increasingly—but by no means, universally—being recognized as a vehicle for reform itself (Kerchner and Mitchell 1986; Johnson 1987; McDonnell and Pascal 1988). The very meaning of collective bargaining is changing as a consequence.

THE ORIGINS OF EDUCATION BARGAINING

To understand where collective bargaining in public education may be headed, we must understand where it came from. Except for restrictions on the right to strike and the substitution of various third-party impasse procedures, most of the features of collective bargaining in public education were borrowed from the private sector: district-wide bargaining units; the periodic negotiation of comprehensive agreements that last for fixed periods of time; legal restrictions that limit bargaining to so-called "bread-and-butter" issues and that require the parties to negotiate "in good faith"; multi-step grievance procedures for the resolution of disagreements that may arise during the life of an agreement; and the use of binding arbitration to resolve such mid-contract disputes, if the parties are unable to resolve them on their own.

Why did education bargainers embrace a set of arrangements derived from the private sector? The simplest answer is that neither teachers, nor administrators, nor those "experts" who helped design the first public sector bargaining laws may have recognized that they had any alternative. The features of "traditional bargaining" had become so embedded in people's minds as "the way collective bargaining is conducted" that it didn't occur to many people that a different system might be feasible.

These features were—and still are—so common in the private sector today that it was easy to forget that most of them were less than half a century old when they were transplanted into public education. In fact, they were invented specifically for labor-management relations in America's burgeoning factories, and at the time they were developed represented sharp departures from an even earlier form of collective bargaining.

Craft unionism, which was the "traditional" form of unionism until the 1930s, was based on principles that were fundamentally inconsistent with the factory system. It was based on the principles: (1) that workers had to be members of a union before they could be hired, (2) that it was the union's responsibility to train workers and to certify when they were ready to be employed, (3) that foremen or immediate supervisors had to be members of the union and subject to union discipline, and (4) that the union would control the work process through its unilateral specification of work rules. All four of these principles were fundamentally incompatible with the unskilled labor markets, standardized mass product markets, machine technologies and hierarchical managerial systems on which factory systems were based. With hindsight, it is clear that these principles had to be abandoned for unions to make inroads into the industrial sector of the economy.

And that is exactly what happened. The workers in smokestack industries abandoned the notion that a "real" union must control hiring, training, immediate supervision and the work process itself, and acknowledged that control of such processes was the prerogative of management. Workers got somewhat higher wages, more job security, and increasingly detailed agreements, with substantive and procedural protections against favoritism and arbitrary exercise of management authority.

Management, in turn, got a more stable workforce, prepared to accept its directions. The higher wages and benefit packages linked contractually to fixed job descriptions, job ladders and seniority had the effect of lowering quit rates and tying workers with specialized skills to the employer, in what one scholar called a new "industrial feudalism" (Ross 1958; Block 1978). Seniority clauses governing reassignments, promotions and layoffs all protected more-experienced workers from the threat of competition from junior workers, thus eliminating an obstacle to the informal sharing of job knowledge among workers (Thurow 1975). Layoff and recall procedures provided employers with a way of temporarily reducing employment during slack periods, without permanently losing the knowledge and skills of the workers who were laid off (Medoff 1979).

The union's formal acknowledgement of management authority was embodied in several provisions of the parties' negotiated contract. The discipline procedures in industrial union contracts established the principle that a worker's basic obligation to his or her employer was obedience: insubordination (not incompetence) was the primary grounds for discipline and/or dismissal. The grievance procedures in such contracts provided top management with information about shop-floor problems and first-line supervisory behavior that top managers would never have gotten through their own management hierarchies.

The linchpin in these arrangements was contained in the arbitration procedures of the parties' negotiated agreements, in the often-overlooked provision that specified that the terms of their agreement would remain in place for a fixed period of time, and in the union's promise not to call strikes during the life of the agreement. Together, these provisions helped establish the central principle of labor-management relations in the industrial setting, namely, that it is "management's right to manage" and that any rights employers have not given up, either by express contract language or by mutually acknowledged past practice, remain rights which employers are free to exercise as they see fit for the duration of the agreement (Elkouri and Elkouri 1976).

The structure of this deal reflected the strategic relationship between laborer and employer in factories. Industrial unions took advantage of the fact that the effective operation of factory systems depended upon the willingness of workers to voluntarily accept orders from their supervisors. The systems were simply too complex (and their dependence upon large numbers of workers was too great) to pretend that obedience could be coerced from each individual, especially if workers were prepared to act collectively in the face of such coercion. The benefits and guarantees which soon began to fill industrial union contracts were the price an employer had to pay to secure the necessary obedience.

The structural arrangements that provided the starting points for collective bargaining in public education in the 1960s, then, were features that originally had been developed to reflect the types of markets, technologies and management systems of America's mass production industries. We make no claims to have made an exhaustive historical analysis, but there are reasons to believe that the policy makers and bargainers who launched education bargaining did not simply overlook that fact, but actually may have found the factory parallel attractive. It was natural for teacher unions to adopt factory union strategies in the 1960s, because the administrators and school board members whom they faced insisted on acting like factory managers. Indeed, one of the basic reasons so many teachers chose to join unions was that the prevailing logic of education management was itself patterned on the industrial model (Callahan 1962; Cole 1969).

School boards and administrators have had an on-again, off-again love affair with industrial management models for most of this century, from the first two decades, when school reformers used "scientific management" principles to give the new discipline of educational administration a body of supposed expertise (Callahan 1962), to the late 1950s, when post-Sputnik reformers issued repeated calls to overhaul the structure and management of school systems. What, in most systems, had been collections of largely autonomous units dominated by building principals were now to be "rationalized," by centralizing the control of educational policies and programs in the hands of district superintendents and central office staff experts (Tyack and Hansot 1982).

If schools were to be run like factories, with hierarchical controls and centralized planning, evaluation and policy-setting mechanisms, then teacher unions would necessarily have to act like factory unions, resorting to roughly the same sorts of strategies for protecting the interests of their members. Like their industrial sector counterparts, teacher unions often challenged particular management decisions and insisted that management put in writing policies that administrators might have preferred to leave to their own discretion. At least in the early years of bargaining, teacher unions played essentially the same reactive role as their industrial counterparts, insisting that it was management's job to set policy and manage; the union's job was to negotiate and then police protections against abuses of that authority.

In fact, teacher unions have provided district-level administrators with many of the same benefits that industrial managers gained from collective bargaining: access to information about school-level problems, orderly procedures for disposing of various personnel issues, and grounds for insisting that school principals adhere to policies prescribed or agreed to by central administrators. Indeed, case studies of school district power relationships indicate that collective bargaining has provided central administrators with one of their most effective tools for centralizing management authority and power in their own hands. Not only has it helped them control their subordinate managers; it also has helped them insulate themselves—and their staffs—from school board "interference" in their day-to-day decision-making, by insisting that board members and administrators must present a "united front" in the face of union pressure (Bacharach 1981). The structures, processes and myths of industrial unionism complemented and in some ways even supported the top-down managerial ideology that existed in most school systems when teacher unions first won recognition, just as they fitted the factory management systems of the 1930s.

Until recently, top-down models of factory or bureaucratic management were the only models that offered any coherent explanation of how school boards and administrators might coordinate what goes on in their schools. Since coordinating the flow of students through the system—and assigning teachers, specialists, support personnel, curriculum requirements, material resources, space and time schedules to serve students as they pass through— are jobs that have fallen to boards and administrators to perform, it is not surprising that so many boards and administrators would find those top-down models so attractive.

But those models are now under severe attack. The factors that make coordination so difficult and therefore so necessary—multiple constituencies with various demands, work techniques with uncertain consequences, unpredictable situations demanding quick responses, constant interaction with others, and direct contact with organizational clients or customers with many different needs—also generate pressure on boards and administrators to allow their teachers a wide degree of latitude over how they organize, plan, execute, and monitor what goes on in their individual classrooms. Indeed, debates over how school systems should be managed (and debates over how they should be "reformed") almost always hinge on the relationship between the need to allow individual teachers discretion and the need to coordinate their individual efforts. Metaphors and strategies that focus on the former evoke images of autonomous professionals or craftspersons; those that focus on the latter evoke images of assembly lines and purposeful bureaucracies. Neither set of metaphors or strategies captures the truly demanding task of school management, which is somehow to satisfy both sets of needs *simultaneously*. It is this dilemma, we would argue, that lies at the heart of the debates over educational reform and the future of collective bargaining in public education. In fact, as we will note, essentially the same dilemma lies at the heart of debates over management and bargaining in *all* sectors of the economy.

RETHINKING MANAGEMENT AND BARGAINING

The top-down strategies which have ostensibly guided school management for most of this century have never made complete sense in public education and have never been strictly observed. At one moment teachers are treated like workers on an assembly line, at another like bureaucrats executing general directives, at still another like independent professionals who are expected to figure out for themselves what it is they should be doing. Observers who have styled themselves as realists have assumed that school systems must be satisfied with constant tension and watered-down compromises between two needs that are equally important and inherently in conflict with each other. Like a fitted sheet one size too small for the bed it is expected to cover, the management approaches employed by school systems could always be adjusted to fit one need or another but never (it seemed) the whole system. Researchers confirmed that teachers and administrators in most systems had informally negotiated "zones of influence," each acknowledging the other's primacy within their respective zones. Teachers would agree to respect administrators' decisions over matters outside the classroom, and administrators would respect decisions that teachers made within their classrooms, so long as the latter did not cause problems for anyone else. The arrangement did not serve the need for coordination or the need for teacher discretion well, but it did allow both needs to be served (Lortie 1975).

These laissez-faire arrangements, we would argue, are now beginning to collapse under the weight of new and more complicated public pressures. School systems that could rely upon "reform" coming in manageable doses— for "rigor" one year, "equity" another, "cost cutting" the next—are now being subjected to demands to satisfy all these demands at once. For the nation's governors, who have been more responsible than anyone for keeping reform at the forefront of public attention, the primary motivation has been to revitalize their states' economies and to forge an "education strategy" for doing so (Osborne 1988). "Excellence" (of some sort) was to be expected of an ever-growing proportion of school graduates.

These new market pressures are forcing school boards to rethink their human resource management policies, just as analogous pressures are forcing private sector employers to reassess theirs. Michael Piore, an economist who has paid special attention to the relationships between product markets, work processes and models of unionism, points out that the logic that once dominated the design of manufacturing work processes—the logic of a detailed, explicit division of labor and of top-down control—assumed that it was feasible to separate the planning of work from its execution. That is, it was feasible to assign the planning function to managers, supervisors and staff experts, and to assign relatively fixed sets of routine duties to individual "line" employees (Piore 1982, 1985).

Piore points out that such a division of labor is practical only in settings where large volumes of standardized products are to be produced, using production methods that are reasonably stable over long periods of time, and that these conditions are now breaking down in large sections of the manufacturing economy. Increasingly stiff international competition and product specialization, improved transportation systems, and new computerized production technologies are all undermining the economies of scale that America's mass production giants once enjoyed. The top-down management techniques and sharp horizontal divisions of labor that were sources of efficiency in an earlier era have grown increasingly inefficient in today's more specialized, varied and variable product markets (Rosenfeld 1988).

These market changes affect both the design of individual jobs and the planning and coordination of work across groups of workers. The more frequently products or services are modified, the more often the tasks necessary to make those products or provide those services change. As tasks change, so must the duties assigned to each employee, rendering jobs with fixed sets of responsibilities obsolete. The more rapidly job duties change, moreover, the less likely it is that staff experts at higher organizational levels will be able to anticipate and decide what all those duties ought to be. Employers, thus, have increasing need of employees who are willing and able to adapt to different work demands and who can determine for themselves what work needs to be performed (Rosenfeld 1988).

But granting individual employees more discretion increases the problems of coordinating their separate activities. Granting employees more independence restricts management's access to information about existing or anticipated problems in the work process, right when other developments are making it imperative that such problems be anticipated and resolved before production begins. In simpler times, manufacturers could resolve such problems by centralizing authority and tightening management control over individual workers, but it is their own efforts to relax such controls that are partially responsible for their current planning and coordination dilemmas. Thus, manufacturers have shown growing interest in computerized information systems that help them keep tabs on the flow of materials and products through their systems. But manufacturers have also expressed interest in mechanisms like self-managed work groups and quality circles that require employees to work cooperatively to identify and solve problems that once were the responsibility of managers to address.

All of these developments point to new forms of work organization and management, as well as changes in the kinds of training that workers receive. Managers throughout the economy are attracted to job enrichment programs, "pay for knowledge" compensation systems, and other strategies aimed at breaking down narrow job definitions and assigning individual workers and groups of workers wider sets of responsibilities and more discretion over how they perform their work (Kochan 1985; Schonberger 1986). They are attracted, as well, to schemes for involving workers in decision-making beyond their immediate work assignments (Walton 1985).

As these developments take hold, industrial unions throughout the economy are being forced to reconsider strategies that have served them well for half a century. As Piore points out, the same factors which are forcing a reassessment of traditional management approaches are undermining traditional "job control" unionism as well. A unionism that is premised on fixed job categories, close links between specific duties and compensation, and detailed rules on how job assignments are made—and on a "common law" that prevents managers from holding workers accountable for mistakes in the organization and planning of work—is bound to be threatened by current economic changes.

But many private sector unions are also discovering new *potential* in the new kinds of dependence that their members' employers are experiencing. Managers are becoming increasingly dependent upon their employees for information about production processes. Managers also need more flexibility in the ways they organize and manage the work that is done. Union tactic that assume that management expects only blind obedience from employee may be undercut by such new management approaches, but tactics that tap these new forms of dependence might serve as the bases for renewed union strength.

Few employers are more dependent than school boards and administrator on their employees' discretion, professional judgment and willingness to cooperate in translating general policies into concrete action. Few employees have as much responsibility as teachers for planning and evaluating the result of their day-to-day activities, much less for planning, directing and evaluating the activities of others. In most settings, these activities are still defined a management responsibilities, even if employees are being invited to share some of them. In public education, they represent the very core of the work of teachers (Conley, Schmidle, and Shedd 1988).

The fact that teachers plan, direct and evaluate the work of others—that is, the work of their students—does not make them supervisors or managers in the traditional labor relations sense, because their "subordinates" are no employees and the decisions they make are not, strictly speaking, "personnel policies." But teachers are supervisors and managers in the more generic sense of those terms: they are responsible for translating general policies into particular objectives; planning, supervising and adjusting work activities securing needed resources; and evaluating both individual performance and the overall success of their work plans (Shedd and Bacharach 1991).

If teacher unions are threatened by the demise of top-down management strategies, they are also in a good position to take advantage of that demise For one thing, they are not threatened by the declining employment base that is making it difficult for private sector industrial unions to convince their members to even think of "cooperating" with management. For another, pressing for collective teacher involvement in school and district decision-making offers the possibility of overcoming the split between "union" and "professional" factions within their own organizations, by shifting the focus of thinking about "professional" issues away from individual autonomy. Perhaps most importantly for the unions, such a shift might allow teacher unions to finally take advantage of a source of potential influence—or to put the matter more bluntly, a source of power—that industrial union principles have always required them to overlook: the fact that their members, as individuals, already manage much of what goes on in school systems themselves. The prospect that a reassessment of union strategies might allow them to end the internal bloodletting, secure new monies for education, and build a stronger, more unified organization has provided union leaders with a powerful incentive to try.

NEW STRUCTURES IN EDUCATION BARGAINING

The basic structure of the agreements that education bargainers will negotiate in the future can be expected to reflect the structure of the overall labor-management relationship in public education, just as the structures of craft and industrial union contracts reflected the relationships which produced them. While teachers will insist on playing a more active role in setting educational policies and programs, boards of education and administrators will almost certainly insist that fixed-term, fixed-length agreements are cumbersome and therefore inappropriate vehicles for addressing those issues. Teachers and their representatives, in turn, will demand guarantees that their involvement in policymaking is more than token. The result—already emerging in many systems—will probably be an increasing reliance on comprehensive negotiations to establish the structure and ground rules for joint decision-making, with longer intervals between each negotiation, fewer restrictions in master agreements, and more explicit procedures for securing "waivers" of contract provisions.

What is more speculative but more intriguing is the possibility that some school districts and teacher unions might go further and eliminate the provision that prevents one party from "reopening" negotiations before the end of a contract without the other party's consent. That provision is a key element in the industrial sector deal that protects the employer's "reserved right" to make management decisions unilaterally. If a union were free to demand that negotiations be "reopened" at any time, the principle that management retains unilateral discretion over issues not covered by the contract would be meaningless. It is not clear that school districts either need or necessarily would want such protections, since they force unions to file grievances and arbitration appeals (or in some states, demands for single-issue "impact" negotiations) over issues generated by the changing circumstances of school system management. Giving either party the right to reopen negotiations on any or all provisions of a district-wide agreement would provide managers with increased flexibility and would remove one of the principal objections to expanding the scope of bargaining.

In addition to changes in the scope of bargaining, changes in the structure of agreements, and changes in the bargaining process itself, many observers expect teacher unions and school systems to negotiate changes in the structure of the teaching profession itself. Indeed, many of the recent debates over education reform have focused on the development of so-called "career ladders" that draw distinctions between the duties of teachers at different "career levels" and that pay teachers according to the level of the ladder that they occupy. We agree that such systems are likely to be discussed and experimented with over the next several years, but the line of argument we have developed here casts a different light on their prospects for success.

Drawing close connections between specific sets of duties and different level of compensation is a basic feature of the top-down systems in industrial work settings. It is that feature, in fact, that managers in the manufacturing setting are now struggling to overcome and that is forcing unions in those setting to reassess some of the basic tenets of industrial unionism. To suggest that public education should move toward more formal differentiation of teaching duties would be to suggest that it should move closer to, not farther from the industrial model, with its detailed rules on who has a right to bid on what duties, what career level gets what new duties, when the assignment of "some higher level duties requires a temporary promotion, and so forth.

Many of today's reformers characterize job differentiation as a way of involving more teachers in decisions that have typically been reserved for administrators. But the unified salary schedule that most school systems us is not an obstacle to such involvement, whereas a differentiated salary schedul would be: formal differentiation would mean that only a limited number of teachers could be involved in such activities, and any teacher would be entitled to refuse to accept responsibilities outside the job description for his or he career ladder position (Bacharach, Conley, and Shedd 1986).

If there is any aspect of current salary practices in school systems that doe represent an obstacle to increased teacher involvement in management, it i the ad hoc practice of treating formal assignments outside the classroom and outside the normal work day as "extra" duties and of paying for each such set of duties separately. That practice is inevitable, of course, as long as th "normal" teacher work day ends roughly when the normal school day end and as long as the work year for teachers is approximately the same as th school year. Those practices are real obstacles to developing a broader concep of teachers' basic professional responsibilities.

Most teachers, in our experience, devote much more than forty hours pe week to their profession, but much of that time is spent at home, reviewin, student work and planning lessons. Such activities, performed in isolation, go officially unrecognized. If teachers' formal work day or work year wer lengthened without a corresponding increase in the school day or school year or if new staffing arrangements were developed that allowed teachers to rotat assignments and share duties with each other, then the basis for a new "deal between teachers and their employer would be created. Boards and administrators would be in a position to insist that many duties that presentl call for extra compensation would henceforth fall within the scope of teacher basic responsibilities. Teachers would be in a position to demand assurance that they would have greater control over how they spend their time outsid the classroom.

The willingness of teacher unions and employers in public education to ever entertain such radical departures from traditional practices probably says mor about the pressures that school systems are under than it does about the specifi formulas that the parties will agree to live by in the future. It undoubtedly will take some time for them to work out and finally accept new ground rules, just as it took employers and industrial unions time to work out all the details of what today is recognized as the "traditional" labor-management formula.

But the historical parallel gives reason to have confidence in the basic argument outlined here. Economic developments, changes in public expectations, and changes in the ways in which organizations like school systems are being managed are once again undermining the bases of one form of unionism and are creating new forms of power in the employment relationship. Put simply, employers throughout the economy—but above all, in public education—are becoming increasingly dependent on their employees' detailed knowledge of work processes and client needs, on their individual willingness and ability to exercise discretion and judgment, and on their willingness to work cooperatively with one another in the face of constantly changing work situations.

The important question is not whether employers will try to make adjustments to these new forms of dependence—they must do so to survive—but whether unions will be able to develop strategies that allow them to marshall the power inherent in that dependence. If they can, they will have created a new form of union that has the potential of being every bit as vigorous and powerful and as appropriate to their setting as craft unions and industrial unions were to theirs. There are good reasons to believe that is exactly what is happening today in public education.

But all these changes are likely to cost money and generate struggles for power **within** school systems. Getting "from here to there" is likely to pose serious, perhaps insurmountable, obstacles.

Nevertheless, we are optimists. Negotiations like those between the Rochester, New York school district and its AFT local, which incorporated many of the Carnegie concepts, reflect a political courage, a willingness to take risks, and a capacity to sustain both cooperation and conflict that bode well for the future of public education and unions. The leaders in Rochester have been willing to confront directly the magnitude of problems we face in public education, and have taken some lumps from their clients and constituents for having done so. All of us interested in improving the quality of education must be equally willing—not to set aside different interests—but to find creative ways of reconciling differences and meeting the multiplicity of demands which our public school systems now confront.

ACKNOWLEDGMENTS

The names of the authors appear in alphabetical order.

NOTE

1. See National Education Association/National Association of Secondary School Principals (1986); also, American Federation of Teachers Task Force on the Future of Education (1986).

REFERENCES

American Federation of Teachers Task Force on the Future of Education. 1986. *The Revolution that is Overdue: Looking Toward the Future of Teaching and Learning.* Washington, DC: American Federation of Teachers.

Bacharach, S. B. 1981. "Consensus and Power in School Districts." *Final Report Under NIE Grant No. G 78 0080.* Ithaca, NY: Cornell University.

Bacharach, S. B., S.C. Conley, and J.B. Shedd. 1986. "Beyond Career Ladders: Structuring Teacher Career Development Systems." *Teachers College Record* 87 (4): 563-574.

Block, R.N. 1978. "The Impact of Seniority Provisions on the Manufacturing Quit Rate." *Industrial and Labor Relations Review* (31): 474-81.

Callahan, R. 1962. *Education and the Cult of Efficiency.* Chicago: University of Chicago Press.

Carnegie Forum on Education and the Economy. 1986. Task Force on Teaching as a Profession. *A Nation Prepared: Teachers for the 21st Century.* New York: Carnegie Forum on Education and the Economy.

Cole, S. 1969. *The Unionization of Teachers.* New York: Praeger.

Conley, S. C., T. Schmidle, and J.B. Shedd. 1988. "Teachers Participation in the Management of School Systems." *Teachers College Record* 90 (2): 259-280.

Elkouri, F., and A. Elkouri. 1976. *How Arbitration Works,* 3rd ed. Washington DC: Bureau of National Affairs.

Futrell, M.H. 1986. "Statement of Support with Reservations." P. 117 in *Carnegie Forum on Education and the Economy.*

Gabler, J. 1987. "National Board to Certify Teachers is Established." *Chicago Tribune,* p. 3.

Hoffman, D. 1983. "New Political Push; Reagan Emphasizes Education Issue." *Washington Post.*

Johnson, S. M. 1987. "Can Schools Be Reformed at the Bargaining Table?" *Teachers College Record* 89 (2): 269-280.

Kerchner, C.T., and D. Mitchell. 1986. "Teaching Reform and Union Reform." *The Elementary School Journal* 86 (4).

Kochan, T. A. 1985. *Challenges and Choices Facing American Labor.* Cambridge, MA: The MIT Press.

Lortie, D.C. 1975. *Schoolteacher: A Sociological Study.* Chicago: The University of Chicago Press.

McDonnell, L. M. and A. Pascal. 1988. *Teachers Unions and Educational Reform.* Santa Monica, CA: The Rand Corporation.

Medoff, J.L. 1979. "Layoffs and Alternatives under Trade Unions in U.S. Manufacturing." *American Economic Review* (69): 380-395.

Mitgang, L. 1990. "Union President Starts War of Words with School Administrators." The Associated Press Wire Reports.

National Commision on Excellence in Education. 1983. *A Nation at Risk.* Washington, DC: Government Printing Office.

National Education Association/National Association of Secondary School Principals. 1986. *Ventures in Good Schooling: A Cooperative Model for a Successful Secondary School.* Washington DC: National Education Association and National Association of Secondary School Principals.

Olson, L. 1987. "Combative Bennett Charges into Final Year." *Education Week* 7 (2): 1, 16.

Osborne, D. 1988. *Laboratories of Democracy: A New Breed of Governor Creates Models for National Economic Growth.* Cambridge, MA: Harvard Business School.

Piore, M. 1982. "American Labor and the Industrial Crisis." *Challenge,* 5-11.

_____. 1985. *"Computer Technologies, Market Structure, and Strategic Union Choices." In Challenges and Choices Facing Americam Labor,* edited by Thomas Kochan. Cambridge, MA: The MIT Press.

Rosenfeld, S. A. 1988. "Commentary: Educating for the Factories of the Future." *Education Week,* 48.

Ross, A. M. 1958. "Do We Have a New Industrial Feudalism?" *American Economic Review* (48): 903-920.

Shanker, A. 1986. "Statement of Support." P. 118 in Carnegie Forum on Education and the Economy.

Schonberger, R.L. 1986. *World Class Manufacturing; The Lessons of Simplicity Applied.* New York: The Free Press.

Shedd, J.B. and S.B. Bacharach. 1991. *Tangled Hierarchies: Teachers as Professionals and the Management of Schools.* San Francisco, CA: Jossey-Bass.

Thurow, L. 1975. *Generating Inequality: Mechanisms of Distribution in the U.S. Economy.* New York: Basic Books.

Tyack, D. and E. Hansot. 1982. *Managers of Virtue: Public School Leadership in America, 1820-1980.* New York: Basic Books.

Walton, R. E. 1985. "From Control to Commitment in the Workplace." *Harvard Business Review,* 77-84.

COMMENTS

David S. Honeyman

There has been a historical relationship between industry and education and the methods used in labor relations, collective bargaining, and negotiations. In tracing the effects of the industrial labor model on education, the authors of "Collective Bargaining Amidst Education Reform" develop several important points for school personnel to consider as we have now moved through the second wave of educational reform and on into the third: the era of "Choice" and decentralized accountability and control.

As the authors indicate, these issues involve the several practices of collective bargaining which are obstacles to educational reform, including the adversarial relationship, inconsistent salary structures, and the shifting of power and control within the school district. Currently there is an emerging dependence on the knowledge base of the teacher and an awareness by effective administrators of the need to nurture a cooperative spirit with staff. As the authors state, "There is an emerging reliance on comprehensive negotiations to establish the structure and ground rules for joint decision making ... and more explicit procedures for securing waivers of contract provision." The current wave of educational reform requires a rethinking of the bargaining cycle in American education.

At the Center for Education Finance at the University of Florida, we have developed and tested a model for integrated collective bargaining (Honeyman and Wood 1990). This model is part of a comprehensive presentation of site based management which includes discussions of finance, budgeting, instruction, law, and collective bargaining for principals, teachers, and parents at the building site. The collective bargaining and negotiations section is based on the premise that the contract must reflect this emerging concern for organizational decentralization and consists of three main parts: the "living" contract, the "working" contract, and "waivers and exemptions" to the working contract.

Briefly, the living contract defines the nature of the bargaining relationship. It identifies the bargaining unit, specifies those aspects of a contract which will have a long-term effect on the school district, and, generally, addresses state rules and regulations. For example, the living contract would include instructional contact time, the length of the school day, the calendar, duty free lunch, and so forth. Usually the living contract is settled and not bargained until statute changes require reconsideration.

The working contract, effectively the master living contract, is negotiated periodically and defines those aspects of the agreement which are more likely to require change from year to year and from building to building. Salaries, fringe benefits, pay for additional duties, start times, and so on are included in the working contract. This working contract allows for building level flexibility to alter the contract language based on the needs of the school site.

The method for requesting changes to this working contract for a site is the waiver process as contained in the living contract. Once the local school site determines the need for a waiver of some provision of the working contract, a waiver request is submitted; and, if approved, the working contract for that site is amended. This results in multiple working contracts, a process which effectively "debargains" the contract without violating state law or applicable Employee Relations Board guidelines and allows for increased local autonomy.

The details of any collective bargaining agreement should not impede the development and delivery of innovative educational strategies for students. This approach to collective bargaining, the living contract, working contract, and waivers, can allow such flexibility. With a thorough understanding of finance, law, and the contract, the local site council can concentrate on the improvement of the instructional program and make recommendations for change knowing there is a process to facilitate their needs.

REFERENCE

Honeyman, D.S. and R.C. Wood. 1990. *Site Based Management: Building a Successful Program.* Gainsville, FL: University of Florida, Center for Education Finance.

THE STRUCTURE OF K-12 SCHOOL FINANCE IN THE UNITED STATES: CONSTRAINTS AND IMPLICATIONS FOR EDUCATION REFORMS

Vincent G. Munley

INTRODUCTION

Most of the papers in this volume present interesting and challenging ideas about the relationship between educational performance and economic performance, in particular about how strengthening public elementary and secondary education might help the United States to increase its output of goods and services. In a sense they explore pathways to a goal of inarguable merit. My objective here is much more modest. I will examine how the existing system for financing K-12 public schools in the United States imposes constraints on this dialogue, and more specifically how it might influence proposals for reform. To complete the metaphor, I will try to map out some important features of the fiscal terrain over which these pathways must traverse.

Because the topic of improving education has attracted the attention of several disciplines, it is important to point out that I am an economist. Different disciplines tend to focus on public policy issues from their own unique perspectives; and failure to appreciate the basis (and perhaps biases) of a different viewpoint can inhibit interdisciplinary exchanges. Because many of the ideas—introducing competition through parental choice, increasing classroom productivity through decentralized management practices, and so on—currently offered for improving education come from economics, an economic perspective may offer valuable insights to all the participants in this dialogue.

Economists generally analyze public policies according to the dual criteria of efficiency and equity. Efficiency, simply stated, requires that resources are allocated to their most highly valued use. Corollary to this is the proposition that dollar votes in the marketplace determine the relative value of different uses, so that at any point in time the existing pattern of income and wealth influences judgments about the relative efficiency of policy alternatives. Equity judgments, on the other hand, evaluate the fairness of the economic outcomes derived from policy alternatives. Equity judgments can never be as precise as efficiency judgments, because what ultimately defines "fair" will always rest upon each person's individual set of values.

The proposed educational reform that has generated the most attention to date is parental choice. This proposal also portends the most significant adaptations and modifications to the existing system for financing public K-12 education. Hence, the major focus of the analysis presented here is directed toward this proposal. Some background information is necessary first, however. To accomplish this I will examine briefly the economic justification for elementary and secondary public schools and the financing structure that is currently in place to support them. This discussion leads naturally to some interesting questions about how reform proposals relate to the two-decade-old (and still very active) legal issue of ensuring some measure of equality in educational opportunity across local school districts.

PUBLIC PROVISION OF K-12 EDUCATION

It is worthwhile to consider briefly the *economic* rationale for providing elementary and secondary education through the public sector. There are, of course, other important social reasons for public provision. And while these motivations have economic implications in a broad sense, I want to focus here on the purposes that most participants in this discussion would consider fundamentally economic in nature.

Standard economic analysis classifies goods and services as private or public according to the manner in which we consume them. In the case of a purely private good, one person's consumption exhausts the commodity, thereby excluding anyone else from consuming it. Things like a glass of milk, a pair of contact lenses, or a half-hour individual consultation with a physician are good examples of this type of good. A purely public good, on the other hand, is characterized by non-excludability or jointness in consumption. A given level of national defense is the prototype example of this type of good, since once it is provided we all "consume" it equally.

Orthodox economic analysis suggests that efficiency is best achieved for private goods when they are provided in free and competitive markets. In this situation each individual chooses his or her personally most preferred consumption level of every good, thus guaranteeing an overall efficient result. For purely public goods the situation is more complicated, however, because everyone jointly consumes whatever total output level is forthcoming. Achieving an efficient provision requires each person to reveal truthfully his or her preferences for the good, and in turn pay for the share of the total cost that this preference implies. In theory, private transactions in a free market could produce this result. In practice, though, the likelihood of free rider problems arising makes determining and obtaining this type of solution extremely difficult, if not impossible.

As a result, governments provide most public goods; and in democracies the output level for each is chosen, either directly or by elected representatives, through the political process. In a federalist system such as the United States, different levels of government have primary responsibility for various fiscal tasks. How these tasks are assigned can have a direct effect on the efficiency of resource allocation by the public sector.

Pursuit of efficiency suggests the following rule: Different public goods should be provided by that level of government which corresponds most closely to the distribution of the population that jointly consumes each particular good (see Oates 1972). For example, the federal government provides national defense because individuals throughout the country jointly share its benefits.

Jointness in consumption holds for other public goods, however, only over a more restricted geographic area. Police protection and parks and recreational services are good examples. For such goods different jurisdictions can provide alternative output levels; and individuals will jointly consume with their neighbors the level that their own local jurisdiction provides. In this setting individuals are free to select that jurisdiction which provides an output closest to their own most preferred level. In an idealized situation where every individual can locate in a jurisdiction that provides precisely his or her ideal output level, the result would be economically efficient for exactly the same reason that free and competitive markets provide efficient resource allocation in the case of private goods (Tiebout 1956).

How does the provision of elementary and secondary education fit into this framework? To answer this question it is necessary to examine the consumption characteristics of education. In the first place, the output of elementary and secondary schools does not fit neatly into the private good-public good dichotomy. It clearly has characteristics of both, and for this reason K-12 education is often refered to as a "quasi-public" good.[1] A high quality local school system provides direct benefits to students, and indirect benefits to their parents, in the form of better preparation for their future life with the promise of greater economic success (Card and Kruger 1992). In this respect education has the characteristics of a private good. This suggests that, at least from the narrow perspective of achieving economic efficiency, it would make sense to relegate the provision of education to the private sector.

Not all of the benefits of education accrue exclusively to current students and their parents, however. A high quality local school system enhances the cultural, economic and social fabric of a community; and consumption of this enhanced local environment is shared jointly by all citizens. If education provision were left entirely to free markets, families might well ignore this public good dimension in determining their own private consumption of educational services. This would then lead to an inefficiently low overall output level from society's perspective. This argument suggests that collective provision of elementary and secondary schools through the public sector can be justified solely on the basis of economic efficiency.

Another rationale for providing basic education through the public sector derives from the unique role that this service performs for society. In his classic treatise on public finance Musgrave (1959) specifically cites education as an example of a class of "merit" goods that are:

> considered so meritorious that their satisfaction is provided for through the public budget, over and above what is provided for through the market and paid for by private buyers. ... The satisfaction of merit wants, by its very nature, involves interference with consumer preferences (p. 13).

Even if we decide that the public sector should provide basic education, several questions remain about how this service should be financed and organized. And its private good, quasi-public good, and merit good aspects, respectively, all offer guidance about the answers to these questions—guidance that at times is contradictory.

The private good characteristic suggests that education should be organized by local jurisdictions and that the level of expenditure per pupil should probably vary from school district to school district. Due to both differences in preferences about education and differences in the ability to afford higher taxes to pay for this service, families will differ in their judgment about what is the optimal private output level. Local organization provides a mechanism for creating a situation where many districts in a region offer alternative "packages" of tax prices and corresponding output levels. This in turn allows families to select through their location decision a level of educational services close to what they would have purchased if this service were not publicly provided. In a technical sense local organization can help minimize the efficiency loss which results from joint provision of a good with private consumption characteristics.

The quasi-public nature of education likewise offers guidance about the appropriate size of school districts. If capturing the common benefits of a well educated population in the decision calculus used to determine the output level of this service is at least a partial justification for public provision, then it makes sense to define school districts as coterminous with the communities over which these benefits are common. Accomplishing this, of course, is much easier in theory than in practice. In rural areas such communities are typically well defined; and school districts bounderies generally reflect their borders, except in cases where this would result in organizational systems too small to take advantage of whatever scale economies exist for the provision of education. In suburban and urban settings, on the other hand, neighborhoods tend to run together and overlap in such a way that defining school districts as coterminous with well defined and distinct communities is an impossibility.

Yet another wrinkle plaguing any attempt to define school district bounderies as precisely coterminous with communities that share the common benefits of education arises from the mobility of today's society. At any point in time a community benefits from the advantages of having well educated residents, including current students. However, communities also benefit from the quality of education provided to residents who moved into the area after completing their elementary and secondary school work. This suggests that achieving an overall efficient output level may require internalizing or in some way compensating for these cross-community benefit exchanges. Such reasoning argues for less decentralization in the organization of education.

The merit good characteristic of education also argues for more centralized control over its provision. If education is, because of the role that it plays in preparing individuals for life, of such basic merit that everyone has a right to a certain quality level, then the state or federal government should ensure that local districts do not provide less. This reasoning is the basis for the series of legal challenges over equity in education that have been argued in state courts over the past three decades.

This discussion suggests that an economic perspective offers valuable insights into the tradeoffs that exist in deciding how to organize public education. Since no single best structure is readily apparent, we turn to an examination of what is currently in place.

THE STATUS QUO

Substantial diversity exists in the economic and political institutions which govern the provision of elementary and secondary education in the United States. The federal government provides only about seven percent of the revenues devoted to financing this public service. The primary focus of both federal funds and federal policies for K-12 education is on students with special needs.[2]

The relative fiscal roles that state governments and local school districts play in providing resources varies considerably from the case of Hawaii's single statewide school system to New Hampshire where locally raised revenues account for about 90 percent of the total funds expended. The organizational structure that characterizes public school administration likewise varies considerably. In some states schools are administered by independent local education authorities, usually called school districts, with autonomous taxing power. The dimensions of these districts ranges widely, from states like Utah and West Virginia which each have well under 100 districts to states like California and Texas which each have over 1000 districts. In other states schools are administered by other municipal governments—typically cities or counties—through the general public fisc.

While there is substantial variation in the institutions which govern elementary and secondary schools across the U.S., there are also important fundamental features for which a common pattern emerges. This is especially true with regard to the way in which both local districts and state governments raise revenues to support public schools. Since reform proposals may affect, or be affected by, these common features, it is worthwhile to examine them.

Locally Raised Revenue

The property tax is the dominant revenue source for all local public expenditures, including elementary and secondary education. Municipal governments typically provide police and fire protection, local road maintenance, sanitation service, parks and recreation, and in some cases the operation of hospitals. In states where general municipal governments also have responsibility for providing educational services, schools compete directly with other services for resources through the budget process. In the majority of states where K-12 education is provided by fiscally autonomous, politically independent school districts, all other local public services are still financed through the general municipal fisc.

How should we judge local property taxes in terms of the twin economic criteria of efficiency and equity? The efficiency criterion measures the degree to which a particular tax promotes productive resource allocation. Taxes that resemble user fees, such as levies on gasoline that are dedicated to highway maintenance, generally receive good marks according to this criterion. Individually derived benefits correspond closely to the levy incurred by each user; and the aggregate benefit justifies the resources devoted to providing it.

The equity criterion, on the other hand, assesses the fairness of a revenue structure used to finance public expenditures. Judgments about fairness ultimately depend upon each person's own value system. Most observers, though, give high equity marks to taxes whose burden falls proportionately more heavily on individuals with greater ability to pay. According to this view a progressive income tax is a good example of an equitable tax.

How well the property tax measures up to the equity criterion depends upon two related factors. The first concerns how the incidence of property taxes is distributed across income classes. For a long time economists and policy makers were convinced that the property tax was moderately regressive over a wide range of income classes. More recent analysis, however, suggests that, in general, the property tax is mildly regressive or proportional over low ranges of income and somewhat progressive over higher income ranges.[3]

A second factor, which in turn has significant implications for resulting incidence patterns, concerns the administration of a property tax. Many state tax codes have provisions that create differential effective property tax rates by either (1) explicitly taxing different classes of property at different rates, or (2) applying a uniform rate to property with differential assessed-to-market values. This allows, for example, agricultural land to be taxed at a lower rate than residential property, which in turn may be taxed at a lower effective rate than commercial, industrial or utility property.

How local property taxes measure up with regard to the efficiency criterion depends upon the nature of the service to which the revenues are dedicated. In the case of police and fire protection, the benefits derived by property owners increase—at least in rough measure—with the level of service provided. Thus, property taxes receive high marks by this criterion. In the case of elementary and secondary education, the correspondence between benefits to property owners and the level of expenditures is less apparent. As noted above, current students and their parents are the most direct beneficiaries of increased school quality; and the relationship between the number of children that a household currently has in public schools and the size of its property tax bill is unclear. Thus, it is difficult to draw firm conclusions about how well property taxes for financing public education measure up.

State Revenue

Except for Hawaii, where there is a single statewide school system, state governments contribute their share of elementary and secondary school monies through formula-allocated grants to local districts. Several states dedicate certain revenues, such as lottery proceeds or a fixed percent of the sales tax, for distribution to local school districts. In almost all cases, however, general fund appropriations constitute the marginal dollars that states distribute in this way.[4]

In quantitative terms, the most important revenue sources for state government general funds are (1) sales and general business receipts taxes, and (2) corporate and personal income taxes. Levies on both sales and general business receipts are ultimately consumption taxes. Because consumption expenditures as a percent of income tend to fall as income rises, economists generally conclude that these taxes are somewhat regressive. This judgment must be conditioned, however, on two important caveats. The first regards provisions in many state tax codes that exempt certain items from sales taxation. These items are typically necessities whose consumption makes up a proportionately larger share of household budgets for low income families. Such provisions reduce the regressive nature of this tax. The second caveat regards the structure of taxes on bequests and inheritances. Since income not spent on consumption must eventually go to one of these ends, a complete analysis should consider these levies simultaneously. And if the same rate applies to all three taxes, the net effect is similar to a proportional tax on income.

Taxes on corporate income fall most heavily on the owners of capital; and, since capital ownership generally increases more than proportionately with income, most analysts conclude that this tax is progressive. The majority of state personal income tax structures are also progressive in nature. An overall equity judgment about state taxes used to support elementary and secondary education, therefore, depends primarily on the relative extent to which an individual state utilizes each of these major levies. My own interpretation of the evidence about the incidence patterns of alternative taxes is that, overall, the levies used to generate state revenues are probably slightly more equitable than local property taxes. This judgment is, however, certainly arguable.

State Aid To Local Districts

In order to make judgments about the efficiency or equity attributes of state appropriated monies for elementary and secondary education, it is necessary to consider not only how revenues are raised but also the way in which they are disbursed. There is considerable variation in the way that individual state aid programs treat specific items such as capital outlays, transportation services, and teacher pension and social security contributions. A common feature of all state formulas, however, is that they distribute funds for basic instructional expenditures in a way that provides more money per pupil to districts with less property wealth and/or income per pupil. The reason is that a major purpose of aid to local districts in virtually every state is to promote equalization in spending per pupil between rich and poor districts.

The heavy reliance on property taxes by municipal governments can give rise to significant disparities in the amount of effort that is required for school districts to raise local revenues to support K-12 education. Variations in property value per student arise from differences in the amount of commercial and industrial property in the local tax base as well as differences in the value of local residential property. When this happens a property-rich district may be able to raise substantially more revenues per student at a lower tax rate (and hence a lighter tax burden to local residents) than a property-poor district can raise at a higher tax rate. When local districts autonomously determine school budgets in such an environment, the likely result is that expenditures per pupil—and hence the quality of education, if more dollars can buy better education—will be markedly higher in property-rich than in property-poor districts. And this is indeed exactly what we usually observe.

Critics first challenged this system in federal court in the case of *Rodriguez* v. *San Antonio Independent School District,* claiming that it violated the equal protection clause of the fourteenth amendment of the U.S. constitution. In 1973 the U.S. Supreme Court ruled, however, that the structure of the Texas school finance system did not represent a violation of this amendment. The effect of this ruling was to relegate the issue of equity in school finance to the state court systems.[5]

The first successful challenge in a state court was the *Serrano* v. *Priest* decision in 1974. The court ruled that the existing system of school finance in California was in violation of the state's own constitution. This decision paved the way for similar litigation in other states. The outcomes of these challenges varied and often hinged on specific provisions in individual state constitutions.[6] And even though not all challenges were successful, the net effect of this widespread litigation was to spur state legislatures to develop allocation programs that promoted equity in spending across local school districts.[7]

State aid programs designed to promote equity in school spending fall into two broad categories: foundation programs and power equalization programs. Under the first a state legislature establishes a foundation level of expenditure per pupil.[8] The state may then allocate to each district a flat grant per pupil equal to this amount. A much more common procedure, however, is for the state to specify a local share of the foundation expenditure for each district. This is typically the revenue raised by each district at a statewide uniform property tax rate. Since the amount of this share varies across districts depending on total value of property in the local tax base, the state grant is proportionately greater for less wealthy districts.

If every district in a state spent exactly the foundation level, then the fiscal result would be analytically equivalent to a single statewide school system or full state funding of K-12 education. Local districts would organize educational services and manage their provision. They would also administer what would essentially amount to a legislated statewide property tax. This situation, however, is not common.[9] Most states with foundation programs allow local districts to exceed the foundation level of expenditure by raising additional local revenues. And several states actually allow local districts to spend less than the foundation level if they impose a local levy lower than the uniform property tax rate specified by the program.

Table 1. State Aid Formulas

Alabama	FG	Montana	F(RLE)
Alaska	PE(ENR)	Nebraska	FG
Arizona	F(ENR)	Nevada	F(RLE)
Arkansas	F(RLE)	New Hampshire	F(ENR)
California	FSF	New Jersey	GTB/Y
Colorado	GTB/Y	New Mexico	FSF
Connecticut	GTB/Y	New York	PE(RLE)
Delaware	FG	North Carolina	FG
Florida	F(RLE)	North Dakota	F(RLE)
Georgia	F(RLE)	Ohio	F(RLE)
Hawaii	FSF	Oklahoma	F(RLE)
Idaho	F(RLE)	Oregon	F(ENR)
Illinois	F(ENR)	Pennsylvania	PE(ENR)
Indiana	F(ENR)	Rhode Island	PE(RLE)
Iowa	F(RLE)	South Carolina	F(RLE)
Kansas	PE(ENR)	South Dakota	GTB/Y
Kentucky	FG	Tennessee	F(RLE)
Louisiana	F(RLE)	Texas	F(ENR)
Maine	F(ENR)	Utah	F(RLE)
Maryland	F(RLE)	Vermont	F(RLE)
Massachusetts	F(ENR)	Virginia	F(RLE)
Michigan	GTB/Y	Washington	FSF
Minnesota	F(RLE)	West Virginia	F(RLE)
Mississippi	F(RLE)	Wisconsin	GTB/Y
Missouri	F(RLE)	Wyoming	F(RLE)

Legend:
F — Foundation
GTB/Y — Guaranteed Tax Base / Yield
PE — Percentage Equalizing
FG — Flat Grant
FSF — Full State Funding
RLE — Required Local Effort
ENR — Local Effort Not Required
Source: Salmon et al. (1988)

A power equalization program creates an environment where the revenue generated by a local school district depends only on the tax rate that it selects, and not the value of its property tax base. The state legislature does this by defining either a guaranteed tax base or a guaranteed tax yield. Because tax yield equals the tax rate multiplied by the tax base, specifying either the yield or the base at any tax rate effectively establishes the other as well. State aid then equals the difference between the amount guaranteed by the program and the revenue raised locally.[10] This program promotes equity since the amount of state aid that any district receives is inversely proportional to its property wealth. In a sense a power equalization program makes the price of education the same for every school district regardless of local property values.

Table 1 presents a compilation of state aid programs published by the American Education Finance Association.[11] A program designated as a Flat

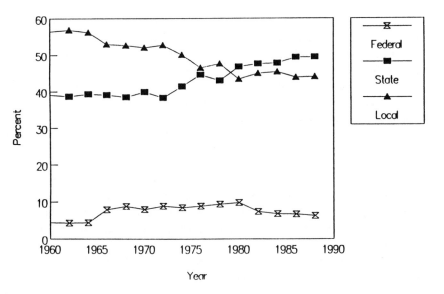

Source: *Digest of Education Statistics* (1988).

Figure 1. K-12 Revenue Sources

Grant (FG) within this classification scheme corresponds to a foundation program where the state provides the entire foundation level of spending per pupil. Inspection of the table reveals that foundation programs are much more common than power equalization programs. Notice also that although most foundation programs specify a wealth-based local share of foundation spending per pupil, eleven states do not actually require school districts to impose a local levy that will raise this amount.

State efforts throughout the last two decades to increase equity in school district spending patterns have had another important effect. At the same time that they implemented more redistributive aid programs, states also increased their level of support for elementary and secondary schools. This altered substantially the mix of resources provided by state governments and local school districts. As Figure 1 indicates, while the percentage of revenues provided by the federal government has fluctuated between four and ten percent, the dominant source of funds has shifted in recent years from local property taxes to state appropriations.

GENERAL IMPLICATIONS FOR REFORM PROPOSALS

Increased reliance on state funds and equalization of spending per pupil across districts represents greater centralization in the public sector provision of K-12 education. This trend has implications for both the efficiency of public sector resource allocation and proposals to improve the quality of education in the United States; and in many ways these implications are related.

The discussion above suggests that increased centralization may promote efficient resource allocation from the perspective of the merit good and quasi-public good characteristics of education. At the same time it exacerbates the inefficiency associated with the collective provision of a service that has a significant private good component.

But what can we say about how this emerging fiscal structure is likely to affect the quality of education? The answer depends on several factors: the impact that changes in spending has on the quality of education, the impact that increased centralization has on the total amount of dollars spent on education, and the impact that increased fiscal centralization has on the way that the provision of education is organized.

The most fundamental question concerns the relationship between spending and school quality. In another paper in this volume Gary Burtless examines in detail the relationship between school spending and measures of both educational output and future earnings capacity (Burtless 1993). He concludes that better schools do significantly affect future earnings capacity, but that how education is organized may be more important than dollars spent in determining the quality of education. Eric Hanushek, basing his findings on an exhaustive survey of available evidence, takes an even more pessimistic view about the relationship between spending and educational quality. He concludes that, at least over the range within which most public schools now operate, there is little evidence that additional spending increases school effectiveness. He further argues that the net effect of state policies to address the equity issue has been to increase total spending on schools with no apparent accompanying benefit (Hanushek 1986).

I think that this evidence suggests that the pursuit of equity in school finance and the pursuit of educational excellence are to some extent incongruent. It also seems inarguable that the dialogue about how to increase the quality of education must take as given our equity-based system. Our tradition of ensuring access to educational opportunity is a longstanding one; and state court decisions continue to reaffirm it. At the same time I believe that there is a need to examine carefully what equity in educational opportunity entails. For different interpretations of its meaning can have consequential ramifications on endeavors to improve the quality of education in the United States.

While few individuals would dispute that access to educational opportunity is a propitious social goal, specifying exactly what this goal *requires* in terms of public policies is problematic. Does it simply mean that state governments must provide enough aid to poor districts so that they can provide adequate educational services? If so, what is the definition of adequate? This is more than a rhetorical question; it is one that state legislatures must grapple with in each budget cycle as they weigh tradeoffs between additional dollars for local schools, spending on other programs, and increased taxes.

Or does equity compel states to ensure that every district provides exactly the same educational services and/or expenditure per pupil? This is a much stricter interpretation of equity. It has as its basic premise the proposition that students in one district are implicitly penalized if students in another district are given additional opportunities. This interpretation suggests that state legislatures must not only establish a minimum level of educational opportunity, but they must also institute a ceiling on the spending ability of wealthy districts.

I find this latter definition of equity perturbing, and I believe that to some extent this is because I bring an economist's perspective to the question. If we live in a free market system, is it right for us to allow some families to provide their children with more expensive clothes, better recreational opportunities and sports cars, but not to allow these same families to provide them with additional resources for education? Such a position seems unreasonable to me. At the same time I perceive that a large segment of the education community feels comfortable with this notion, precisely because its equity basis is so pure.

Whatever philosophy we adopt about the meaning of equity may affect the viability of several prominent proposals for school reform. One current proposal that offers great promise and appears to have widespread support is better school management through decentralized decision making. The idea behind this approach is that teachers and their principals are more likely to accomplish their missions when left to their own devices and not encumbered by bureaucratic constraints. I see the increased centralization that accompanies a strict definition of equity as incompatible with this strategy. In the first place, the raison d'etre for decentralized management is to allow schools to be different from each other. And it seems incredible to expect that the differences that emerge will all result in the same level of spending per pupil. Secondly, experience suggests that when state governments provide a greater share of the resources for public programs they tend to become more, not less, involved in their organization.

Another popular reform strategy is the magnet school. The distinctive characteristic of a magnet school is that it offers specialized programs and unusual opportunities for learning. This is fundamentally at odds with a strict interpretation of equity requirements. The very concept of a magnet school implies that it offers something that is not available elsewhere. Moreover, the special programs of magnet schools typically cost more to provide than traditional instruction. They are different, and at present their facilities are limited. In fact, the opening of a magnet school has resulted in parents camping out in queues for days in order to secure an opening for their child (Sylvester 1989). Equity policies may affect educational output in the U.S. in ways other than through their impact on current reform proposals. A strict equity rule requires ceilings on locally raised revenues. When this happens the only way for citizens to influence the flow of resources to schools is through state capitals. In this environment there is a less well-defined relationship between tax dollars and the private benefits that accrue to parents and students. And implementing policies that diminish parents' fiscal authority over schools may beget an unintended side effect by making them less involved in other aspects of the education process. This would be unfortunate since virtually every study of the determinants of educational success concludes that parental involvement is the single most important factor.

What can we infer from present policies concerning the meaning of equity? Most states currently permit discretionary local spending. Power equalization programs by their very nature allow school districts to determine the local levy. And the majority of foundation programs allow districts to spend in excess of (and sometimes less than) the specified local share.

In response to successful equity challenges to school financing arrangements, courts typically have ruled only that the existing structure was in violation of a state's constitution. They then permitted the state legislature to develop a more redistributive aid program. Recent decisions, however, suggest a trend toward more proscriptive solutions. Only one year after the Texas Supreme Court, in *Edgewood* v. *Kirby,* mandated the state to decrease spending disparities between rich and poor districts, a district judge ruled that the reform enacted by the Texas state legislature was not comprehensive enough (*Education Week*, October 3, 1990). And in *Abbott* v. *Burke,* the New Jersey Supreme Court ruled that the state must ensure that spending per pupil in the state's poorest cities matched that of its most affluent suburbs (*New York Times,* June 6, 1990).

Perhaps the best way for states to avoid judicially imposed school finance regimes is to make sure that their legislated programs do not leave them susceptible to successful challenges. As Table 1 illustrated, existing state programs are designed to promote equity. They falter when they fail to provide enough resources and/or enough redistribution to eliminate substantial spending disparities between rich and poor districts.

The proposal for educational reform that clearly has received the most widespread attention to date is parental choice. Its benefits have been discussed at length in sources ranging from an op ed piece in the *New York Times* by Governor Perpich of Minnesota to a series of writings by John Chubb and Terry Moe.[12]

Parental choice differs from other proposed reforms in that it mandates a fundamental reconfiguration in the institutions which govern the provision of public education. For this reason it may be more compatible with equity-driven fiscal centralization than proposals for magnet schools and school based management.

Under parental choice a student's parents are free to select the public school that he or she will attend. The arguments in favor of this option are compelling. It allows parents and children to decide which school is best, taking into account how differences in school offerings can best match the different needs of individuals. It also places competitive pressures on school administrators. By taking away the captive audience of local residents, it forces schools to be more efficient and to produce a superior product—just as a competitive market forces firms in the private sector to do the same. Frequently cited examples of the success that accompanies parental choice options are the Minnesota state-wide plan, the Cambridge, Massachusetts school district plan, and District 4 plan in the Harlem section of New York City's school system.

What are the implications of choice systems for the public finance of elementary and secondary education? To answer this question requires an analysis of the political economy of local public sector decision making.

Consider first how choice affects school district revenues. In the Cambridge and New York City cases cited above, there is no effect on revenues. When choice is defined *within* a school district, both local revenues and state revenues per pupil are the same regardless of which school a student attends. This type of choice plan will achieve its purposes, of course, only when districts are large enough to have several schools from which students can choose.

Table 2 presents the distribution of the number of schools per district for each of the 50 states.[13] Inspection of this table suggests that most districts have fewer than 10 schools and many have only one or two. A district with fewer than 10 schools probably operates one or perhaps two high schools, two or three junior highs or middle schools, and a few elementary schools. Choice will be limited within these districts and nonexistent in districts that operate only one or two schools. Creating effective choice for students residing in these areas probably requires allowing interdistrict transfers.

Operating an interdistrict choice plan is more involved and is likely to come about only through state government initiative. The Minnesota plan provides an excellent example. In Minnesota, state aid follows a student who chooses a school in a different district. The local share of foundation level spending can also follow this student since the Minnesota state aid program requires local effort (refer again to Table 1.) As discussed above, a required local share for a foundation program is analytically equivalent to a legislated statewide property tax. Under this form of aid program, implementing a statewide choice plan is relatively straightforward. Because the total foundation amount is earmarked for a student, it can naturally go to the school that he or she selects.[14]

Discretionary local spending introduces greater complexity to the question about how to allocate revenue in the presence of interdistrict choice. Any

Table 2. Distribution of the Number of Schools
in U.S. Local Public School Systems

	20 or More	10-19	3-9	2	1
Alabama	9	29	83	6	2
Alaska	6	11	18	15	5
Arizona	6	16	77	40	91
Arkansas	4	9	93	226	1
California	63	124	386	166	412
Colorado	15	12	80	69	4
Connecticut	5	21	87	13	39
Delaware	2	6	7	2	2
Florida	26	14	37	6	12
Georgia	14	27	124	10	11
Hawaii	1	0	0	0	0
Idaho	2	12	58	31	15
Illinois	10	38	488	185	307
Indiana	11	36	180	62	13
Iowa	7	12	223	197	12
Kansas	7	16	186	97	18
Kentucky	6	35	103	30	4
Louisiana	23	30	13	0	0
Maine	0	11	94	18	106
Maryland	15	5	8	3	10
Massachusetts	9	26	169	44	120
Michigan	24	47	351	91	77
Minnesota	5	14	126	266	22
Mississippi	1	16	114	24	19
Missouri	9	23	183	251	95
Montana	1	3	38	40	462
Nebraska	4	9	64	218	608
Nevada	3	4	9	1	0
New Hampshire	1	5	56	24	72
New Jersey	9	30	247	114	201
New Mexico	5	11	47	25	0
New York	5	43	372	164	166
North Carolina	32	41	63	4	58
North Dakota	1	3	28	182	68
Ohio	11	43	470	88	8
Oklahoma	7	16	202	235	176
Oregon	8	15	95	64	135
Pennsylvania	8	60	368	68	11
Rhode Island	3	4	22	5	6
South Carolina	12	26	49	5	6
South Dakota	3	6	134	34	9
Tennessee	12	43	69	9	9
Texas	54	43	531	377	107
Utah	11	12	17	0	0
Vermont	0	1	24	29	195
Virginia	21	34	63	14	3
Washington	17	26	120	69	65
West Virginia	21	18	16	0	0
Wisconsin	10	20	251	105	56
Wyoming	3	10	33	2	8

Source: Government Organization (1987, Table 16).

additional spending by districts over and above a foundation program's required local effort fits this category. And all locally raised revenue is discretionary under power equalization programs and foundation programs that do not require local effort. School district residents decide how much they will spend this way either through budget referenda or through their elected representatives.

If a student chooses to attend school in another district, should his or her share of the home district's discretionary local revenue go with the student? Or should this money stay with those students who remain in the home district? This is not an easy question to answer. Its resolution depends on a judgment about who owns the property rights to these funds. Do they belong to the student or do they belong to the taxpayers? Policy makers in state capitals must ultimately resolve this issue. How they do so will affect local expenditure decisions.

Consider first the case where local funds follow transferring students. In all likelihood citizens who decide local budgets will not wish to send their tax dollars to another district to subsidize these students. The net effect therefore will be for all individual districts to reduce discretionary spending below what it otherwise would have been.

But what if discretionary local revenues stay put? The resident district must forego the state aid and required local effort that follows this student; but other local revenues are now spread over fewer students. In one sense a district which loses a student is better off, since the same local revenues can now be used to provide more educational services for the students who remain. The same situation is not true, of course, in a receiving district. Citizens there must use part of whatever discretionary revenues they raise to help educate nonresident students. This may eventually lead net importing districts to spend less money on local schools than they would have otherwise. It is conceivable that this could result in a net reduction in the flow of resources to education.

All of this presupposes that parental choice will prompt a substantial amount of transferring. It is important to recognize that the benefits to be derived from choice do not require this. The potential of transfers is really all that is necessary to create the competitive environment that achieves its objectives. And most parents place significant value on having their children attend neighborhood schools. It is nonetheless interesting to examine how the potential for active interdistrict transferring might exert stress on the existing structure of school finance arrangements.

Table 3 presents the same data as Table 2 but for only those states where discretionary local spending is most significant. These are the states that Table 1 lists as having power equalization programs and foundation programs not requiring local effort. The distribution of the number of schools that a district operates is important because it allows us to identify the magnitude of districts where effective choice requires interdistrict transfers. This is not the only

Table 3.   Potential Fiscal Stress Areas

Average School District Size (sq. mi.)		Distribution of the Number of Schools in U.S. Local Public School Systems				
		20 or More	10-19	3-9	2	1
13	New Jersey	9	30	247	114	201
21	Massachusetts	9	26	169	44	120
30	Connecticut	5	21	87	13	39
55	New Hampshire	1	5	56	24	72
57	Illinois	10	38	488	185	307
90	Pennsylvania	8	60	368	68	11
103	Michigan	24	47	351	91	77
118	Maine	0	11	94	18	106
119	Indiana	11	36	180	62	13
130	Wisconsin	10	20	251	105	56
251	Texas	54	43	531	377	107
271	Kansas	7	16	186	97	18
317	Oregon	8	15	95	64	135
399	South Dakota	3	6	134	34	9
523	Arizona	6	16	77	40	91
589	Colorado	15	12	80	69	4
10,662	Alaska	6	11	18	15	5

Sources: Government Organization (1987, Table 16), *Digest of Education Statistics* (1988, Table 69).

important element, however. School district size is also important since the cost of attending another school will depend upon how far away it is. Table 3 therefore ranks these states according to mean geographic area. Inspection of the table reveals that states where school districts are small both in terms of their geographic area and the number of schools that they operate are concentrated mainly in the northeast and north central United States.

What policies might we suggest for enhancing choice opportunities in these states? The obvious answer is for state governments to provide additional aid to districts that accept transferring students. The amount of this aid should cover all additional costs that a district incurs. The total expense associated with this policy will likely be quite modest relative to most existing state K-12 educational expenditures. This is especially true if, as most analysts expect, the potential for choice is sufficient to achieve its objectives so that actual transfers will not be widespread.

CONCLUSION

A major consequence of the pursuit of fiscal equity in school finance has been the relative growth in state government revenues dedicated to K-12 schools.

At the same time, increased state fiscal responsibility is a natural solution to any fiscal stress that may develop if parental choice leads to a significant number of interdistrict transfers. This may seem like pure serendipity to proponents of parental choice.

There is a more compelling justification for using increased state aid as a vehicle to implement parental choice plans, however. It is a reason that will resolve a major practical impediment to choice proposals, one that its proponents have neglected and its critics apparently have not yet discerned. Proponents of parental choice typically forge their arguments on a market-based analysis of providing education.[15] These arguments neglect the lack of an analogy in public schools to the role of the entrepreneur in free markets. Competition works in free markets because entrepreneurs are willing to risk losing their own resources in return for the gain that they will realize if they succeed. And the evidence is overwhelming that this profit motive is effective. But who are the potential losers in districts when students transfer? At first glance, unless so many students leave that a district is unable to operate with reasonable scale economies, the only apparent losers are school officials. For eventually they must explain to voters why resident students prefer the educational services provided elsewhere. In the end, however, it is local property owners who are at risk. This is especially true for capital expenditures. School facilities are expensive and the ultimate lien on the general obligation bond indebtedness of school districts is local property.

Local property owners certainly have a strong incentive to force school officials to perform efficiently lest they incur the cost of empty classrooms. There is no profit motive, however, to create an incentive for them to incur this risk in the first place. School districts are public enterprises that provide education as a service to local residents. If parental choice introduces the possibility of economic failure, but does not provide any reward for economic success, we can expect the new education market that develops to be a thin one. It will not be in voters' own self interest to approve new bond issues, and eventually existing facilities will wear out. Unless parental choice plans allow for-profit schools similar to for-profit hospitals, and I have not yet seen any such proposals, some other mechanism is necessary to ensure that there will be schools around from which parents can choose.

One possibility is to allow existing non-profit private schools and parochial schools into the choice process. The city of Milwaukee introduced a choice plan in the fall of 1990 that includes private schools; and Chubb and Moe (1990) favor including parochial schools as well. I personally don't believe that there is at present a sufficient number of private non-profit schools to solve this problem; and it seems clear that issues about the relationship between church and state, and not economic necessity, will determine whether parochial schools can participate.

I believe that we must look to state capitals to solve this dilemma. If governors and legislatures were willing to finance a significant share of new capital outlays throughout their state, they could effectively reduce the risk to local property owners of debt financed, under-utilized facilities in the event that a choice plan induced pupils to abandon their district. Such a policy might consist of shifting present dollars of state aid from operating expense subsidies to capital expenditure subsidies, or it might involve increasing the level of state aid to support more fully capital outlays. I will leave it to others to speculate about whether or not our elected officials are likely to embrace such a policy.

NOTES

1. In an early discussion of this issue Buchanan (1960) referred to goods of this nature as quai-public goods.

2. See the paper in this volume by Raymond Bell for a more detailed discussion of federal policies toward elementary and secondary education.

3. See Fisher (1988) for an excellent discussion of this issue, including how the degree of within- and across -state variation in local tax rates can affect the conclusion we reach about the degree of progressivity or regressivity of this tax.

4. See Munley (1990) for a detailed discussion of many of the conclusions mentioned briefly in this paper.

5. In the purest sense, the term equity in the school finance literature means equality of educational opportunity. Because educational opportunity, or school quality, is very difficult to measure, equity has usually been defined operationally in terms of expenditures per student. The courts have likewise adopted this definition. See Rubenfeld (1979) and Berne and Stiefel (1984).

6. For an overview of individual state court decisions on this issue see van Geel (1982) and Briffault (1987).

7. It is interesting to note that litigation continues over this issue. State courts in Kentucky, Montana, New Jersey, and Texas have recently ruled that existing school finance systems were in violation of their respective state constitutions. Similar litigation has been initiated, or is pending, in at least a dozen other states.

8. Some state programs explicitly adjust the foundation expenditure level to take into account regional price differentials which affect school district costs.

9. New Mexico and Nevada are examples of where this occurs.

10. A strict interpretation of a power equalization program would require property-rich school districts to remit to the state any local revenues exceeding the amount guaranteed. Such recapture provisions are extremely rare because of the obvious political ramifications.

11. See Salmon et al. (1988).

12. See Perpich (1989); Chubb and Moe (1988, 1990a, 1990b).

13. These data represent all public school systems and not just those that provide only elementary and secondary education. For several states this number exceeds somewhat the number of K-12 school districts as reported in Digest of Education Statistics. Since most non K-12 districts are involved in special purpose education, such as community colleges, Table 2 probably overstates slightly the proportion of one- and two-school districts.

14. Some states define foundation spending in terms of instructional units rather than per pupil. Since these programs typically define instructional units in terms of numbers of students, allocating any student's share is straightforward.

15. See, for example, Chubb and Moe (1988, 1990a, 1990b).

REFERENCES

Bell, R. 1993. "The American System of Education." In *The Economic Consequences of American Education,* edited by A.P. O'Brien and R. J. Thornton. Greenwich, CT: JAI Press.

Berne, R. and L. Stiefel. 1984. *The Measurement of Equity in School Finance.* Baltimore, MD: Johns Hopkins University Press.

Briffault, R. 1987. "State-Local Relations and Constitutional Law." *Intergovernmental Perspective* 13 (3/4): 10-14.

Buchanan, J.M. 1960. *The Public Finances.* Homewood, IL: Richard D. Irwin.

Burtless, G. 1993. "Current Proposals for School Reform: An Economist's Appraisal." In *The Economic Consequences of American Education,* edited by A.P. O'Brien and R.J. Thorton. Greenwich, CT: JAI Press.

Card, D. and A. Kruger. 1992. "Does Schooling Matter? Returns to Education and the Characteristics of Public Schools in the United States." *Journal of Political Economy* 100, 1-40.

Chubb, J.E. and T.M. Moe. 1988. "Politics, Markets, and the Organization of Schools." *American Political Science Review* 82 (4): 1065-1087.

———. 1990a. *Politics, Markets and America's Schools.* Washington DC: The Brookings Institution.

———. 1990b. "Choice Is Panacea." *The Brookings Review* 8 (3): 4-12.

Digest of Education Statistics. 1988. National Center for Education Statistics, U.S. Department of Education, Table 107.

Fisher, R.C. 1988. *State and Local Finance.* Glenview, IL: Scott, Foresman, and Co.

Hanushek, E.A. 1986. "The Economics of Schooling." *Journal of Economic Literature* 24 (3): 1141-1177.

Munley, V.G. 1990. *The Structure of State Aid to Elementary and Secondary Education.* Washington, DC: Advisory Commission on Intergovernmental Relations.

Oates, W.E. 1972. *Fiscal Federalism.* New York: Harcourt, Brace and Jovanovich.

Perpich, R. 1989. "Choose Your School." *New York Times,* A17.

Rubinfeld, D. 1979. "Judicial Approaches to Local Public Sector Equity." In *Current Issues in Urban Economics,* edited by P. Mieszkowski and M. Straszheim. Baltimore, MD: John Hopkins University Press.

Salmon, R., C. Dawson, S. Lawton and T. Johns. (eds.). 1988. *Public School Programs in the United States and Canada.* Blacksburg, VA: American Education Finance Association.

Sylvester, K. 1989. "Schools of Choice: A Path to Educational Quality or Tiers of Inequity?" *Governing* 20, 50-54.

Teibout, C.M. 1956. "A Pure Theory of Local Expenditures." *Journal of Political Economy* 64, 416-24.

U.S. Department of Commerce. 1987. *Government Organization.* Washington, DC: Bureau of the Census.

van Geel, T. 1982. "The Courts and School Finance Reform." Pp. 71-106 in *The Changing Politics of School Finance,* edited by N.H. Cambron-McCabe and A. Odden. Cambridge, MA: Ballenger Publishing.

COMMENTS

Elliott J. Dubin

Professor Munley's paper, "The Structure of K-12 School Finance in the United States: Constraints and Implications for Education Reforms," presents a clear and concise exposition of the economists' perspective of two major issues currently facing public elementary and secondary education: improving the quality of education and assuring equity in the distribution of education services. This paper should prove valuable to nonexperts in the area of education because it presents information on and analyses of the economic role and nature of primary and secondary education, sources of funding, state aid formulas, and proposals to reform education in a clear and concise manner. However, the main value of this paper is that it shows that the two issues are interrelated. In fact, the author concludes that the pursuit of equity in school finance, usually defined as reducing the differences in per pupil expenditures across school districts (within a state) and the pursuit of excellence in education, often are at cross purposes.

A major portion of the paper is devoted to explaining why education is generally provided through the public sector. The author states that because of the "public good" aspects of education, parents would purchase less than the socially optimal level of education for their children.[1] Similarly, local communities would provide less than the socially optimal level of education since some of the benefits "spill over" their boundaries into other geographic areas (e.g., the state and nation). While it is true that the "public good" attributes of education are a factor leading to the underproduction and underconsumption of education, the investment nature of this function is also a factor in society's provision of less than the socially desirable level of this service.

The reason education is considered an investment is its long-term nature. Unlike other services provided by the local community (police and fire protection, roads, etc.) which provide benefits for the community immediately, the benefits of education begin to accrue only after the pupil leaves school and begins to participate in the economic, political, social, and cultural life of the community. That is, parents and the community must bear the cost of providing education services for a period of 12-13 years (from ages 5-6 until high school graduation) before any benefits are realized. Thus, pupils and their parents incur the risk that their investment in education will not generate the expected "payoff." Similarly, local communities would provide less than the socially optimal level of education because they cannot fully recapture the benefits of providing this service as long as individuals are free to migrate from a community which provided a high quality of education.

The discussion of the major sources of revenues currently used by all types of governments to finance public elementary and secondary education presents some interesting insights concerning the efficiency and equity of funding sources. As Professor Munley correctly points out, education is generally considered a "merit good" by economists. This is a good or service that exhibits characteristics of both private goods and public goods.[2] Because of the private good characteristics of education, some portion of the costs of its provision should be financed by user charges or fees (charges that approximate prices for private goods and services) to maximize efficiency in production and consumption of education services. As is pointed out in the paper, none of the major sources of revenues currently used to finance public education (property taxes, sales taxes, and individual and corporate income taxes) approximates a user fee. The absence of an analog to a market price may lead to overproduction or underproduction of K-12 education.

The methods of financing K-12 education may also violate standards of intergovernmental equity, if one believes that those who ultimately benefit should also pay for this service. One of the primary benefits of education is higher lifetime earnings. A portion of this benefit can be recaptured through the imposition of progressive taxes on income or wealth. However, the heaviest user of progressive income taxes is the federal government, which currently provides between 6 and 7 percent of public school revenues. State governments also use progressive income taxes as well as regressive-to-proportional sales taxes to finance their share of public school revenues. The paper correctly considers these revenue sources as more equitable than local property taxes because they are more closely related to the level of benefits received.

In his discussion of state aid for education, Professor Munley points out two salient facts: (1) state funds have supplanted local funds as the main source of public school revenues; and (2) state aid formulas have become more redistributive: that is, relatively more aid per pupil is allocated to low-wealth school districts. The author also points out that the increasing reliance on state ınds to finance education can reduce the overall efficiency of resource ıllocation, and act as an obstacle to improving the quality of education. This ıst point is most important because it reveals why achieving greater equity ı education finance and improving education outcomes are so difficult to chieve simultaneously.

Most proposals to improve the quality of education, as stated previously, ıvolve decentralizing management and decision-making: that is, changing the ʋay education services are produced. However, increasing reliance on state ınds to provide education services will inevitably lead to greater centralization ıf school management. State legislators and governors will become more ınvolved in the organization and administration of education because they must ɛvy taxes to finance this function and, therefore, will be held politically ıccountable for the results.

There are other issues and questions of education finance that the paper did ıot address. For example, because of the public good characteristics of K-12 ɛducation and the interstate mobility of the population, should the federal ;overnment provide a greater share of the funds for general education? Should he federal government provide more funds for primary and secondary ɛducation to reduce interstate differences in per pupil expenditures? If one ıelieves that the answers to these questions are yes, another question arises: ʋhat would be the impact on the efficiency of resource allocation and the ıossibility of improving the quality of education?

This paper performs a valuable service for those interested in the areas of ɛducation finance and education reforms, especially policymakers who must lecide how education resources are to be allocated. Using well-reasoned ırguments, Professor Munley points out that it is probably not possible ımultaneously to achieve a more equitable distribution of education resources ıcross school districts, to improve the quality of education, and to increase he efficiency of allocating education resources. Possible reforms such as chool-based management, magnet schools, and parental choice—all of which, ı is believed, would improve the quality of education—generally require lifferences in per pupil expenditures. Considering the lack of empirical ɛvidence linking higher school spending with improved educational outcomes, his seems quite logical. Thus, the problems facing American education will ıot be solved either by only increasing the level of resources devoted to ɛducation, or by only changing the methods by which education services are ırganized and administered.

NOTES

1. The "public good" aspects of education include (1) the increased productivity of a student ıver his/her lifetime that is not fully recaptured by the student in terms of higher lifetime earnings;

and (2) an enhanced social, economic, cultural and political fabric of the community that provided high quality education.

2.   The private good aspects of primary and secondary education are (1) those receiving education (pupils and their parents) derive direct benefits from this service; and (2) there is no "free rider" element in the consumption of this service i.e., individuals can be prohibited from receiving this service.

EUROPEAN SCHOOL SYSTEMS AND FINANCING:
LESSONS FOR THE UNITED STATES

Nicholas Barr and Howard Glennerster

THE ISSUES

This section is concerned mainly with a brief overview of the objectives of education. The next section discusses important analytical issues including the major (and unanswered) question of the relation between the extent and form of expenditure on education and the growth of output in an economy. These two sections assist analysis of the European experience and draw out lessons (positive and negative) for the U.S. system of school education and higher education, which are discussed in the following two sections. A final section summarizes the main conclusions.

The objectives of education policy (as of policy more broadly) include efficiency, equity, and social solidarity. Efficiency has at least two aspects: *macro efficiency* addresses the issue of the fraction of national resources to be devoted to education; *micro efficiency* is concerned with the efficient division of that total between different types and levels of education.

The efficiency goals embrace both the contribution made to output by education viewed as an investment good and its benefits as a consumption good; and efficiency should relate both to the allocation of a given stock of resources and to the dynamic efficiency issue of the effect of education on economic growth.

Private Benefits

Public Benefits

Production	Consumption	Production	Social Goods
Preparation for work, enhanced earning capacity. (Rate of return to education as a measure.)	Education of one's children with social equals. Present pleasure, potential future non-monetary gains from extended leisure pursuits. Simple capacity to acquire knowledge. (Largely immeasurable.)	General benefit from a highly trained labor force with skills not specific to one firm. Scientific and other research with commercial or industrial applications. (Largely immeasurable.)	Respect for law and order, socialization into existing norms and values; transmitting cultural heritage; occupational mobility and positions open to the most able; an informed electorate, mutual benefits derived from living in a culturally rich society; promoting equal access to education and a sense of social justice; social cohesion and a sense of shared citizenship; promoting social and racial equality. (Some can be measured.)

Private/Public Values

Conservative/Liberal values

Figure 1. An Education Value Map: Potential Benefits from Education

Equity is concerned with how education is distributed. Though the aim can be disputed, we take it as an objective throughout the paper that policy should seek to make education available on the basis of relevant educational criteria (e.g., desire for additional education and the ability to absorb it), independent of irrelevant criteria such as race or sex (so-called horizontal equity). An additional equity aim (vertical equity) is that the availability of education should depend as little as possible on family wealth, and should be financed so as to further that objective.

The social solidarity objective relates to the contribution of education to the formation of society broadly, as opposed to its inculcation of individual-specific skills. Aims here include the development of shared values (e.g., the importance of freedom of speech, the rule of law, and the like).

Beyond such general aims, it is impossible to state a set of universally agreed goals for education. Education produces a mixture of present consumption benefits and future ones, of future production benefits for the individual and for society in different measure. More controversially it also produces social goods which may vary from instilling a respect for law and order to creating a shared sense of common citizenship. Some may see education primarily in terms of a private investment while others put more emphasis on the social goals. Yet there is also fundamental disagreement about which social goals education should pursue. We illustrate these divergent value dimensions in Figure 1. It is important to emphasize these different goals because they imply a set of tradeoffs which politicians are reluctant to debate openly.

Thus there is no necessary agreement about which aims should be pursued nor, where aims are in conflict, about the relative weight which should be accorded to each. In part this is because people have different values: and in part it is because important outcomes cannot be measured; for reasons discussed in the next section, the *public* benefit from education (a major focus of the conference) is a case in point.

THE THEORETICAL BACKDROP

Three salient issues are discussed in turn: the optimal size of the education sector; the optimal degree of subsidy; and the problem of capital market imperfections.

The Optimal Size of the Education Sector

Quantitative evidence on the socially efficient volume of investment in education (the macro efficiency objective) by type of education (the micro efficiency objective) would be an invaluable guide to policy. There are many reasons why such evidence is not available, not least the problem that many key variables cannot be measured. One problem, however, the so-called screening problem, stands out.

The investment case for education rests on the (usually unstated) assumption that it leads to increased productivity. The screening hypothesis argues that education is *associated* with increased productivity, but does not *cause* it (the large literature on this and other aspects of the education literature is surveyed by Blaug [1976]).

The distribution of earnings depends on factors like sex, race, family circumstances, natural ability and the quantity and quality of education (Blaug 1970). The screening hypothesis is a special case which argues, first, that education beyond a basic level does not increase individual productivity and, second, that firms seek high-ability workers but are unable, prior to employing them, to distinguish them from those with low ability. The problem is analytically identical to adverse selection in insurance markets, or more generally to "lemons" (Akerlof 1970), in the sense that one side of the market has more information than the other. Individuals therefore have an incentive to make themselves distinctive by some sort of signal (Spence 1973). According to the screening hypothesis postprimary education fills exactly this function: it gives a signal to prospective employers, which it is in the *individual's* (though not necessarily in society's) interests to acquire. Just as an individual's good health may be due more to a naturally strong constitution than to medical care so, according to this view, is productivity the result of natural ability rather than post-primary education.

There are various counter-arguments. Wherever education overlaps with vocational training, there is a direct contribution to productivity. The strong form of the hypothesis also assumes that there is only one type of job. In practice skills and job characteristics are heterogeneous, so that it is necessary to match workers and jobs, giving education an additional social return as a matching device.

Whether there is *some* validity in the hypothesis is an empirical matter. The verdict is undecided and likely to remain so. Individual productivity is determined in part by measurable factors like age, sex and educational qualifications; it also depends on vital but unmeasurable influences like natural ability and family background. Attempts to quantify the determinants of productivity which omit the unmeasurable factors are statistically flawed.[1] The theoretical conclusion, given the present state of knowledge, is that it is not possible to make quantitative statements either about the size of the educational sector or about the contribution of education to economic growth.

The best that is possible is to look at rather rough-and-ready empirical data. United Kingdom evidence (Glennerster and Low 1989) shows a greater than unitary income elasticity of private education spending in Britain between 1974 and 1985; state spending over the period did not rise with income. To the extent that private preferences are efficient, this suggests that the U.K. government is underspending. Such an observation, however, though possibly telling us something about static efficiency, tells us nothing about the relation between education and economic growth.

Subsidies for Education

To argue for subsidies for education is to presuppose either an equity or an efficiency argument for doing do. The horizontal and vertical equity goals have already been asserted. The efficiency case for subsidies must rest on one of two arguments: that education, though benefiting the individual recipient, also confers benefits on others (the so-called externality argument) (Blaug 1976); or that, for technical reasons, it is not possible to borrow enough to pay for education (the problem of capital-market imperfections) (Becker 1964).

Education has at least one unarguable external benefit. By raising a student's earnings, it increases his or her future tax payments; in the absence of any subsidy, an individual's investment would confer a "dividend" on taxpayers in the future. This is inefficient, in that investment in education would be inefficiently small, and is therefore the minimum case for a subsidy.

Does education create external benefits over and above this tax dividend? It is part of the conventional wisdom that it does. *Cultural benefits,* which have a close link with the social solidarity objective, arise out of shared experiences and common values. Any society has to consider its appropriate balance between cultural diversity (which, at least in the West, is desirable in itself, and which contributes to the vitality of a society) and cultural homogeneity (which is necessary if a society is to be more than a collection of isolated individuals). Again, it is not possible to answer the issue definitively because the issue raises fundamental value judgements and because key variables cannot be measured.

To the extent that the existence, preservation, development and transmission of a common culture benefits everyone and is fostered by the educational process, a clear case exists for subsidy, a case which is no less strong for the absence of quantifiable evidence. In addition, because cultural benefits derive not just from education per se, but from being educated together with everyone else, there is an efficiency case for education to be publicly organized, an argument which is at its strongest for pre-university education.

Production benefits arise if education not only makes someone more productive, but also contributes to the productivity of others. At the most basic level, my productivity is increased if I can assume that other people can read. Similarly, if colleagues learn the same word processing package they contribute to each other's productivity as well as to their own. The link between education and economic growth arises also in this context (Blaug 1970) but, again, cannot be demonstrated quantitatively, mainly because of the screening problem.

The externality justification for educational subsidies is strong in presumptive terms, but cannot be demonstrated empirically. Because of the "tax dividend" point there is an unarguable efficiency case for *some* subsidy; but it is not possible to show quantitatively how much. The remaining argument for subsidy, and particularly for the near-100 percent subsidy implied by tax-funded education which is free at the point of use, must rest on its contribution to equity and social solidarity.

Capital Market Problems

Loans for education are particularly relevant to later arguments about higher education. There are problems for both lenders and borrowers.

Demand-Side Problems

Loans organized like a conventional mortgage or bank overdraft are risky from the individual student's viewpoint and are therefore likely to deter applicants, particularly those from the most disadvantaged backgrounds. This is both inefficient (because it wastes talent) and inequitable (because it reduces social mobility).

It is sometimes argued (U.K. Department of Education and Science 1988) that people from poorer backgrounds will borrow to buy a house, so why not to buy education? Apart from the tax advantages, when someone buys a house, (a) he knows what he is buying (since he has lived in a house all his life), (b) the house is unlikely to fall down, and (c) the value of the house is likely to go up. When people borrow for education, (a) they are not fully certain what they are buying (particularly if they come from a family with low educational attainments), (b) there is a perceived risk of failing to complete the qualification, and (c) though the *average* private return to education is positive (U.K. Department of Education and Science 1988), there is considerable variance around it (Bennett, Glennerster, and Nevison 1992). For all three reasons, borrowing for educational purposes is much more risky than borrowing to buy a house and the risks are likely to be greater for people from poorer backgrounds and for women.

Supply-Side Problems

Long-term loans are risky also to the lender. There is no collateral (contrast the case of lending for house purchase). If the legalization of slavery is ruled out, the private sector will make long-term unsecured loans only with a government guarantee. A second form of risk to the lender is asymmetric information, in that students are better-informed than lenders whether they aspire to careers in arbitrage or the arts.

Because the loan guarantee is expensive, total lending will tend to be policed: either loans are rationed, or the worst risks are excluded. There are also high administrative costs, particularly for more risky students: lending institutions have to keep detailed records of each borrower; and the cost of chasing repayments is also substantial, the more so because the loan is unsecured. We return to these capital-market issues in the context of student loans.

LESSONS FROM EUROPE: SCHOOLS

The 1950s and 1960s

Some of the most important changes for the present economies of Western Europe occurred some 20-30 years ago when they decided for social reasons to broaden the base of their education systems. To understand the process, it is helpful to pick up the story earlier.

The Early Postwar Period

In the period of reconstruction after the Second World War the countries of Western Europe developed essentially divided or selective systems of education beyond the age of 10, 11, or 12. Building on their traditions they extended access on a limited but competitive meritocratic basis to academic schooling—grammar school, lycee, or gymnasium. Where Britain differed, most notably from Germany, was that it never created a second layer of technical schools for the skilled workers in the economy. Instead, for the remaining 80 percent of the population, it extended elementary education to the end of a child's fourteenth year, after which children left school and, in practice, left education altogether. Vocational education and job training were to be undertaken by employers, if at all. This left Britain with the best trained academic elite and the worst trained general labor force in Europe.

The reason for this outcome lies deep in British social history. Essentially such a system was in the narrow self-interest both of the professional elites and the organized skilled working class. It gave both direct control and restricted entry to the group and kept up their rewards. It also reflected the deep-seated belief of the elite that only a very small part of the population would ever be capable of extended intellectual effort. These attitudes were mixed into a lethal, anti-productive cocktail by the opposition to industrialism and vocational education to be found throughout the governing elite, among romantic conservatives and socialists alike (Wiener 1981).

Policy in the 1960s

It was not until the 1960s that these restrictive assumptions began to break up. An American sociologist (Turner 1971) draws a broad distinction between education systems. In those like the American, most people were expected to go as far as they could, and individuals removed themselves from the system. This contrasted with systems which made an early selection of a few who were forecast to do well and on whom extra resources could be lavished. In strict efficiency terms (i.e., ignoring other objectives) this is a cost-effective way to educate, so long as (a) predictions about individual ability are good, (b) we knew what kind of skills to teach, and (c) the number of people needing a high level of skill is small. Increasingly it was realized that these assumption were losing whatever validity they may once have had.

Early research on the effectiveness of the selective systems in both Sweden and Britain (U.K. Department of Education and Science 1970) suggested that large numbers of children were failing to gain entry who, at least at the margins, were not distinguishable from those who were being selected, and the social class bias in the choice was considerable. Perhaps as significant, governments began to realize that the assumptions about the future labor force implicit in the past models were not valid. The abandonment of selective patterns of schooling began in Sweden in the early 1960s and in Britain in the mid-1960s, followed by France but only partly by West Germany. The Germans had never made the mistake of dividing their children into a small elite and then the mass of others. There was always a large and prestigious second sector of the technical high school providing high-quality and well-resourced preparation for the skilled job market.

These reforms were always controversial, and were opposed by those who argued that mixing academic and other children in the same school would drag down the standards of the most able. The dire example of the American high school was often quoted. In fact, the Europeans were perhaps fortunate in that they began with selective academic schools and merged them with, or expanded them to become, institutions which catered for the whole ability range. In the case of British comprehensive schools, for example, comparisons were always drawn between the standards they were achieving and those achieved by the old grammar schools. This was unfair, but it did mean that the pressure was always on them to hold to these standards for the most academic, and to bring other children up to them wherever possible. They also had to develop new courses for the less academic and develop qualifications for them, to avoid a situation in which only academic children left school with any qualifications.

Research on the outcome of this revolution in traditional European school structures bears out the argument that the existence of the previous selective system created beneficial pressures for quality in the new, less selective, institutions. In Scotland and in England and Wales the results suggest that the standards achieved by the most able children have neither improved nor fallen at all significantly, but the results achieved by the average and below-average child have risen. This was the burden of the early Swedish research. A Scottish study of school leavers in 1975/1976 coincided with the changeover

(Gray, McPherson, and Raffe 1983). It was possible to compare the achievements of those in comprehensive, selective and mixed areas. The results show that overall those in the comprehensive areas did best. The top-ability pupils did slightly better in the selective system, those lower down the ability range did much better in the comprehensive system. The uncreamed comprehensive schools had much less social class differentiation and less truancy. Many more of those who left school did so with a qualification of some kind. A second, and U.K.-specific, reason for this outcome was the other material policy change of the period in the United Kingdom—the raising of the minimum school-leaving age from 15 to 16 years in 1972.

The third major policy change, which affected all countries in Europe (as it did the United States), was the expansion of higher education. As discussed later, the United Kingdom had always had a tiny but expensive system of university education. Despite resistance from many university teachers at the time, Conservative and Labour Governments managed to expand the university sector in the 1960s. Possibly even more important, the Labour Government of the 1960s introduced a whole new sector of higher education dedicated to vocational and applied scientific education. These polytechnics, as they were called, were public-sector institutions, unlike the universities which remained private institutions and formally autonomous. Though to some extent copying the universities more than some of their originators would have wished, they constituted a quite new tradition in British higher education and provided the universities with much-needed competition.

Another innovation was the creation of the Open University, which amalgamated the traditions of public service broadcasting with the high standards associated with universities. It has become the largest university in Britain, teaching on the BBC air space and employing a network of local teachers.

The Results

In the period since the early 1970s, this combination of changes has transformed the British labor force's human capital content, as the figures in Table 1 show. The number of individuals with no educational qualifications fell by nearly one third between 1974 and 1985, from 61 percent to 43 percent of all 16-49 year olds. Those with some vocational qualifications rose slightly from 13.5 to 15.5 percent. Those with Ordinary levels (the standard expected of good academic students at 16), rose sharply from 13 percent to 19 percent, and those with Advanced levels from nearly 5 percent to nearly 8 percent over the decade.[2] Though involving only a narrow range of subjects, Advanced levels involve study in depth and are equivalent at least to the first year of American undergraduate studies. Recent figures show an even sharper rise.

Table 1.   The Qualifications of the British Labor Force
1974-1985

Qualification	1974 Percent	1985 Percent
No qualifications	60.7	42.6
Vocational qualifications	13.5	15.5
Ordinary level[a]	13.2	19.1
Advanced level[a]	4.9	7.9
Other high level	5.1	8.2
Degree	2.7	6.7
All 16-49 year olds	100	100

Notes: [a] See Gray, McPherson, and Raffe (1983).
Source: Howard Glennerster and William Low, "Does It Add Up: Education and
the Welfare State" in John Hills (ed.), *The State of Welfare,* (Oxford
University Press, 1989).

Turning to higher education, it should be remembered that there is a dual
effect. The changes of the 1960s increased the throughput of the education
system. In the mid-1950s roughly 6 percent of the late teenage group entered
full-time higher education. The changes we have described more than doubled
that figure to about 14 percent by the early 1970s. There it stopped for reasons
discussed later. That age group was historically large. Moreover as this new
higher plateau of young people moved into the labor force, the less well-
educated previous generations were moving out. In just over a ten year period
the proportion of the labor force with university degrees more than doubled.

In short, the economic gains in productivity of the United Kingdom achieved
in the 1980s may rest on educational foundations laid in the much-condemned
1960s.

After the Oil Crisis

One of the characteristics of the past decade and a half in Britain and to
an extent also in Continental Europe has been an explicit shift of declared
Government policy towards the productive goals of education. The paradox
is that the expenditure restraints of the period have had the opposite effect.

Both Labor and Conservative Governments responded in similar ways, so
far as education is concerned, to the economic crisis of 1976 and after.
Education spending was cut back, the harshest cuts falling on higher education.
In Britain in the decade after 1975 state expenditure on the 18 to 24 year old
age group fell in real terms by about 25 percent.

In schools various schemes were introduced to subsidize links between school
and work place. One of the largest changes occurred in the training of young
people who left school at 16 with no training in industry. The economic crisis,

Table 2. Average Years of Education of Population Aged 15-65

	Secondary Education			Higher Education		
	1950	*1973*	*1984*	*1950*	*1973*	*1984*
France	3.04	4.11	4.89	0.18	0.47	0.90
Germany	4.37	5.11	5.17	0.14	0.20	0.31
United Kingdom	3.27	3.99	4.50	0.13	0.25	0.42
United States	3.40	4.62	5.10	0.45	0.89	1.62

Source: Maddison (1987, pp. 649-698).

exacerbated by cutbacks in public expenditure in the early 1980s, effectively destroyed the old apprenticeship schemes run by firms (which had always been a largely male and industrial and craft phenomenon). The Government, concerned about the consequences of large numbers of unemployed young people, began its own national training scheme. In its first years this was largely a form of subsidized employment but it gradually improved to have some real training content and to last for two years. By the mid-1980s, the cost of these schemes was 0.3 percent of GDP.

Compared with the training schemes and systems of vocational schools in countries like Germany and France, however, they are still mediocre. A series of studies (Prais 1981; Prais and Wagner 1983, 1985, 1988) has accumulated detailed evidence not only of this deficiency but also of its impact in the work place. The century-long neglect of the training of young people in Britain remains a major weakness, as does the early age which children leave school (Micklewright, Pearson, and Smith 1989). Government remains of the view that training is the job of the private sector, and the private sector remains of the view that it would be best if their competitors did the training and they poached the results. One can hardly fault their short term logic. The topic is discussed further in the next section.

In higher education, expenditure on institutions was cut relative to the size of the age cohort; in addition, student support from the state to finance them through college was reduced. The private costs of staying out of the labor force and going to university rose. The private rates of return to higher education fell and the demand for higher education declined, or at least stopped rising, from the early 1970s through to the early 1980s. More of the 18-21 age group were forced by cuts in university intake, to go to the cheaper and more vocationally oriented polytechnics, notwithstanding a large rise in the age group. In the 1980s, returns on higher level qualifications rose steadily and demand to enter higher education rose again towards the end of the 1980s (Bennett, Glennerster, and Nevison 1992). Despite this the United Kingdom continues to have a low participation rate (see Table 2).

LESSONS FROM EUROPE: HIGHER EDUCATION

Drawing on the analytical arguments set out earlier, this section establishes a series of building blocks out of which to construct a policy for funding higher education and, in the light of that discussion, assesses experience in the United Kingdom and elsewhere to suggest lessons for the United States. Discussion focuses on the finance of higher education, with no discussion of delivery. Thus there is no discussion of the role of the federal and state governments in organizing higher education, both for reasons of space and because it is on the funding side that the most obvious scope for improvement lies.

Implications for Policy Design

Background Issues

The funding paradox. Higher education faces a painful and unavoidable tension. Large taxpayer subsidies for tuition fees or living expenses can restrict the size of the higher-education sector because of the desire to contain public spending. Where qualified students have no automatic entitlement to a place in higher-education (e.g., Britain), the constraint takes the form of a restriction on student numbers. The result is a high-quality system, but one which turns away at least some qualified applicants. In countries where students have an entitlement to a place (France, Germany, Italy), the impact of cost containment is mainly on quality (e.g., enormous lectures, little contact with faculty, etc.). With less public funding per student (e.g., the United States), there are no externally imposed supply-side constraints, and no qualified applicant is turned away. However, unless limited taxpayer funding is sufficiently redistributive, students from lower-income backgrounds will be deterred from applying.

Thus high subsidies can harm access on the supply side, but their absence can harm it on the demand side. This is the dilemma which a well-designed funding system should alleviate.

Funding higher education institutions. In Europe most (though not all) higher education institutions are substantially tax funded. In much of mainland Europe tuition fees are minimal, and students have to find support only for their living expenses. In the United Kingdom, fees are substantial but are paid out of taxation for U.K. students[3] (students from outside the European Community generally have to pay fees in full). The European debate has been concerned with the possibility of vouchers, particularly to liberate higher education from excessive planning.[4] In this area the United States has avoided many of the problems of planning through its large private higher-education sector. Problems remain, however, in that American state universities and similar institutions are argued to cause inefficiency by tieing the fee subsidy to a take-it-or-leave-it package (Peltzman 1973). The design of a system which minimizes distortion in students' choice between the public and private higher-education sector, though important, is not discussed further, partly because any policy must be firmly rooted in specific U.S. institutions, and partly because in this area, in can be argued, Europe can learn from the United States.

Student Loans

Student loans and types of repayment. It is precisely to resolve the sort of capital-market problems discussed earlier that income-contingent loans were originally advocated, that is, a loan with repayment in the form of x percent of the individual's annual income. This type of loan is in sharpest contrast with loans organized like a mortgage or bank overdraft, with repayment in fixed installments over a fixed period. The arguments for income-contingent loans are powerful, and worth spelling out. An early proposal by Friedman (1962), in considering the government's role in vocational and professional training, explicitly recognized capital-market imperfections, in particular the riskiness of student loans (e.g., the absence of any security). He pointed out that:

> [t]he device adopted to meet the corresponding problem for other risky investments is equity investment plus limited liability on the part of shareholders. The counterpart for education would be to "buy" a share in an individual's earning prospects; to advance him the funds needed to finance his training on condition that he agree to pay the lender a specified fraction of his future earnings.

The Friedman proposal draws its inspiration from the benefit principle (he who benefits should pay). A different approach starts from a predisposition towards free, tax-financed education, abandoning that model only because of the extent to which higher education, because it is used mainly by students from better-off backgrounds, is financed regressively. It was pointed out early that,

> in the United Kingdom, higher education is now financed as a social service. Nearly all the costs are borne out of general taxation.... But it differs radically from other social services. It is reserved for a small and highly selected group.... It is exceptionally expensive.... [And] education confers benefits which reveal themselves in the form of higher earnings. A graduate tax would enable the community to recover the value of the resources devoted to higher education from those who have themselves derived such substantial benefit from it (Glennerster, Merrett, and Wilson 1968, p. 26).

A key conclusion is that the benefit principle and the ability to pay approach both lead to the same policy prescription.

Subsidies for loans.   Almost all student loan systems are subsidized, creating a mixture of loan and implicit grant. Though the intuitive appeal is understandable, intuition in this case should be resisted. The resulting system is inequitable because the loan subsidy is indiscriminate rather than targeted, and its cost is considerable. Equity goals are better served if the loan scheme charges a market or near-market interest rate, and saved resources are channelled into redistributive grants or scholarships.

Interest subsidies are also inefficient because the interest rate should not give an inefficient bias to a student's choice between supporting him or herself through current earnings or out of future earnings. Interest subsidies give an incentive to borrow an inefficiently large amount: poor students will borrow because they need the money, rich students to profit from the difference between the subsidized interest rate and the market rate.

Even without the incentive to excessive borrowing, subsidized loans are expensive, creating supply-side constraints: either the amount each student can borrow is rationed; or the number of student places is restricted.

Repayment over a long period.   The efficient duration of a loan should not exceed the lifetime of the asset in question. Thus it is possible to get a three-year car loan, but a 25 year home loan. An educational qualification is a lifelong asset; it is therefore efficient if students have the option of repaying their loan over their working lives. A long repayment period also has equity advantages: by spreading repayment, monthly payments are smaller, minimizing the deterrent effect of the loan on access.

The role of private funds.   Under appropriate conditions (market or near-market interest rates, secure repayment or government guarantee), the private sector could lend the money students borrow and could expand the system to meet demand, as with house purchases.

In theoretical terms it should not matter from which sector students borrow. Suppose it is efficient to expand higher education, and that students borrow from public funds. If additional public borrowing crowds out private investment, it will only be less-efficient private investment which is crowded out—a result which is itself efficient.

That theoretical conclusion, however, is valid only under stringent assumptions: in particular government and taxpayers must be rational and well-informed about the future. Neither is true. Public funding requires that taxation is higher than would otherwise be the case, with possible disincentive effects; and higher public spending may affect financial and foreign-exchange markets. If students borrow from private funds no issue of taxation or incentives arises—we do not, after all, argue that the large and growing mortgage debt discourages work effort.

There are also political issues. There is virtually unanimous support for the principle of academic freedom, and considerable support for the view that excessive reliance on public funding threatens that freedom (the argument was keenly felt, *inter alia* at the University of California during the later 1960s and early 1970s).[5] It follows that diversifying the sources of funding contributes to the independence of higher education.

Other Aspects of Student Support

The role of tax-funded grants and scholarships. Though many countries have grants of some sort to assist living expenses, it is questionable whether heavy reliance on grants is the best form of support. The U.K. system shows the potential pitfalls.[6] The public spending constraints of the 1970s and 1980s discussed earlier led to erosion of the basic grant, a problem exacerbated by the failure of many parents to contribute to student support. In consequence, a non-trivial number of students fell below the official poverty line. However, though many students are poor, their parents, disproportionately, are well-off. Thus the grant and tuition fees are paid on average by the average taxpayer but are typically enjoyed by individuals whose parents have above-average incomes. The result is that the grant system is regressive.[7] In addition, the taxpayer costs per student are high by international standards, exerting downward pressure on the size of the system (as noted earlier, Britain has close to the lowest entry rate into higher education of any industrialized country). The U.K. grant system, in short, leaves students in poverty, is regressive, and creates pressures to keep the system small.

The role of compulsory family support. Student support in most countries relies heavily on parents (Johnstone 1986). When education was a concern mainly of the social elite, this approach was both natural and appropriate. The reliance on *compulsory* parental support is open to question today, when higher education is both a mass phenomenon and an economic necessity.

The arguments in favor of parental contributions are, first, that they save public spending, thus allowing a larger higher education sector. Second, since parental support is generally means tested it can be argued that it is equitable. Third, students cannot easily borrow from the private sector; but parents can borrow, and so parental contributions can be thought of as an indirect form of private-sector loan. Parental contributions, on this view, are an intergenerational attempt to correct a technical failure in capital markets. A counter-argument is that a well-constructed loan scheme is a more efficient and equitable way of correcting the market failure.

There are other counter-arguments. Parental contributions may constrain the size of the higher-education system because attempts to enlarge it by increasing parental contributions can lead to a revolt amongst middle-class parents (as happened in Britain in 1985). Parental support can also be patchy, as in the United Kingdom, though anecdotal evidence suggests that it works better in other countries.

This is not an attack on the idea of parents helping their children, merely on the idea of building a system of student support on the *assumption* that parents will contribute. With a well-constructed (e.g., not heavily subsidized) loan system, students and their parents can make their own choices; parents who wish to help their children can do so; and children whose parents refuse have other options.

The role of employers. Since employers benefit from the education of their employees, it is efficient for at least two reasons that they contribute to its costs. It forces them to face the costs of trained manpower (given the declining number of younger workers over the next 20 years, an increasingly scarce resource). It might be argued that the employer contribution will be passed on to consumers. That, too, is efficient: it makes them face the costs of the scarce resources involved. It is efficient if a poor coffee harvest drives up the price of coffee; and it is efficient if employers, and through them consumers, pay higher prices after a poor brain harvest.

An employer contribution also helps to minimize an important market failure mentioned earlier in the context of training. Employers resist making donations on any substantial scale to education and training because the resulting graduates might subsequently work for another firm. Each firm thus faces an incentive to leave educational donations to other firms, that is, a free-rider problem, which is as relevant to lower as to higher levels of education and training. One solution is a user charge, possibly in the form of an additional payroll tax for each trained person employed. An employer thus pays only for individuals who are currently contributing to his profits and whom he finds it worthwhile to continue to employ. Given the free-rider problem it is no surprise that industry nowhere contributes any longer on a substantial scale.

Lessons from the United Kingdom[8]

A Government loan proposal was published in November 1988 (the day after the U.S. Presidential election, hence with minimal fanfare) with the stated objective of reducing the taxpayer cost per student. Under the scheme:

- Students take out a loan to supplement the maintenance grant; the grant is frozen in nominal terms (i.e., the real grant will fall as prices rise) and the loan component will increase; the process will continue until student support comprises 50 percent grant and parental contribution, and 50 percent loan.

- Entitlement to certain social security benefits, most notably income-tested assistance with housing costs, is withdrawn.
- The loan bears a zero real interest rate.
- Repayment commences at the start of the tax year after the summer in which the student leaves higher education. It takes the form of (usually) ten installments (i.e., mortgage-type repayments), suspended for those earning below 85 percent of the national average.
- Students borrow Treasury money, but in the original proposal both the issuing of the loan and the collection of repayments were to be administered by the banks.

The scheme is open to fundamental criticism. First, for the reasons set out earlier, mortgage-type loans are likely to harm access. Second, students borrow Treasury money, thus ruling out public expenditure savings for a long time; on the Government's own figures (U.K. House of Commons 1989) the scheme produces no cumulative net saving for at least 25 years. The scheme frees no resources for expansion, and at the same time risks harming access. Even in its own terms it achieves no desirable objective.

Nor was the scheme liked by the banks, who were unwilling to put customer relations at risk by collecting repayments and also were worried about the burden of administrative costs. For both reasons they contemplated participation only if repayments were collected by an arms-length institution, the Student Loans Company, owned jointly by the banks, whose costs would be met by government. In December 1989, however, after a year of discussion, the banks pulled out. The Government decided to run the Student Loans Company itself. The scheme took effect in October 1990.

An alternative U.K. proposal (Barnes and Barr 1989; Barr 1989) was designed with two explicit objectives: expansion of higher education, and improved access for students from poorer backgrounds. Its key characteristics are:

- The loan would bear a real interest rate of 3 percent.
- Repayment would take the form of an addition to the individual's National Insurance Contribution (NIC) (currently 9 percent of earnings for most employees).
- The additional repayment would be "switched off" once the individual had repaid the loan plus interest. Thus no-one would repay more than he or she had borrowed.
- Because repayments (1) bear a realistic real interest rate, and (2) are secure, it is possible for the money which students borrow (subject to a partial Treasury guarantee) to come from the private sector.

The scheme has various advantages.

- *Expansion and access* are enhanced. Income-contingent repayments do not discourage applicants; and low earners, women working in the home, and unemployed individuals are automatically protected.
- *Administration* is simple and cheap because it "piggy backs" on to an existing system, and uses a well-established tax base.
- *Security of repayment:* defaults are minimal: NICs are hard to evade; and, because they give title to future benefits, there is little *incentive* to evade. Security allows repayment over a lengthy period, thus making a low contribution rate possible, and also facilitates private-sector funding.
- *Private-sector funds:* the possibility of funding loans largely from the private sector opens up the possibility of immediate public-expenditure savings, thus freeing resources for expansion and other measures to improve access.
- *The avoidance of distortions:* it is argued that student loans with income-contingent repayments, because they have a redistributive element, will create adverse selection problems, in that only students who think that they are poor risks will choose to join. There are several counterarguments. First, risk-averse students may prefer to belong to an income-contingent scheme even if they think that they are good risks. Second, students are constrained by imperfect capital markets, and are not able to choose to opt out of the income-contingent scheme. Third, adverse selection, even if it takes place, may not be a major problem: if students opting out of a state loan scheme join a private-sector scheme, they release public resources which can then be used for other purposes. Fourth, the UK proposal just described even in principle raises no problems of adverse selection: no student repays more than he or she has borrowed (thus high earning graduates are not penalized); the implied subsidy to low-earning graduates is paid out of general taxation.

Lessons from Other Countries

Higher education funding in a variety of countries is surveyed in detail by Johnstone (1986) to which volume, notwithstanding subsequent changes, readers are warmly referred. This section is somewhat more eclectic, looking for the most part at the reform process in countries with specific lessons for the United States, particularly the United Kingdom, Sweden, Germany and (slightly exceeding the remit of the paper) Australia and New Zealand. The section concludes with a reform proposal emanating from within the United States.

Sweden

Sweden first introduced a substantial loan scheme in 1965. The measure was intended to expand higher education in the face of public-expenditure constraints, and to equalize participation across socioeconomic groups. The package provided support at 140 percent of the official subsistence level, comprising a grant (25 percent of the total) and a tax-funded loan. The grant was fixed in nominal terms, so that the loan became more important over time. Means testing against parental income was abolished.

After a two year grace period, an individual's first repayment was his total debt divided by the repayment period (normally the number of years to his fifty-first birthday). Thereafter the nominal annual repayment was increased each year by the rate of inflation. The system was thus a publicly-funded mortgage loan with a zero real interest rate. In 1975 the interest rate was changed from the rate of inflation to a (generally higher) nominal rate of 4.2 percent.

By the early 1980s:

- Inflation had eroded the fixed grant so that the loan element had increased to 94 percent of student support; indebtedness for a three-year degree could reach over $20,000.
- There was increasing complaint that student support was inadequate.
- The earlier improvement in the social composition of students was reversed. Because of worries that this was causally related to the previous two points:
- A review of student support was established, leading to reform in 1989.[9]

The main characteristics of the 1989 reforms were:

- Total student support was increased by about one fifth, from 140 percent of subsistence to 170 percent.
- The grant element was increased from under 6 percent to about 30 percent of the total and was indexed, thus restoring a stable relativity between grant and loan.
- Repayment terms were tightened somewhat: the grace period was reduced, and the interest rate set at half the market rate (generally higher than the previous rate of 4.2 percent).
- Loans are no longer funded from taxation, but out of borrowing by the National Debt Office; only the interest subsidy and written off loans are a budgetary charge.
- Repayments are 4 percent of gross income two years earlier, and cease once the loan has been repaid.

The reforms explicitly or implicitly acknowledge a number of lessons.

- *Interest subsidies:* the extent to which loans are subsidized has been steadily decreased by reducing the grace period and by gradual increases in the interest rate.
- *The balance between grant and loan:* there was general agreement that the balance had tipped too far towards loans, acknowledging the need for multiple sources of support.
- *Parental contributions:* means testing against parental income was abolished in 1965, and against a spouse's income in 1982.
- *Private funding:* loans continue to be publicly funded, but the 1989 transfer of loans to the government loan account is at least a step in the right direction.
- *Income-contingent repayments:* large loans with mortgage-type repayments were associated with lower participation by the lower socioeconomic groups. The 1989 reforms therefore introduced explicit income-related repayments.

France

France offers a different model. Like Sweden (for all students) and the United Kingdom (for the great bulk of home undergraduate students), students pay negligible fees. In sharp contrast with both countries, however, it offers little assistance with living costs. There is a maintenance grant with very limited scope: its maximum value in 1987-1988 was about $1750, and only about 15 percent of students receive any grant at all. There is also a minimal loan system involving less than 1 percent of the undergraduate population (U.K. Department of Education and Science 1988). France is therefore an example of a system where students have a guaranteed right of admission, pay virtually no fees, but receive virtually no help with their living costs. It is included here for the sake of completeness, but is not directly relevant to countries like the United States in which fees are a substantial part of the landscape.

Australia

Though straying somewhat beyond the strict remit of this paper, the Australian and New Zealand experience is more directly relevant to the United States. The Australian government appointed a Committee on Higher Education Funding in 1987, whose terms of reference included expansion and improved access. The Committee's Report (the Wran Report) was published in May 1988 and, as amended, took effect in January 1989.

The core of the reform package was a Higher Education Contribution Scheme, whereby students became liable for a contribution of about one fifth of the average tuition fee (i.e., the contribution does not vary across subjects). Students have the option of paying the contribution on enrolment (at a 15 percent discount). Otherwise the contribution is paid out of a loan at a zero real interest rate. Repayment is suspended for individuals with earnings below the national average. Thereafter, repayment is 1 percent of taxable income, rising to 2 percent and, at the highest incomes, to 3 percent, collected through the tax system.

Though often represented as a tax, the scheme is properly thought of as a loan for two reasons: it is voluntary in the sense that the fee charge can be paid upon enrolment; and the additional contribution is "switched off" once the charge has been paid. Several points are noteworthy. The revenue from the scheme will finance expansion of higher education. Repayments are based on individual ability to pay explicitly to avoid compromising access. Though the contribution is argued to be more equitable than the previous tax-funded system, the change should not be overstated: the effect of the interest subsidy is to reduce the contribution from 20 percent of average tuition costs to closer to 10 percent (Hope and Miller 1988).

New Zealand

The Hawke Report on Postcompulsory Education and Training in New Zealand echoed earlier concern over New Zealand's low enrolment in higher education, and its underfunding. One of its main conclusions was that:

> [t]he most attractive way of obtaining private funding ... is that recommended by the recent Wran Committee in Australia.
>
> The Working Group, with the exception of Treasury, favours [the scheme] being seen as a means of acquiring additional resources for [higher education].
>
> The particular merits of the Wran proposals are that it provides for funding from students independently from their family..., while ensuring that repayments are required only when they have income levels which enable them to be sustained.

The Hawke Report went beyond the Wran Report in one important respect by rejecting interest subsidies. It proposed a real interest rate of about 3 percent, except for individuals caring for children, who would pay a zero real interest rate (i.e., in the latter case real debt would not increase during time out of the labor force).

The Hawke proposal was thus a tax-funded income-contingent scheme without substantial interest subsidy, intended to encourage expansion without harming access. Though endorsed, with modifications, by the government, the scheme was not implemented. The New Zealand government failed to follow Australia's example by imposing the collection of repayments on the tax authorities. When the tax authorities demurred, the government turned to the banking sector. The banks, however, were reluctant to become involved, both because the scheme was controversial and because the government was not prepared to give unconditional loan guarantees. In September 1989 they pulled out and the scheme was shelved.

The United States

The problems are well-known. Five stand out (Reischauer 1989).

1. *Complexity:* it is unduly kind to talk about a loan "system":

[t]he complex range of grants and loans from federal, state and campus sources is a major administrative problem for most institutions. Students seldom understand all that is available (U.K. Department of Education and Science 1988).

2. *Mortgage-type repayments* apply almost without exception.
3. *Interest subsidies* are pervasive.
4. *High default rates:* Stafford Student Loans (the largest scheme) give a federal guarantee to loans to students by banks. The banks therefore have little incentive to chase defaulters. The result, in combination with the absence of any mechanism for suspending repayments when income is low, is high default rates (U.S. Department of Treasury 1988).
5. *Cost:* the combined effect of interest subsidies and defaults is that the system is costly and of only questionable benefit in encouraging participation from the lower-income groups.

During his Presidential campaign, Michael Dukakis proposed a new scheme. Students would borrow from banks; the federal government would guarantee the loan. Repayment would be a percentage of the individual student's subsequent income, collected alongside the social security contribution. It was claimed that this "Pay As You Went" scheme would save public money, be equitable, administratively simple, and with few defaults. The scheme went down with the Dukakis campaign.

Reischauer (1989, pp. 34–42) offers a more fully articulated social insurance approach to student loan policy. Students would borrow from a federal trust fund, it being left open whether the funds would be federal or private. Repayment, in the form of an addition to withholdings under the Federal Insurance Contributions Act (FICA), would be a percentage of the individual's income, varying with the amount borrowed. The loan would bear a positive real interest rate. Reischauer argues that real repayments are largely unaffected by fluctuations in nominal interest rates, since such fluctuations generally reflect the rate of inflation which in turn is captured by the buoyancy of wages; thus higher inflation causes higher interest rates, but also, through higher wages, leads to higher repayments. In the basic model it is assumed that repayment will be over an entire working life. Reischauer calculates that under those circumstances a 1 percent additional contribution would repay a loan of $4000.

The scheme is an income-contingent loan scheme with no substantial interest subsidy, and with the possibility of private-sector funding. Its main difference from the schemes discussed earlier is that the additional contribution is not "switched off" once the loan has been repaid, thus introducing redistribution within cohorts of students.[10] The use of the social security mechanism, it should be noted, is not an option in Australia and New Zealand, which have no explicit social security contributions.

CONCLUSIONS

Developments in the theoretical literature on the economics of information over the past twenty years have greatly enhanced our understanding of market failure. For instance, it is now possible to show why actuarial insurance is not readily applicable to risks like unemployment (Barr 1987). With hindsight, it is easy to explain the catastrophic failure of unemployment compensation in Britain in the 1920s and early 1930s, and to understand the forces which led to the U.S. Social Security Act of 1935 taking the form it did. The moral of the story is that policy will not work unless the underpinnings are right. The development of education illustrates the same point.

So far as school education is concerned, two results stand out. First, for efficiency reasons which are quite independent of arguments about social justice, systems should cater to the entire ability range, not just the intellectual elite. Second, as the German example shows, the academic system should be buttressed by a broad-ranging and rigorous system of training.

When applied to higher education, the theoretical arguments can be interpreted as supporting a regulated, competitive system with largely private-sector institutions, supported by substantial public funding. In this respect the United States has progressed further than Europe.

On student loans, however, the United States has much to learn from other countries. The theory predicts that undue reliance on a model of voluntary private loans (as for house purchases) will lead to precisely the sort of problems experienced in the United States, notably high default and impediments to access. A number of schemes elsewhere address these problems.

The Swedish reforms took effect in January 1989. The Australian reform began on the same date; from the same stable, New Zealand considered a very similar set of proposals in 1988 and 1989. The Dukakis/Reischauer proposals were a 1988/1989 phenomenon. The British alternative proposals grew at the same time. All four sets of proposals—Swedish, Antipodean, American and British—have the same objectives, expansion and improved access; all derive, implicitly or explicitly, from earlier arguments; and all, following the same logic, reach broadly the same conclusion, most particularly that loan repayments should be income contingent.

ACKNOWLEDGMENTS

Financial help to one of the authors (Nicholas Barr) from the Esmee Fairbairn Charitable Foundation, and the Suntory-Toyota International Centre for Economics and Related Disciplines, London School of Economics and Political Science is gratefully acknowledged.

NOTES

1. It is a standard proposition in econometrics that omitted independent variables, unless they are orthogonal to the included variables, will cause biased ordinary least squares estimators. Similar problems generally arise with maximum liklihood estimation. The assumption of orthogonality is untenable in the present example, since educational attainments (measurable) and family background (largely unmeasurable) are strongly related.

2. Ordinary levels involved public examination, normally at or around age 16, and normally comprising 5-7 subjects in both arts and science. Advanced level is normally taken in 2-3 subjects at or around age 18, often in related areas (e.g., mathematics, physics and chemistry, or French, German, and English). Ordinary levels have now been replaced.

3. Though the public accounting is complex, the effect is that U.K. students studying at U.K. universities and polytechnics pay no tuition fees.

4. For a critique of U.K. government policy and a specific U.K. voucher proposal, see Barnes and Barr (1988).

5. It is interesting to speculate whether the National Guard would have been sent to drop tear gas from a helicopter on anti-Vietnam war protesters if the demonstration had been at Stanford rather than the University of California, Berkeley.

6. For a critique, see Barr and Low (1988).

7. For a similar result for the publicly-funded University of California, see Hansen and Weisbrod (1969, 1978).

8. The institutions discussed in this section are those of England and Wales. Arrangements in Scotland and Northern Ireland differ slightly, but not enough to affect the argument.

9. For a survey of the Swedish system, see Morris (1989).

10. In principle, this raises problems of adverse selection; but see an earlier discussion in the context of student loans in the United Kingdom.

REFERENCES

Akerlof, G. 1970. "The Market for 'Lemons': Qualitative Uncertainty and the Market Mechanism." *Quarterly Journal of Economics* 84: 488-500.

Barnes, J. and N. Barr. 1988. *Strategies for Higher Education: The Alternative White Paper.* Aberdeen: Aberdeen University Press.

Barr, N. 1987. *The Economics of the Welfare State.* London: Weidenfeld and Nicolson.

―――――. 1989. *Student Loans: The Next Steps.* Aberdeen: Aberdeen University Press.

Becker, G. 1964. *Human Capital.* New York: National Bureau of Economic Research.

Bennett, R., Glennerster, H., and Nevison, D. 1992. "Investing in Skill: To Stay on or Not to Stay on." Oxford Review of Economic Policy, 8(2).

Blaug, M. 1970. *An Introduction to the Economics of Education.* London: Penguin.

————. 1976. "The Empirical Status of Human Capital Theory: A Slightly Jaundiced Survey." *Journal of Economic Literature* 14: 827-855.

Friedman, M. 1962. *Capitalism and Freedom.* Chicago: University of Chicago Press.

Glennerster, H. and W. Low. 1989. "Does It Add Up: Education and the Welfare State." In *The State of Welfare,* edited by J. Hills. Oxford: Oxford University Press.

Glennerster, H., S. Merrett, and G. Wilson. 1968. "A Graduate Tax." *Higher Education Review* 1: 26.

Gray, J., A.F. McPherson, and D. Raffe. 1983. *Reconstruction and Secondary Education: Theory, Myth and Practice Since the War.* London: Routledge and Kegan Paul.

Hansen L. and B. Weisbrod. 1969. "The Distribution of Costs and Direct Benefits of Public Higher Education: The Case of California." *Journal of Human Resources* 4: 176-191.

————. 1978. "The Distribution of Subsidies to Students in California Public Higher Education: Reply." *Journal of Human Resources* 13: 137-139.

Hope, J. and P. Miller. 1988. "Financing Tertiary Education: An Examination of the Issues." *The Australian Economic Review* 4: 37-57.

Johnstone, B. 1986. *Sharing the Costs of Higher Education: Student Financial Assistance in the United Kingdom, the Federal Republic of Germany, France, Sweden and the United States.* New York: College Examination Board.

Micklewright, J., M. Pearson and S. Smith. 1989. "Has Britain an Early School Leaving Problem?" *Fiscal Studies* 10: 1-16.

Morris, M. 1989. "Student Aid in Sweden: Recent Experience and Reforms," In *Financial Support for Students: Grants, Loans or Graduate Tax,* edited by M. Woodhall. London: Kogan Page.

Peltzman, S. 1973. "The Effects of Government Subsidies in Kind on Private Expenditures: The Case of Higher Education." *Journal of Political Economy* 81: 1-27.

Prais, S.J. 1981. "Vocational Qualifications of the Labour Force in Britain and Germany." *National Institute Economic Review* 98: 47-59.

Prais, S.J. and K. Wagner. 1983. "Some Practical Aspects of Human Capital Investment: Training Standards in Five Occupations in Britain and Germany." *National Institute Economic Review* 105: 46-65.

————. 1985. "Schooling Standards in England and Germany: Some Summary Comparisons Bearing on Economic Performance." *National Institute Economic Review* 112: 53-76.

————. 1988. "Productivity and Management: The Training of Foremen in Britain and Germany." *National Institute Economic Review* 123: 34-47.

Reischauer, R. 1989. "Help: A Student Loan Program for the Twenty-First Century." In *Radical Reform or Incremental Change? Student Loan Policies for the Federal Government,* edited by L. E. Gladieux. New York: College Entrance Examination Board.

Report of the Committee on Higher Education Funding. 1988. *The Wran Report.* Canberra: AGPS.

Spence, M. 1973. "Job Market Signalling." *Quarterly Journal of Economics* 87: 355-374.

Turner, R.H. 1971. "Sponsored and Contest Mobility and the School System." In *Readings in the Theory of Educational Systems,* edited by E. Hopper. London: Hutchinson.

U.K. Department of Education and Science. 1970. *Public Schools Commission, 2nd Report. Vol. 2.* London: HMSO.

U.K. Department of Education and Science. 1988. *Top-up Loans for Students,* Cm 520. London: HMSO.

U.K. Department of Education and Science. 1989. *Aspects of Higher Education in the United States of America: A Commentary by Her Majesty's Inspectorate.* London: HMSO.

U.K. Department of Education and Science. 1988. *Top-Up Loans for Students,* Annex C. London: HMSO.

U.S. Department of Tresure. 1988. *Budget of the United States Government: Fiscal Year 1988, Appendix.* Washington, DC: United States Government Printing Office.

U.K. House of Commons. 1989. *Official Report, Written Answers.* 24: col. 441. London: HMSO.

Wiener, M.J. 1981. *English Culture and the Decline of the Industrial Spirit 1850 to 1980.* Cambridge: Cambridge, University Press.

COMMENTS

Jimmy Weinblatt

This paper presented several interesting facts on the various educational systems in Europe and elsewhere and gave an interesting analysis of the issue of student loans. I would like to share some of the thoughts I had while reading the paper.

The authors indicate that there is a general disagreement regarding the goals of education. Are these goals mainly concerned with equity, efficiency, or social solidarity? Probably all three of these considerations are involved, but the effect that education has on them is not clear. As mentioned in the paper, these goals are difficult to measure, and thus it is difficult to determine the optimal level of education. The general feeling is that there is a need for more education. Thus, the net benefit of more education is assumed to be positive. Still, there is an awareness of a budgetary reality that does not allow for an increase of public resources. Therefore, there is a need to use the existing government resources in a way that would stimulate learning, increase the number of students, and be more equitable.

I think that the goal of the reforms and proposals presented in the paper is to have more education with possibly less public spending. I am not sure that this is feasible, however.

In spite of the disagreement on the goals of education and despite the inability to determine the optimal amount of education, politicians have to decide on the size and the structure of education, and they do so either consciously or unconsciously.

The lack of consensus is characteristic of most issues of policymaking. Is there a consensus on the size of defense? Health? Welfare programs? As with

163

other policy issues, decisions on education are made at the practical level of budget appropriations, and it is through these appropriations that policy makers reveal their preferences.

There is no need to aim at a consensus that cannot be achieved. There should be a logical and efficient mechanism of decision making. Questions regarding the nature of this mechanism belong to the field of public choice, which is not within the scope of this conference.

The authors assume that the current level of education is suboptimal and that the government in the United Kingdom is not spending enough on education. They support this argument by mentioning that although the income elasticity of education is greater than one, state spending has not grown at the same pace as income.

Another possible explanation for the relative decline in government appropriations for education is that the government wants to enhance the growth of private education. This is consistent with trends toward privatization and with the process of switching production of public goods from the government to private enterprise.

Research in general and economic research in particular do not provide good insights on issues concerning the impact of education on such goals as economic growth, equity, and social solidarity. I would like to say a few words about each of these goals.

1. *Economic growth.* Economic growth is related to technological progress and to the quality of labor and capital. My own research on the Israeli manufacturing sector indicates that most of the growth in total factor productivity is attributable to the rate of growth in investment, mainly to the introduction of younger and more productive equipment. Similar results have been found for Canada and for the United States. Technological change is certainly enhanced by education. The question is what type or level of education is needed for that purpose. For example, it is not necessary to provide widespread higher education to generate technological progress. This could possibly be achieved more efficiently by providing education in science and technology to the best students. But, this is contrary to the suggestions of the paper.

2. *Equity.* The 1980s was a decade of decrease in equity in the U.S. and probably in some European countries. Still, it is possible that the level of formal education rose at the same time. There were other factors more powerful in the short and the long run that affected equity. If we aim at equity, it might be more efficient to achieve it by other means.

3. *Social Solidarity.* I have no evidence, but my intuition is that education significantly contributes to the development of values and abilities that are essential for democracy, social stability and social prosperity. I would add that for consumers also education is extremely important not only for rational and

intelligent present consumption, but for future consumption too. Even though there are measurement problems, economic research could provide valuable insights here. I personally believe that this is the field where widespread education at all levels can have the greatest effect.

The authors seem to support the granting of student loans that are partly subsidized for the purpose of overcoming imperfections of the capital market. They do not believe that mortgage-type loans as exist in the United States are efficient, and therefore suggest income contingent loans to follow the principle of "He who benefits should pay."

The idea of linking the payment to the benefit from education is good. However, how can we say what part of income should be attributed to education? Since we do not know, all we will do is impose a surtax on people with higher education, the burden of which would probably fall on those students from poor families.

THE CANADIAN EDUCATIONAL SYSTEM

Judith A. McDonald

INTRODUCTION

Over the past decade, domestic and international demographic and economic developments have conspired to make education a top concern for policymakers and voters in Canada. Canada shares three problems with most other western industrialized economies: slower growth, structural change in employment, and the need for reduced government spending to deal with a massive national debt. Canada has been growing at an increasingly slower rate over the last two decades.[1] And, according to many researchers,[2] western economies are in for a long period of economic stagnation and mounting scarcity. There have been broad structural changes in employment over the post-war period: the government and service sectors have grown, while manufacturing and resource sectors have shrunk. The world market is increasingly competitive, and Canadian manufacturing is being seriously challenged. One of the tasks facing Canada is to increase its investment in technology and research and to improve the training and adaptability of its labor force. However, at the very time that education is more important than ever to help Canada deal with the required adjustments ahead, the educational system finds itself plagued with crises of its own. There are widespread cutbacks in education financing and many concerns about quality.

This paper will examine both the Canadian elementary-secondary school system and the post-secondary sector. First, facts and figures will be presented.

167

Next, the financing of both the elementary-secondary and post-secondary sectors will be discussed. Finally, there will be a discussion of some of the benefits of education as well as key policy issues. Throughout the paper comparisons will be made between Canada and the United States, so that Canada's situation can be put in perspective.

GENERAL OVERVIEW

According to the European Management Forum,[3] Canada leads the world in per capita public expenditures on education, and has a relatively large proportion of the population participating in higher education. Expenditures for all levels of education in 1983 were equal to 7.7 percent of GNP, thus surpassing the United States (6.9% of GNP), the United Kingdom (5.8%) Japan (5.8%), France (5%), Australia (5.9%), and most other industrialized countries. In the 1980s, only a few countries (Sweden [9.5% of GNP], Norway [9%], and U.S.S.R. [7.8%]) exceeded this level of expenditure.[4]

Canada's educational system consists of 15,410 public, private and federal elementary and secondary schools and 268 post-secondary institutions in all 10 provinces and 2 territories.[5] During the 1989-1990 academic year, education in Canada was a $43.5 billion enterprise; and an estimated 5.9 million Canadians, about a quarter of the population, were enrolled full-time in educational institutions. Of this student population, elementary and secondary schools accounted for 5,074,300; non-university, post-secondary institutions for 315,150; and universities for 513,900. The total enrollment in universities including both full-time and part-time students, consisted of 716,110 undergraduates and 100,100 graduate students.

As discussed in a study by the Centre for Policy Studies in Education (1988 p. 4), educational policies and institutions in Canada have to be understood in the context of the historical development of federalism. Education is a provincial matter and the Constitution Act, 1982 (formerly the British North America Act, 1867) grants the provinces the right to make educational legislation. Unlike most other countries, Canada has no Ministry of Education at the federal level. Because each province and territory has authority over education, there is no national policymaking process for education. Thus Canada is essentially made up of twelve education systems. Provincial autonomy in education allows for adaptation to local conditions and is strongly defended across the country. Some feel that national policies could not be flexible enough to accommodate regional preferences. The legal, administrative and financial provision for public education from elementary school through university is the responsibility of each provincial or territorial government, not the local or municipal governments. A department (or ministry) of education implements government policy and legislation for education in each province

Table 1. Schooling by Level Completed, 1981
(percent of population age 25 and over)

Less than Grade 9	Some Secondary	Some Non-University	University or More
Canada			
24.8	37.6	20.3	17.3
United States			
16.8	51.2	15.1	17.1

Source: West (1988, pp. 18-19).

ind territory. The policies and powers of the government are embodied in a School or Education Act(s) and University and College Acts. The provinces and territories have also created a sub-organization of local units of administration, "school boards," to assist them in fulfilling their educational functions. School boards are charged with the responsibility for operating elementary schools (generally grades 1 to 6 or 8) and secondary schools generally grades 7 or 9 to 12, 13 in Ontario) in their jurisdiction. Within each province there is significant local autonomy. Still the educational systems in the different provinces have much in common, although each has unique features. Differences generally can be traced to the traditions and goals of the founding settlers in each province.[6]

The federal government is directly involved with education only in that it provides educational services to native students, children in the Northwest Territories and Arctic Islands, children of armed forces personnel, and inmates of penitentiaries. Federal expenditures for these programs constitute about 3 percent of total spending on elementary-secondary education. However, the federal government's provision of funds to the provinces gives it an indirect influence over other aspects of education.

How Educated is the Canadian Population?

In 1984, the maximum level of education reached by 70 percent of the population (age 15 or higher) was either elementary or secondary school.[7] About half of all Canadians ended their education with some exposure to high school, while roughly 30 percent of the population had some post-secondary schooling. The fact that the Canadian population is becoming increasingly educated is shown by an increase in the median years of schooling from 10.6 years (1971) to 11.8 years (1981).

According to West (1988), relatively more Canadians obtain post-secondary schooling than Americans. This can be seen from the third and fourth columns of Table 1. However, in 1981, the median years of schooling were 12.5 in the

United States and 11.8 in Canada. Bertram (1966) identified Canada's income relative to that of the United States as a function of the education of the two countries. (Canada's average income is about 10% lower than that in the United States.) Bertram suggested that at least part of this income difference could be explained by Canada's lower stock of education. However, Canada has been narrowing this gap: in the United States median years of schooling increased from 12.3 to 12.5 during the 1970s, while for Canada the comparable figures are 10.6 to 11.8.

The Elementary-Secondary School Sector

The number of students grew in the post-war baby boom until one out of four Canadians was in elementary or secondary school in the early 1970s. Now fewer than one in five is in these schools, roughly the situation in the 1950s. The number of teachers grew rapidly during the 1960s, and has remained relatively constant. Consequently, the student/teacher ratio has fallen from 26 (1960) to 18 (1985).

There are three types of elementary-secondary schools in Canada. The public school systems are available in every province and are funded by the governments. The Roman Catholic separate school system is publicly funded in Ontario, Alberta, Saskatchewan, the Northwest Territories and the Yukon. Independent or private schools also exist within each province, and they receive direct funding in British Columbia, Alberta, Manitoba, Quebec and Saskatchewan. Unlike the United States, where the Constitution calls for a separation of church and state, each province in Canada is free to allocate tax dollars to non-public schools.

In 1989-1990, about 4.7 percent of Canada's total elementary and secondary school enrollment was accounted for by private schools. In 1971-1972, this figure was 2.4 percent. This trend towards increasing enrollment in private schools has been met with increased financial support of private schools from public funds.[9] Shapiro (1985), for example, is concerned with this trend. He claims that private schools tend to perpetuate religious and other differences and therefore should not be encouraged through public funding.

According to the Centre for Policy Studies in Education,[10] retention rates in high school are comparatively high: 93 percent of 16-year-olds and 67 percent of 17-year-olds were attending elementary and secondary schools in 1984. The number of high school graduates continues to increase as retention rates rise. For example, 80 percent of those enrolled in grade 12 graduated from high school in 1981-1982. The percentage of students finishing high school has also been rising: for every 100 18-year-olds, there were 55 high school graduates in 1971-1972, and 63 a decade later. However, a substantial fraction of the high school population still does not graduate. Those who do not graduate are more likely to live in rural areas, to be from lower socio-economic homes, and to be Indians or Inuit.

Post-Secondary Education

Post-secondary education consists of two types of institutions: degree-granting institutions (universities and colleges) and non-degree-granting institutions (community colleges, technical institutes, colleges of agriculture and of art, and hospital schools of nursing).

According to the *Corpus Almanac* (1990, p. 7.5), Canada has 68 public, degree-granting universities. Only two-thirds of these institutions were in existence in 1960. The private sector is essentially absent in post-secondary education in Canada. This differs markedly from the situation in many other countries; for example, in Japan roughly 80 percent of college students attend private institutions, and in the United States about 30 percent (West 1988, p. 103). Total university enrollment increased from 113,864 (1960-1961) to an estimated 513,900 full-time graduate and undergraduate students in 1989-1990.

During the 1980s enrollment in post-secondary institutions has been increasing at a faster average annual rate (5%) than in the late 1970s (1%).[11] This is due to the fact that the participation rate of 18-21 year-olds in university education has increased by nearly 20 percent from 1978-1988. This demand increase has come mostly from women, part-timers and foreign students. This fairly continuous growth of enrollment and increase in participation rates over the last two decades is reflected in the median years of education given above. By 1985 the proportion of the adult population with post-secondary credentials was 21.5 percent; in 1981, it was 18.5 percent.

FINANCING EDUCATION

In this section, we will examine how education is financed. At exactly the time when the need for an educated population is increasing, there appears to be widespread financial restraint in Canada's educational system, particularly at the university level (Skolnik and Rowen 1984, pp. 122-150). This restraint may be due to slower growth in the Canadian economy, which reduces government revenue, as well as increased demands on the government, which may only get worse as the baby boom ages. Also, although at the level of elementary and secondary schooling the cost of education per child has increased, there is a general feeling that the quality of education has been falling (Easton 1988, p. 101).

Financing Elementary-Secondary Education

Canadians spend an amount equal to the federal deficit each year on education, and about two-thirds of this is spent on elementary-secondary schooling. Because education is, constitutionally, a provincial responsibility,

Table 2.   Public School Funding by Levels of Government

Year	Total Expenditure on Public Schools (millions, current dollars)	Percent of GDP	Percentage Share of Elementary and Secondary School Funding Financed by Each Level		
			Federal	Provincial	Municipal
1950	328	1.8	3.6	37.8	58.6
1960	1224	3.2	4.1	43.5	52.4
1970	4638	5.4	5.9	57.4	36.7
1980	14730	4.8	2.7	68.8	28.5
1986*	21583	5.4	—	—	—

Note: * Estimated values
Source: Easton (1988, p. 9).

most of the money for education comes from within the province, although federal and local governments also share the responsibility for financing public education. The share of national income spent on elementary and secondary education has fluctuated from about 3.2 percent in 1960 to 5.4 percent in 1970 and 1986 (see Table 2).

As can be seen from Table 2, from 1950-1980, the share of municipal government spending has fallen relative to that of the provincial government. Wilkinson (1986) feels that this change reflects a desire on the part of provinces to redistribute the tax burden so that it falls more equally on all districts and to equalize per student expenditures among districts.

Where the Money Comes From

The money for provincial grants to education comes from the provinces' general revenue funds. Personal and corporate income taxes, retail sales tax (except for Alberta), and excise taxes (such as those on gasoline and alcohol) account for most provincial revenue,[12] with federal transfer payments serving as yet another source.

In the 1980s about 70 percent of total school board revenue came from provincial grants. This percentage varied among provinces, depending on the financial formulas used. For example, Newfoundland, Prince Edward Island, and New Brunswick relied almost entirely on provincial funding for revenue, while in Manitoba and Saskatchewan school boards received between 45-50 percent of their funds from provincial grants and the rest from local property taxation and other local sources.

The other major source of school board revenue is the local property tax. The total equalized assessment (market value) of all property in a school district or municipality forms the property tax base for the local government.

Municipal councils and school boards estimate their financial needs, and then assess a "mill rate" that must be applied to the property base to generate the required amount.

Dibski (1987, p. 76) claims that provinces are relying less on local property taxes as a school revenue source since property taxes are regressive. This can be clearly seen in Table 2, which depicts the growing reliance on provincial taxes—especially income taxes, which are more equitable.

To ensure that the quality of education does not depend on the wealth of the school district, each provincial government structures its school grants system to compensate for the varying local fiscal situations. Local ability-to-pay determines the grants received; for example, a poor school district receives a grant which constitutes a higher percentage of that board's total revenue than a rich district would receive. The grants system is designed so that the total amount of revenue per pupil from grants and taxes, and the mill rates for school taxes, are equalized across the province.

Since Confederation, the federal government has made transfer payments to the provinces from its general revenues. The two main goals of these payments have been equalization of provincial fiscal capacity and cost-sharing of specific social programs (like health, welfare, and post-secondary and vocational education). Once received, these federal funds are spent according to provincial priorities.

Provinces in Canada differ in their ability-to-pay in the same way that school systems differ. To ensure that each province can meet the basic needs of its citizens, the federal government, in cooperation with the provinces, redistributes the wealth of the country using "equalization payments." The Constitution of Canada (1982) outlines an obligation to ensure adequate and equitable funding of all public services, including public elementary and secondary education. The relevant passage is:[13]

> Parliament and the government of Canada are committed to the principle of making equalization payments to ensure that provincial governments have sufficient revenues to provide reasonably comparable levels of public services at reasonably comparable rates of taxation. (Subsection 36.2)

Historical Background

From the late 1950s to the early 1970s, there were substantial improvements in the adequacy and equity of school funding despite historically high levels of educational need and burden. One reason for these improvements was that beginning in 1957 the federal treasury made equalization transfers to those provinces whose own sources of revenue fell below a certain minimum.[14] Brown (1989, pp. 64-81) claims that these improvements were financed by provincial government budget surpluses due to economic growth, a growing provincial share of progressive income tax revenues, and more generous federal revenue equalization payments.

However, since the early 1970s, recessions and stagnation have hurt provincial treasuries. Also, the federal government has been less able and willing to maintain the level of revenue equalization. In 1982, the equalization standard was narrowed from the weighted national average per capita yield of all ten provinces to that of the five middle income or "representative" provinces.[15] In 1985-1986, the federal government made equalization payments totalling $5 billion to all provinces except British Columbia, Ontario, Alberta, and Saskatchewan.[16] In 1987, about 18 percent of all provincial revenue came from this source; and for certain Atlantic provinces, the percentage was closer to 50 percent. The cost is currently about 20 percent of total federal expenditures.

Brown (1989, pp. 64-81)[17] undertook a recent study to see whether the educational goals of the Constitution are being met. To do this, he examined the financial abilities of the provinces, the financial efforts of the provinces to support elementary and secondary education, and the educational outputs (enrollments and graduates) from 1965 to 1986. From Brown's study, it seems that interprovincial differences in the financial abilities of the provinces began to re-emerge in the early 1970s. These were followed, with a lag of about five years, by a re-emergence of interprovincial differences in spending levels for elementary and secondary education. There is also some evidence of growing interprovincial differences in relative effort.

While the evidence of widening interprovincial differences in financial ability, spending levels, and relative effort were quite dramatic in the first half of the 1970s, they were not followed (at least as of the mid-1980s) by a similar re-emergence of interprovincial disparities in enrolment and graduation figures.[18] Brown hypothesizes that the equalization in the quality of inputs and outputs of provincial school systems that occurred throughout the 1960s and early 1970s has not yet been eroded by the re-emergence of interprovincial differences in either financial ability or effort (at least as of 1986). However, these trends toward widening disparity should be a cause of concern. The 1982-1987 federal-provincial fiscal arrangements may mean that the Constitution's goal of educational equality will not be met.

Canada-United States Comparisons

In his 1979 study of the impact of values on school finance, Lawton (1989, pp. 29-40) concludes that Canadians seem to place greater emphasis than Americans on equality in elementary-secondary school financing. He also claims that Canadians appear to be more tolerant of authoritative acts on the part of their governments—for example, governments that increase the size of the school district to capture economies of scale. Lawton claims that the

Table 3.   Coefficients of Variation in Per Pupil Operating Expenditures, 1975

State/Province	Coefficient of Variation	State/Province	Coefficient of Variation
Hawaii	.00	Arizona	.17
Prince Edward Island	.04	Mississippi	.17
Newfoundland	.06	Delaware	.18
Nevada	.07	Colorado	.18
New Brunswick	.09	Arkansas	.18
Utah	.09	Washington	.18
Florida	.09	Nebraska	.19
Iowa	.09	Oklahoma	.20
Louisiana	.10	Maryland	.20
Ontario	.12	Ohio	.20
Alabama	.12	Texas	.20
North Carolina	.12	Kentucky	.20
New Mexico	.13	New Jersey	.20
West Virginia	.13	Wyoming	.20
South Dakota	.13	Tennessee	.21
Indiana	.13	Montana	.21
Rhode Island	.13	Vermont	.21
Nova Scotia	.14	California	.21
Oregon	.14	Connecticut	.21
North Dakota	.14	Illinois	.22
South Carolina	.14	New York	.23
Kansas	.14	Massachusetts	.23
Minnesota	.15	Missouri	.24
Alaska	.16	Virginia	.27
Idaho	.16	Georgia	.28
Wisconsin	.16		
Maine	.16	Average Coefficient	
New Hampshire	.16	of Variation:	
Pennsylvania	.17	for 5 out of 10	
Michigan	.17	Canadian Provinces	.09
		for the United States	.17

Source: Lawton (1989, p. 35).

"technology" of educational finance in Canada and the United States is quite similar.[19] Therefore, the greater equality of expenditure per pupil in Canadian provinces, as shown in Table 3, must be reflecting differences in values. He feels that Canadians place greater emphasis on the needs of society as a whole, while Americans tend to view the individual's needs as pre-eminent.

Table 3 lists in rank order the coefficients of variation[20] in per pupil operating expenditures for five of Canada's ten provinces and for all 50 states. Data for the remaining Canadian provinces were not available; but based on those provinces' histories of forming larger school districts and assuming a high share of the financial burden for education, Lawton concluded that the missing provinces' coefficients of variation would be similar to those for which data are available.

Lawton's 1979 results (which used data from 1975) are admittedly rather dated. However, to the extent that Lawton's finding of greater inequality of expenditure per pupil in the United States reflected different political values, casual observation of court cases reveals a continuation of these differences. While the Canadian court has been ruling on the equitable treatment of groups, the American court continues its traditional concern about the equitable treatment of individuals (p. 38).

Financing Post-Secondary Education

In recent years there has been considerable discussion about the organization of post-secondary education and the appropriate method of federal and provincial funding.[21] These discussions have led to changes in the amount and distribution of financing for higher education in Canada, changes which also reflect the government's concern over limiting spending.

Historical Background

Responsibility for post-secondary education rests with the provinces.[22] Before 1951, the federal government provided direct support for the education of veterans and shared in the costs of occupational training. During the period 1951 to 1967, the federal government provided financial support to universities in the form of a flat subsidy per student. In the following decade, 1968 to 1977, provincial governments were supplied with 50 percent of the operating costs of post-secondary institutions. Between 1972 and 1977 year-to-year increases were limited to 15 percent. Hence, the amount a province received depended on how much it spent. This arrangement stimulated the allocation of resources to the specified programs, but it was criticized on the basis that the federal government was setting priorities and interfering with provincial autonomy.

Where the Money Comes From

Currently, provincial and territorial governments are the major sources of financing to universities. They provide an annual operating grant to each university and also support capital expenditures. A Statistics Canada "Trend Analysis" found that over the period 1975-1985 total university spending as a percentage of GNP was fairly constant at about 1.5 percent, amounting to $7 billion in 1986-1987. During the same period, though, there was some change in the composition of university financing, as shown in Table 4. The average provincial operating grant has decreased from 81.2 percent to 78.4 percent of total university operating income. Research grants (not shown) and tuition fees

Table 4. Percentage Distribution of University General Operating Income by Major Source of Funds, Canada, 1975/76 to 1984/85

	Federal Government	Provincial Governments	Fees	Gifts	Investment Income	Other Sources
1975/76	1.2	81.2	14.5	0.7	0.9	1.5
1976/77	1.2	82.8	13.5	0.5	1.1	0.9
1977/78	1.2	82.1	13.8	0.5	0.9	1.4
1978/79	1.7	82.1	13.3	0.6	1.1	1.2
1979/80	1.4	82.1	13.0	0.7	1.6	1.3
1980/81	1.3	81.9	13.1	0.7	1.6	1.3
1981/82	1.7	80.8	13.6	0.6	2.0	1.4
1982/83	2.0	79.6	14.5	0.7	1.5	1.6
1983/84	2.2	79.3	15.3	0.6	1.2	1.4
1984/85	2.4	78.4	15.9	0.6	1.4	1.3

Source: West (1988, p. 30).

have increased in importance as sources of university funds (from 9.5% to 13.3% and from 14.5% to 15.9% respectively).

Tuition fees account for a small amount of the total cost of post-secondary education (roughly 16% in 1988). In the United States, tuition fees provide about 20 percent of the funds for public schools and 50 percent for private schools. However, Canadian universities have little flexibility in setting tuition fees; these are controlled by the provincial governments. For example, if an Ontario university charged more than 10 percent above the "set formula fee," then the provincial grant to that university would be reduced by the additional tuition revenue (West 1988, pp. 99-102). The Macdonald Commission (1985) and the Canadian Manufacturers' Association (1987) believe that tuition fees and the entire post-secondary education system should be deregulated. The current monopoly situation is characterized as lacking "dynamism" and exacerbating inequality. This will be discussed further in a later section.

The federal government's support for post-secondary education is now governed by the Federal-Provincial Fiscal Arrangements Act (1977) and the Established Programs Financing (EPF) Act (1977). The Fiscal Arrangements Act put the determination of the amounts of many conditional grants on a per capita basis that would increase yearly in relation to GNP growth, rather than to the growth in provincial costs. Under the EPF, provincial governments receive unconditional block funding based on their populations and GNP changes. During 1985-1986, the federal government made $4.5 billion in tax and cash transfer payments to the provincial governments.

The EPF Act of 1977 has generated much controversy and criticism. This has occurred because provincial governments have substantial discretion in the use of these funds: that is, to qualify for this federal grant the province is not required to spend any particular amount on post-secondary education. Consequently, there are now significant differences in the provision of post-secondary education across Canada, and real expenditure per student on post-secondary education has fallen since 1977 in almost all of the provinces (Johnson, 1985). However, to make a claim of "deficiency" in post-1977 fiscal arrangements (as has been done, for example, by Johnson in a special 1985 report to the Secretary of State), one needs to know the optimal share of GNP that should be devoted to post-secondary education. This will be addressed in a later section.

Statistics Canada has produced reports that outline other financial problems faced by the universities. For example, capital expenditures, as a percentage of total university expenditures, fell from 30 percent in 1960 to almost 6 percent in 1984-1985. University operating expenditures rose more slowly than inflation over the period 1975-1976 to 1984-1985. While university real funding rose by 2.5 percent from 1977 to 1984, enrolment rose by 25 percent over the same period. The results have been cutbacks in teaching staff, increased class sizes, reduced support staff, and lowered levels of new equipment purchasing and maintenance (Centre for Policy Studies in Education 1988, p. 50).

THE BENEFITS OF EDUCATION

There exists a substantial body of research showing that both individuals and society as a whole derive significant economic benefits from education. There are non-economic benefits to education as well. Many researchers (Atherton 1989; Hanushek 1986) claim that education "makes people more productive in the labor market, better able to participate in democracy, better consumers, healthier, and so forth—in other words, healthy, wealthy, and wise."

In 1965 the Economic Council of Canada (1965) published its second annual review entitled "Towards Sustained and Balanced Economic Growth." About one-third of this report dealt with the role of education as a major, if not primary, factor in promoting economic growth, increasing equality in the income distribution, reducing regional income disparity, and eliminating poverty. This report led to a substantial shift in resources to the university sector (although in the 1980s universities began to lose resources as noted above), as shown in Table 5. However, the educational expansion of the 1960s and 1970s did not bring about many of the benefits that had been promised in the Economic Council's report.

The relationship between higher education and economic development has long been recognized. Much of a nation's research and development is undertaken at universities, particularly basic research. Moreover, universities are expected to produce professionals who not only conduct research but also find applications for this research.

Table 5. Percentage Distribution of Expenditures
on Education in Canada, Selected Years

	Elementary/ Secondary	Non- University	University	Vocational and Other
1960-61	77.9	3.4	16.0	2.7
1965-66	70.9	2.9	21.7	4.5
1970-71	63.6	5.6	23.3	7.5
1981-85	65.2	7.9	20.3	6.6

Source: Atherton (1989, p. 44).

In this section we will look at the most recent studies on the benefits of education to Canada. Since most of the studies that have examined education's contribution to Canada's growth are out of date (Bertram 1966), the focus instead will be on the relationship of education to unemployment and on the rates of return on education.

Education and Unemployment

The correlation between the level of education and success in the labor market is fairly strong. As would be expected, Canadian men and women with less education are disproportionately represented in the ranks of the unemployed. For example, according to the 1981 census, men with less than grade nine education (22% of the male population) make up 30 percent of total male unemployment (Easton 1988, p. 19). According to the Secretary of State (1986), a 1984 survey of 1982 graduates indicated that the higher the educational attainment, the lower the rate of unemployment for both men and women. This is consistent with the evidence from other countries.

Since unemployment represents not only lost output but also human suffering, and to the extent that education is causally associated with reduced unemployment, the benefits of education go beyond its contribution to national output (Michael 1982) . However, as Easton (1988, pp. 24-25) observes, it makes little sense to consider the value of education as the value of its contribution to growth without subtracting the cost of its provision.

The Rate of Return to Elementary and Secondary Education

Constantatos and West (1988) calculate the returns to elementary and secondary education and emphasize that they differ depending on the cost of raising funds. For elementary schooling in which there is a zero marginal cost to raising public funds, the social rates of return range from 13.6 to 16.8 percent, depending on the amount of lifetime earnings attributed to education (as opposed to other factors, like innate ability). If the "deadweight cost"[23] of raising the funds is included, these returns fall to 9.3 and 12.2 percent. Similar calculations for secondary school yield rates of return between 5.5 and 7.5 percent with a zero marginal cost of public funds.

The Rate of Return to Higher Education

Vaillancourt and Henriques (1986) claim that the private rate of return on higher education is between 7 and 14 percent. The social rate of return is between 6 and 10 percent. They also suggest that the rate of return varies across Canada; for example, the social return is much higher in eastern and central Canada than in the west. Also, as might be expected with a subsidized system of higher education, the social return is always less than the private return. The rate of return on a three-year BA exceeds that on a four-year (honors) BA.

The rate of return to higher education may be falling, however. For example, Mehmet (1977) found that the returns to a university education were 22 percent in 1969 but only 18 percent in 1972. This is consistent with the findings of Dooley (1986) who found that the earnings differential between university and secondary school graduates was falling during 1971-1981. This could be due to improvements at the secondary level or decline at the university level.

West (1988, pp. 64-67) improves upon the work of Vaillancourt and Henriques by allowing for different assumptions about the role played by "ability" in earnings differentials since regression analysis suggests non-educational influences (such as innate ability) account for 20 to 40 percent of the additional earnings of educated workers. West obtains a variety of social rates of return from Canadian university degrees. The lowest is a social rate of return of 6.95 percent, when he assumes that 35 percent of earnings differentials are due to innate ability.

POLICY ISSUES

Trends in Federal-Provincial Relations

As discussed in an earlier section, Brown (1989, pp. 64-81) claimed that slower economic growth, growing needs in the public sector, spending restraints, and limits on federal-provincial transfers (that is, revised federal-provincial fiscal arrangements) have caused interprovincial differences in ability-to-pay, which had been narrowing, to begin widening again. These differences in ability-to-pay have caused interprovincial differences in spending per pupil and provincial-local revenue allocations to education.

This movement towards widening disparity is cause for concern, especially since there is little hope for higher federal funding in the future, given the poor forecasts for Canadian growth. One solution may be to earmark more of the federal funds currently available for education. However, this may hurt other provincial programs, for example, health.

Brown (1989, pp. 76-81) examined some long-term demographic trends and concluded that the expansion of the most productive age group in the population (age 20 to 64) will coincide with a relative decline in the combined young and elderly populations well into the next century. He claims that these generally favorable dependency ratios should permit increases in national output to provide adequate levels of financial support for education and other social services. Since he also projects that there will be a narrowing of interprovincial differences in dependency ratios, it should be easier to fulfill the Constitution's goal of equal access to public services in the future. This goal of equalization of opportunity and tax burden is the most critical at the elementary-secondary level, since society gains the most from this level of education.

Financial Support for Higher Education

As previously discussed, there are many who claim that post-secondary education is underfunded, especially as a result of the EPF Act of 1977. However, comparison with other countries suggests that Canada is relatively well supplied with post-secondary education (at least as of 1981). Recall that by 1981 37.6 percent of Canadians age 25 and over had some post-secondary education whereas the comparable figure for Americans was 32.2 percent (see Table 1). Also, to claim "underfunding" one should have some notion of "optimal" funding. The usual method of determining whether university training pays off socially is to compare the social rate of return from university education with the rate of return on physical capital. Vaillancourt and Henriques' (1986) estimates lead them to conclude that since the social returns are often lower than the return on physical capital (10%) and lower than the private return, provincial governments should reduce their subsidies to universities. West's (1988, pp. 65-67) estimates of social returns (6.95%) compared to his return on physical capital (6.5%) led him to conclude that the social return on human capital was roughly equal to that on physical capital in 1980. If adjustments are made for the deadweight welfare costs of public funds, however, the returns to post-secondary education fall below those on capital.

These results offer little support for those who claim that the EPF Act has had a harmful effect because it has led to a decline in real dollar-per-student spending on university education. In fact, these reductions in spending could well have been called for in order to regain that lower but optimum level where marginal human and physical capital returns are equal.

As mentioned in an earlier section, tuition fees generate a smaller amount of the total costs of education in Canada than in other countries, and universities are given little flexibility in setting these fees. Some have suggested that tuition fees be "deregulated" as a way for universities to obtain more financing given the (admittedly debatable) situation of insufficient funding.

It has also been suggested that tuition be deregulated as a way to improve the productivity and quality of universities. For example, the Macdonald Commission (1985) argued that freeing up the fee structure would result in a much more heterogeneous post-secondary system that would more efficiently serve the needs of different students. The Canadian Manufacturers' Association (1987) claimed that:

> Tuition and university programs must be deregulated to encourage the emergence of excellence and to increase the flexibility and responsiveness to changing economic and competitive conditions.

Vaillancourt and Henriques' estimates of high private rates of return to higher education led them to conclude that tuition fees could be increased in all regions of Canada without much effect on enrollments.[24]

The Quality of Education

Quality is difficult to define and measure, particularly in Canada, where national examinations have never been in place (because of provincial jurisdiction), and province-wide examinations at the end of high school have not been administered since the 1960s. Recently, however, five provinces have re-introduced secondary-school diploma exams.

In Canada, as in the United States, there is concern about declining standards. Some of the reasons for this may be the loosening of requirements in the 1970s (perhaps because more young people were staying in school and expecting to graduate) and financial cutbacks. Wilkinson (1986) notes that the public perceives a deterioration of quality in the traditional skills of mathematics and language. The Ontario Ministry of Education (1981) notes that employers are dissatisfied with the preparedness of the work force. Because there is a widespread perception that quality in the schools has been deteriorating, some method of assessment should be instituted, ideally one that gets at the value added by the educational system (rather than traditional standardized tests).

Government Priorities Toward Education Shifting

Throughout this paper the reduction of funding from federal, local or provincial governments has been noted. Whether or not this indicates a shift in the priority of education is very difficult to say. As argued earlier, perhaps the reduced funding for post-secondary education is optimal from society's point of view.

There is mixed evidence regarding government funding for the elementary and secondary sector. According to Brown (1989, p. 69), spending per pupil has increased from $471 in 1965 to $4729 in 1986. Easton[25] says that between 1961 and 1981 the real cost per student increased faster than the corresponding rate of real per capita national product. In real terms, educating a student today costs more than three times as much as in 1960. Brown (1989, p. 72) found that total spending for public elementary and secondary education as a percentage of total provincial and local government spending fell steadily from 22.12 percent in 1970 to 14.75 percent in 1986. Since the decline in enrollment over the period was about 17 percent, other factors were involved, such as more rapid growth of spending for competing services (for example, health care) and some decline in the policy importance of education (perhaps due to a reduced emphasis on the goal of equality in society).

The Canadian Teachers' Federation (1986) claims that elementary and secondary education has been losing ground to other social programs. For example, although the percent of total provincial-local government spending allocated to elementary-secondary education fell from 17 percent (1975) to 14 percent (1984), the shares allocated to other social services (including higher education) increased from 39 percent to 41 percent. This reduced priority for elementary-secondary education should be investigated further as the returns to the economy for spending on elementary-secondary education are greater than for spending at higher levels.

Encouraging Research and Development

Because the world market is becoming increasingly competitive, it is important for Canada to engage in appropriate research and development efforts. The evidence on this front is not encouraging, however. The Science Council of Canada (1984) expressed concern over the quality of science education, and science and technology are critical to Canada's ability to compete in today's international environment.[26] OECD statistics indicate that Canada has only half as many engineers and scientists per capita as most of its major competitors.[27] The Johnson Report (1985) says that Canada is lacking "the vehicles and the incentives for mobilizing the resources and talents into the kind of 'critical mass' which is called for and found in world-class centres of excellence."

It is important for Canada to develop a national strategy on science and technology.[28] This national plan should address the following key questions: how to improve the quality of science and mathematics education and how to encourage more students to study science, become engineers and scientists and remain in Canada.

CONCLUSIONS

Canada shares many concerns with the United States about the state of its educational system. In both countries there is general financial restraint, which is causing cutbacks in educational support at the very time that an educated labor force is crucial to helping both countries compete internationally. Also, both the United States and Canada are concerned about the quality of their educational systems.

Although Canada has been improving relative to the United States in terms of median years of schooling and the average Canadian student performs better than the average American student on international tests, disturbing trends have been uncovered in Canada which may well halt this improvement. Some key differences between the Canadian and American systems are putting considerable strain on Canada's education resources: most notably the use of public funds for the financing of private elementary-secondary schools, the absence of private colleges or universities, equalization payments from the federal government to poorer provinces, and less variation in interdistrict per pupil expenditures. Hence, in the future the Canadian system may become more similar to that of the United States.[29] However, before this occurs it is critical to discern the source of the relative advantage of the Canadian system. If these differences contribute to the relative superiority of the Canadian educational system, then they should not be done away with.

NOTES

1. From 1966-1973, Canada's GNP, adjusted for inflation, grew at an average of 5.4 percent per year. In the last 7 years, real GNP increased an average of 1.6 percent per year.

2. For example, see Skolnik and Rowen (1984, p. 169).

3. See the Centre for Policy Studies in Education (1988, p. 5).

4. See Dibski (1987, p. 66).

5. Much of the information contained in this section was obtained from Sova (1990, pp. 7-3-7-12).

6. For example, according to Sova, *1990 Corpus Almanac,* p. 7-3, Scottish educational practice had a strong, early influence on English-speaking Canada; Quebec followed the educational traditions of France.

7. These facts and those presented in the next section, "The Elementary-Secondary School Sector," unless otherwise noted, were obtained from Easton (1988).

8. According to Sova, *1990 Corpus Almanac,* Newfoundland provides tax support for educational districts established for religious denominations. Recent legislation in Quebec provides for French-speaking and English-speaking schools, rather than denominational ones. In British Columbia, New Brunswick, Nova Scotia, Manitoba and Prince Edward Island, non-sectarian public education is provided.

9. For example, according to Brown (1983, pp. 1-22) from 1971 to 1980 this funding increased from 18.3 percent to 32.2 percent of total private school expenditures.

10. The statistics found in this paragraph are from the Centre for Policy Studies in Education, *Education and the Economy, The Canadian Case,* 1988, pp. 8-9, Statistics Canada, *The Labor Force, August 1987* and Statistics Canada (1986).

11.   The statistics in this paragraph are from West (1988, pp. 2, 19-22). According to West from 1975-1986 the rate of growth for females in universities was 7 percent. In 1986, 4 out of 10 graduate students were women, as opposed to 3 out of 10 in 1975. Also, in 1986, 49 percent of full-time undergraduates were women.

12.   Many of the facts and ideas in this section are drawn from Dibski (1987, pp. 66-78). For specific, detailed accounts of provincial financing of elementary and secondary school, see Lawton (1987). Other sources of revenue are: royalties on natural resources (for British Columbia, Alberta, and Saskatchewan); profits of crown corporations and public utililties; and fees collected by various government agencies for licenses and services.

13.   This reference was found in Brown (1989, p. 64).

14.   According to Dibski (1987, p. 70), the amount of equalization that a province received depended upon the shortfall between its own revenue and the agreed-upon norm. Therefore, the equalization payments on a per capita basis were much higher for poorer provinces (and represented a greater percentage of the total revenue of these provinces). Those provinces whose own revenues equalled or exceeded the norm received no equalization.

15.   These five "representative" provinces are Ontario, Quebec, Manitoba, Saskatchewan, and British Columbia. Alberta, the most financially able province, was omitted because its high natural resource revenue was thought to distort the "representativeness" of the norm. The four Atlantic provinces, the least financially able provinces, were also dropped from the equalization standard. See Brown (1989, p. 65) and the Macdonald Commission, *Report of the Royal Commission on the Economic Union and Development Prospects for Canada* (1985, p. 181).

16.   According to Dibski (1987, p. 71), equalization and other transfer payments grow year by year and constitute an increasingly important source of revenue for most provinces.

17.   See Brown (1989, pp. 64-81). Brown measures financial abilities by using the tax base (that is, personal income) or total revenue (that is, taxes plus other sources of revenue, for example, government grants). Financial effort is measured by spending per pupil, spending as a percentage of provincial personal income, and spending as a percentage of total provincial and local government spending.

18.   Brown (1989, p. 72) finds that enrolment and graduate figures suggest that real or non-financial educational inequalities among the provinces have either halted the narrowing trend of earlier years or have remained static. For example, the national average of 14- to 17-year-olds attending school increased from 85 to 90 percent between the late 1970s and the mid-1980s. Interprovincial differences over the period were low and relatively stable. Also, there was a narrowing trend in interprovincial differences in student retention between 1978 and 1983. The recession in the early 1980s was probably partly responsible for this result. It may also have been attributable to the narrowing in provincial spending on education, which continued until 1976, and had a continuing, lagged effect.

19.   Both states and provinces have developed various programs to assist the poorer districts. Both foundation programs and power or percentage equalization plans are widely used in both countries. According to Lawton, *The Price of Quality*, New Brunswick and Prince Edward Island have set the foundation level at 100 percent of budgeted expenditures: that is, they have assumed full funding. Other provinces have moved very close to this as well. Salmon, Dawson, et al. (1988, p. 4) reported that 32 states have minimum foundation programs; 15 have some form of variable guaranteed funding; 4 had both types; and 6 have some form of minimum flat grant.

20.   The coefficient of variation is a measure of dispersion which takes all values in a series into account. It is the standard deviation divided by the arithmetic mean, expressed as a percentage.

21.   See, for example, the Macdonald Commission, *Report of the Royal Commission on the Economic Union and Development Prospects for Canada*.

22.   Much of the following discussion, including the statistics, is drawn from West (1988, p. 96) and the Centre for Policy Studies in Education, *Education and the Economy, The Canadian Case*.

23. A "deadweight loss" occurs because taxation causes otherwise profitable transactions to be avoided or encourages otherwise unprofitable transactions to be included.

24. See Vaillancourt and Henriques (1986). They estimate that a doubling of tuition fees would reduce private rates of return by no more than 3 percent for a three-year degree. Also, see West (1988, pp. 100-104).

25. See Easton (1988, p. 39). According to Easton, one-quarter of this increase is due to the change in student/teacher ratios (these have fallen from 26.1 in 1960 to 18.3 in 1986) and about 40 percent is due to increases in teacher salaries. Since the mid-1970s Canadian teachers have been earning about 30 percent more than their American counterparts. Also, the increase in Canadian teachers' salaries has been much faster than that experienced by broad classes of other income earners in Canada.

26. However, according to Robitaille (1985) students in Ontario and British Columbia performed well in mathematics compared to students in other OECD countries.

27. See OECD (1986). Some of the reasons for this may be: the "brain drain," especially to the United States; the aging of the present research population; and a failure to produce sufficient numbers of students with graduate degrees. See Centre for Policy Studies in Education (1988).

28. See the Centre for Policy Studies in Education, *Education and the Economy, The Canadian Case*, pp. 51-52.

29. For example, many critics claim that Canada needs to establish private universities and colleges which would be more "efficient" and less of a strain on public funds.

REFERENCES

Atherton, P.J. 1989. "Recent Developments in the Economics of Education and Their Policy Implications." In *Scrimping or Squandering? Financing Canadian Schools*, edited by S.B. Lawton and R. Wignall. Toronto, Ontario: The Ontario Institute for Studies in Education.

Bertram, G.W. 1966. *The Contribution of Education to Economic Growth*. Ottawa, Ontario: Economic Council of Canada, Staff Study No. 12.

Brown, W.J. 1983. "The Educational Toll of the 'Great Depression'" Pp. 1-22 in *The Cost of Controlling the Costs of Education in Canada*, edited by B.D. Anderson and W.J. Brown. Toronto, Ontario: The Ontario Institute for Studies in Education.

————. 1989. "Education Finance and the Interplay of Competing Goals." Pp. 64-81 in *Scrimping or Squandering? Financing Canadian Schools*, edited by S.B. Lawton and R. Wignall. Toronto, Ontario: The Ontario Institute for Studies in Education.

Canadian Manufacturer's Association. 1987. *The Importance of Post-Secondary Education*. Toronto, Ontario: Canadian Manufacturer's Association.

Canadian Teachers' Federation. 1986. "Elementary and Secondary Education Losing Ground to Other Social Spending in Canada and in Most Provinces." *Link* 10 (2):14.

Centre for Policy Studies in Education. 1988. *Education and the Economy, The Canadian Case*. Vancouver, BC: University of British Columbia.

Constantatos, C. and E. West. 1988. "Education and the Marginal Cost of Public Funds." Unpublished manuscript, Ottawa, Canada.

Dibski, D.J. 1987. "Financing Education." In *Social Change and Education in Canada*, edited by R. Ghosh and D. Ray. Toronto, Ontario: Harcourt, Brace, Jovanovich.

Dooley, M. 1986. "The Overeducated Canadian? Changes in the Relationship Among Earnings, Education, and Age for Canadian Men: 1971-81." *Canadian Journal of Economics* 19, 142-159.

Easton, S.T. 1988. *Education in Canada, An Analysis of Elementary, Secondary and Vocational Schooling*. Vancouver, BC: The Fraser Institute.

Economic Council of Canada. 1965. *Towards Sustained and Balanced Economic Growth.* Ottawa, Ontario: Economic Council of Canada.

Hanushek, E.A. 1986. "The Economics of Schooling: Production and Efficiency in Public Schools." *Journal of Economic Literature* 24, 1141-1177.

Johnson, A.W. 1985. *Giving Greater Point and Purpose to the Financing of Post-Secondary Education and Research in Canada.* Ottawa, Ontario: Secretary of State's Office.

Lawton S.B. 1987. *The Price of Quality, The Public Finance of Elementary and Secondary Education in Canada.* Toronto, Ontario: Canadian Education Association.

————. 1989. "Political Values in Educational Finance in Canada and the United States." In *Scrimping or Squandering? Financing Canadian Schools,* edited by S.B. Lawton and R. Wignall. Toronto, Ontario: The Ontario Institute for Studies in Education.

Macdonald Commission. 1985. *Report of the Royal Commission on the Economic Union and Development Prospects for Canada.* Ottawa, Ontario: Supply and Services Canada.

Mehmet, O. 1977. "Economic Returns on Undergraduate Fields of Study in Canadian Universities: 1961 to 1972." *Industrial Relations,* 32 (3).

Michael, R.T. 1982. "Measuring Non-Monetary Benefits: A Survey." In *Financing Education: Overcoming Inefficency and Inequity,* edited by W. McMahon and T. Geske. Urbana, IL: University of Illinois Press.

OECD. 1986. "Research and Development, Invention and Competitiveness." In *OECD Science and Technology Indicators.* Paris, France: OECD.

Robitaille, D. 1985. *An Analysis of Selected Achievement Data from the Second International Mathematics Study.* Vancouver, BC: Student Assessment Branch, Ministry of Education.

Salmon, R., C. Dawson, S.B. Lawton, and T.L. Johns. 1988. *Public School Finance Programs in the United States and Canada.* Blacksburg, VA: American Education Finance Association and Virginia Polytechnic Institute and State University.

Science Council of Canada. 1984. *Science for Every Student: Educating Canadians for Tomorrow's World.* Ottawa, Ontario: Supply and Services.

Secretary of State and Statistics Canada. 1986. *The Class of 82: Summary Report on the Findings of the 1984 National Survey of the Graduates of 1982.* Ottawa, Ontario: Ministry of Supply and Services.

Shapiro, B.J. 1985. *The Report of the Commission on Private Schools in Ontario.* Toronto, Ontario: Ministry of Education.

Skolnick, M.L., and N. S. Rowen. 1984. *"Please Sir, I Want Some More"—Canadian Universities and Financial Restraint.* Toronto, Ontario: The Ontario Institute for Studies in Education.

Sova, G. ed. 1990. *1990 Corpus Almanac and Canadian Sourcebook.* Toronto, Ontario: Southam Business Information and Communication.

Statistics Canada. 1986. "Trends in Long-Term Unemployment by Industry and Occupation." In *The Labor Force.* Ottawa, Ontario: Supply and Services, Catalogue 71-001.

The Ontario Ministry of Education. 1981. *Report of the Secondary Education Review Project.* Toronto, Ontario: Ministry of Education.

Vaillancourt, F. and I. Henriques. 1986. "The Returns to University Schooling in Canada." *Canadian Public Policy* 12 (3): 449-458.

West, E. 1988. *Higher Education in Canada, An Analysis.* Vancouver, British Columbia: The Fraser Institute.

Wilkinson, B.W. 1986. "Elementary and Secondary Education Policy in Canada: A Survey." *Canadian Public Policy,* 535-572.

CURRENT PROPOSALS
FOR SCHOOL REFORM:
AN ECONOMIST'S ASSESSMENT

Gary Burtless

INTRODUCTION

Informed observers agree that American schools are in trouble. United States high school and junior high school students stand near the back of the class in international rankings of student knowledge and achievement. The mediocre quality of American education is apparent in a wide variety of measures of student performance. None of these measures is perfect, but most of them point in the same direction: High school graduates know less than they once did and far less than typical graduates of high schools in other industrialized nations.

Many people believe that the failings of the U.S. school system will profoundly handicap the nation in its race to maintain economic parity with other countries. In its recent report on American education goals, the National Governors' Association stated bluntly that "Education is the key to America's international competitiveness" (National Governors' Association 1990). Economists have offered abundant proof that unskilled, undereducated workers are falling further behind the economic mainstream. The authors of the influential *Workforce 2000* report argue that the structure of the economy is changing in a way that eliminates jobs for the less skilled while boosting demand for highly educated workers. Their labor market forecast suggests steady, strong growth in occupations requiring advanced education and skill but a sharp slowdown in the number of workers meeting the minimum skill requirements for those jobs (Johnston 1987). U.S. schools thus face a fundamentally new task: Educating all students for an economy that no longer rewards unskilled labor.

The goal of this paper is to evaluate the likely success of several broad ·strategies of school reform. I approach this goal in a rather indirect way. First, I consider what economists have had to say about the link between schooling and the broader economy. Most economists, like the authors of the *Workforce 2000* report, are convinced that investments in schooling provide a tangible reward in the form of higher pay and worker productivity. Much of the evidence in support of this view comes from detailed analyses of the relation between schooling attainment and students' later experiences in the labor market. More rarely, economists have analyzed evidence on the relationship between investments in school quality and later success in the job market. Both kinds of research are evaluated in the next section of the paper.

Of equal relevance to the school reform debate is the large and growing literature on student performance inside schools. While economists are not sure they understand the relationship between school performance and later job market success, most parents are persuaded that their children must learn specific knowledge and problem-solving skills in order to succeed in their careers. If this is true, one important finding of the school performance literature leads to a profound puzzle. Analysts studying student achievement in individual schools find no reliable or consistent relationship between heavier investments in schools and student performance. But economists analyzing the labor market report substantial extra earnings gains for workers educated in more expensive schools. The middle section of the paper considers some of the main findings from the school performance literature.

In the concluding section, I consider the implications of different strands of economic research for school reform. Like several other economists, I find it unlikely that investment in more school resources will significantly alter student achievement. Only a reorganization of current resources offers much hope for meaningful improvement.

EDUCATIONAL ATTAINMENT, EDUCATIONAL QUALITY, AND EARNINGS

The level of schooling and the quality of educational experience decisively affect the productivity and earnings of individual workers. The strong relationship between educational attainment and earnings capacity has been recognized in the economics profession for several decades. Theoretical and applied economists have sought since the early 1960s to explain how and why education affects the distribution of personal earnings. The most influential model to explain this relationship rests on the theory that educational investments in human beings are similar to physical investments in plant and equipment. Just as investment in buildings or machines involves an initial expenditure which must be weighed against some future stream of financial benefits, investments in workers involve an initial sacrifice of time and money that is eventually offset in the form of higher future output or earnings.

Because economists are interested in assessing the efficiency of public and private investments in human capital, they have devoted prodigious energy and resources to measuring the exact payoff from different forms and levels of schooling. In addition, a few economists have sought to determine the contribution of educational investments to overall economic growth and productivity improvement. Such studies typically find that increases in the educational attainment of American workers account for as much as a quarter of the growth in output per person employed (Denison 1985, p. 30). If these calculations are taken as valid, the contribution of educational investment to productivity growth has been greater than the contribution of investment in physical plant and equipment.

Of course, the insight of a rocket scientist is not needed to recognize the positive association between educational attainment and lifetime earnings. As far back as 1950, Paul Glick estimated that a college degree was worth $103,000—the difference between the $165,000 in lifetime earnings received by a high school graduate and the $268,000 earned by a typical college graduate (Aaron 1978, p. 66). Although this naive estimate can be criticized on several grounds, Glick's method of estimating the value of school, with some modification, continues to be applied to this day. Analysts compare the average earnings of workers who have attained a particular level of schooling with the average earned by workers who attain the next higher level. The difference in average earnings, with some statistical adjustment, provides a simple estimate of the value of extra schooling. The benefit of extra schooling, at virtually every age and for virtually every class of workers, appears to be positive.

Figure 1 shows the average 1987 earnings of American men with various levels of schooling. Note that the earnings gap between highly educated and less well educated workers grows larger with age, a pattern that is reflected in the diagram by the steeper slopes of age-earnings profiles for better educated groups. At the youngest ages, workers with high educational attainment do not necessarily have greater earnings than workers with less attainment. By about age thirty, however, the average earnings status of different educational classes is perfectly consistent with their educational rank. From age 30 to about age 50, the earnings gap between educational classes continues to climb.

The numbers shown in Figure 1 in fact understate differences in earnings associated with differences in schooling attainment. The statistics are based on average annual earnings for those workers who reported positive wages or

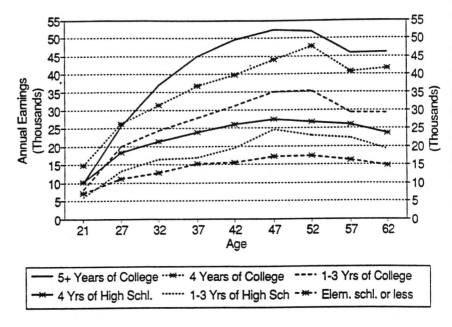

Source: U.S. Bureau of the Census, *Money Income of Households, Families and Persons in the United States: 1987* (Series P-60, no. 162), Table 36.

Figure 1.   Earnings by Age and Education in 1987 Males

self-employment income during 1987. Because schooling attainment is positively correlated with labor force participation and negatively correlated with unemployment, highly educated men are far more likely than less educated men to be employed at a given age, particularly past 50. For example, among men 25 to 34 years old, 97 percent of college graduates had earnings during 1987 while only 83 percent of men with just an elementary school education were in the paid work force. The gap is even wider at older ages. Ninety-five percent of college graduates between 45 and 54 earned wages or self-employment income in 1987. Among less educated men of the same age, only 76 percent without schooling beyond the elementary level had earnings in 1987. Educational attainment not only has a powerful association with the income a worker earns if employed, it has a large effect on a person's chances of holding a job.

The gain from extra schooling is large, but perhaps more significantly it has been growing over the past decade. Among workers with varying levels of education, the annual wage of those with a college diploma has climbed rapidly relative to the wage earned by workers with a high school education or less. Figure 2 shows trends in relative earnings of two broad classes of workers:

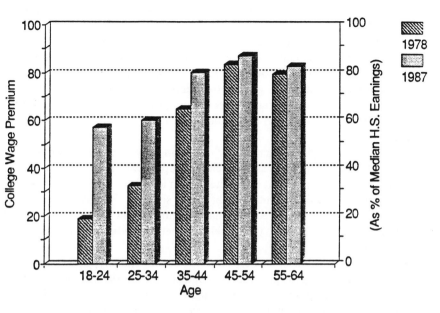

Source: U.S. Bureau of the Census, *Money Income of Households, Families, and Persons in the United States: 1987* (Series P-60, no. 162) Table 36.; and *Money Income of Families and Persons in the United States: 1978* (Series P-60, no. 123), Table 51.

Figure 2. Trends in the College Premium for Men 1978-1987

men with four or more years of college and men with one to four years of high school. After falling slightly during the 1970s, the earnings premium from a college education rose sharply in the 1980s, especially at younger ages. Among male workers aged 25 to 34 in 1978, the average college graduate earned 33 percent more than an average worker who had a high school education or less. By 1987, the earnings premium for college graduates had jumped to 60 percent. The rise in wage differentials has been smaller among women and older men, but is apparent in those groups as well.[1]

These tabulations understate the growing advantage enjoyed by more educated workers because they exclude information about potential workers who have no earnings at all as a result of unemployment or failure to participate in the job market. Unemployment and labor force participation trends since the 1970s have worked to the disadvantage of high school graduates and dropouts. The unemployment rate suffered by less educated workers has risen sharply in relation to the rate observed among the highly educated; their labor force participation rate has fallen. Many economists, including me, believe that these trends can be explained by shifts in the structure of demand for labor of different skill classes. Even as the share of highly educated workers in the labor force has grown, the demand for such workers has apparently accelerated. The result is higher relative unemployment among unskilled workers and higher relative wages for workers with advanced schooling. This pattern confirms some of the qualitative predictions contained in the *Workforce 2000* report (Johnston 1987). Not only is the educational attainment of U.S. workers important in explaining the growth of average wages and productivity over time, it is increasingly important in determining who gains and who loses from changes in the industrial and occupational structure and from innovations in technology.

To be sure, the high and increasing correlation between education and earned income does not prove a causal relationship between the two variables. Education and income could be affected by an identical set of determinants—race, family background, innate ability, and so forth. Because these factors simultaneously affect both educational attainment and earnings, and affect them in the same direction, the correlation between education and earnings might be spurious.

That the correlation is entirely spurious seems unlikely, however. Social scientists investigating the payoff to schooling have typically included statistical controls for the most important social and economic factors that might affect both education and earnings. Thus, recent estimates of the benefit from schooling—unlike Paul Glick's—take into account the impact on earnings of observable factors such as race and family background. These estimates generally imply that the rate of return on investment in additional schooling is positive and in the range of 5 to 15 percent. (That is, if we calculate the dollar investment in schooling as the sum of the direct public and private cost of education plus the wages a student gives up in order to remain in school, the higher wage the student can earn over the course of a career as a result of additional schooling yields a return after inflation of 5 to 15 percent a year.)

Statistical estimates of the value of schooling have been criticized because they usually fail to account for factors that affect both educational attainment and earnings but that are difficult or impossible to measure. One such factor is innate personal ability. Another is school quality. Even though we do not possess good measures of either variable, economists and other social scientists have devised ingenious methods to account for their possible influence in determining the correlation of education and earnings. Griliches and Mason (1972) obtained aptitude scores from tests administered to armed forces enlistees, many of whom had not yet completed their formal schooling. Taking account of the influence of schooling attainment obtained before enlistment as well as general ability as measured on the aptitude test, the two economists estimated the effect on subsequent civilian earnings of the additional schooling soldiers obtained after their enlistment or discharge from military duty. Perhaps surprisingly, they found that the typical bias from ignoring the influence of ability on earnings is quite small—on the order of 10 percent.

This finding suggests that analysts who are forced by data limitations to ignore the influence of general intellectual ability on earnings will not seriously bias their estimates of the effect of schooling on earnings. It thus seems highly probable that economists and other analysts have established a causal link between the level of schooling attainment and individual earnings. Moreover, the size of the estimated effect implies that investments in schooling offer attractive returns in comparison with other investment opportunities, such as new plant and equipment, savings accounts, or bonds.

Of greater direct relevance to the debate over school reform is research on the influence of school quality on earnings. The inherent quality of schools is of course unobserved and probably unmeasurable. Analysts can, however, measure the differential impact of different school systems by ascertaining whether they produce different kinds of effects on outcomes of interest, notably, in-school achievement and post-school earnings. In addition, analysts can frequently discover whether school systems differ in certain measurable ways, for example, in student/teacher ratios, average teacher salaries, length of school year, or the demographic character of their student bodies.

Economists have for some time suspected that differences in the average quality of schools can help explain differences in the return to schooling enjoyed by members of different races. Tabulations similar to those shown in Figure 1, calculated separately for blacks and whites, revealed that black men in the 1950s obtained far smaller earnings gains as a result of additional schooling than white men with the same age and work experience. Because most black workers had been educated in segregated and seriously deficient schools, a natural inference was that black workers with high levels of schooling attainment were disadvantaged relative to similar white workers because of the poor quality of their schooling (Welch 1966, 1967). This inference was apparently confirmed when economists discovered in the 1970s that black-white differences in returns to schooling had shrunk for cohorts of men entering the labor force in the 1960s, by which point the average quality of schooling among young blacks—as measured by its cost—approached that among young whites (Welch 1973a, 1973b).

Differences in returns to schooling enjoyed by blacks and whites provide strong though not definitive evidence that school quality as well as quantity can affect individual earnings. A number of analysts have investigated the effects of state-wide or regional differences in schooling resources on the economic payoff from education. Until the 1950s, states varied widely in average class size, teacher pay, length of school year, and spending per pupil. Several investigators found support for the hypothesis that workers educated in states or regions spending more on educational inputs derived a higher payoff per year of attendance in school. That is, the earnings gain generated by an additional year of schooling is greater for workers educated in states where per-pupil spending is higher.[2]

The most exhaustive and convincing research on this topic is a recent study by labor economists Card and Krueger (1990). Their analysis is based on individual-level 1980 Census data on earnings of men born between 1920 and 1949. After dividing their sample into three large birth cohorts (with birth years between 1920-1929, 1930-1939, and 1940-1949, respectively), Card and Krueger essentially estimated separate earnings functions for men classified by the state of their birth and their birth cohort. This procedure yielded an estimate of the rate of return to additional schooling for each of the cohorts in each of the states. The authors then statistically estimated the relationship between the return to schooling in a given state and several attributes of the state's educational system, including class size, teacher training, average teacher salary relative to the state's mean wage, and length of school year. Using historical data derived from the U.S. Office of Education's *Biennial Survey of Education* and *Digest of Educational Statistics,* the authors calculated average values of these variables for years in which men in their sample were in school.

The statistical results leave little doubt that there is a significant and meaningful relationship between the cost and quality of educational inputs, on the one hand, and earnings gains attributable to educational attainment, on the other. Increases in length of school year and teacher salaries and reductions in the pupil/teacher ratio lead to statistically significant gains in the measured return to additional schooling. Thus, factors that many school reformers hope to improve—teacher pay, time spent in school, and average class size—have been shown to affect the distribution of lifetime earnings. Card and Krueger suggest, for example, that a decrease in the pupil/teacher ratio of five students is associated with a 0.4 percentage point increase in the rate of return to schooling, while a 10 percent increase in teachers' pay is associated with a 0.1 percentage point increase in the rate of return to schooling. (A student educated in the average state can expect to earn wages about 5 to 7 percent higher for each year of schooling received above a minimum threshold of education, usually about two or three years of school.) In addition, the two economists find some support for the hypothesis that average teacher quality, as measured by teachers' educational attainment, can have a beneficial effect on the returns to schooling. Finally, their analysis confirms the earlier finding by Welch that returns to schooling among black workers have converged toward those enjoyed by whites as the average quality of black schooling has improved.

On balance, thirty years of statistical research on the relationship between education and earnings offers abundant evidence to cheer advocates of school reform. Economists have found a strong correlation between educational attainment and more costly school inputs, on the one hand, and lifetime earnings, on the other. Improvements in the quantity and quality of formal schooling appear to cause measurable and substantial differences in the earnings capacity of individual workers.

Not all economists are persuaded that the statistical evidence on individual gains from improved schooling implies that the social gains are as large as the private ones. The job market signalling hypothesis, proposed in the 1970s as an alternative to human capital theory, offers a competing explanation for the association between schooling and earnings. According to the signalling hypothesis, education is simply a screening process that reveals to potential employers characteristics of workers that make them more or less attractive as employees. Workers obtaining the correct set of educational credentials will have greater access to better paying jobs and, as a consequence, will earn more money over their lifetimes (Spence 1974). According to this view, education does not produce ability or productivity; it merely identifies existing talent.

Some critics of the screening hypothesis object that an employer must eventually become informed of the true ability of its workers, regardless of the credentials they bring to a job, which should gradually lessen the value of the credential as time goes on. But, as shown in Figures 1 and 2, the earnings advantage enjoyed by better educated workers actually grows with age. One problem with this objection to the screening hypothesis is that the educational signal, even though it might not cause a worker to be more productive, could be highly correlated with the worker's inherent productivity. The high correlation between educational credentials and later earnings might simply demonstrate that the credential is a successful screen. The fact that the credential is accurate in identifying (or predicting) productivity does not imply that it caused the productivity to occur.

An obvious implication of the job market signalling theory is that the social value of schooling investments can be greatly exaggerated by estimates of the private return to schooling. Even though it is worthwhile for an individual to improve his or her career prospects by investing in extra school credentials, it does not follow that economy-wide production gains will match individual wage gains. No economist has to my knowledge proposed a statistical test that can reliably distinguish between the human capital and job market signalling theories. Thus, school reformers are left with a fundamental uncertainty. Even though they may be confident that educational improvements can increase the earnings gains that students will enjoy as a result of formal schooling, they cannot be equally confident that those improvements will yield equivalent advantages to the broader economy.

SCHOOL DIFFERENCES
AND EDUCATIONAL ACHIEVEMENT

If schooling improves productivity, as the human capital model assumes, the improvement presumably occurs because of what is learned in schools. Schools attempt to impart specific knowledge, but they also seek to improve reasoning and problem-solving skills. We do not know which specific skills or areas of knowledge yield the greatest rewards in the labor market, in the form of either higher wages or greater personal productivity. Hunter (1986) and Schmidt (1988), in recent surveys of the literature on ability and job performance, assert that tests of general cognitive ability, rather than tests of specific aptitudes or job knowledge, have the highest validity in predicting actual job productivity.

While it is sometimes asserted that schooling cannot affect general cognitive ability, because the trait is innate or inherited, a variety of evidence is consistent with the hypothesis that schooling raises general ability. Bishop (1987) notes, for example, that (a) school attendance raises scores on general aptitude tests; (b) average American scores on IQ tests rose by more than one standard deviation between 1918 and 1965; (c) scores on similar aptitude tests have risen more than a standard deviation since World War II in Japan, France, Germany, Belgium, and the Netherlands; and (d) scores for blacks and some other disadvantaged groups have risen in comparison with white scores as additional schooling resources have been invested in minority education.

Whether the effect of schooling on productivity and earnings occurs solely or even mainly because of its effect on general mental ability is unknown. As noted earlier, Griliches and Mason (1972) concluded that inclusion of a measure of general aptitude in a regression predicting earnings did not greatly reduce the estimated effect of additional schooling. They also found that the independent contribution of measured ability in predicting later earnings was quite low, while the effect of schooling attainment was sizable. Other researchers have obtained higher estimates of the effect of general ability on earnings, but few have concluded that its measured effect is as high as that of schooling attainment.[3] If schooling does improve productivity, this set of findings suggests that the improvement occurs at least partly because of changes in personal characteristics not measured on general ability tests.

Nonetheless, aptitude and achievement test scores are by far the most important measures used by educators to gauge the success of their efforts. Test scores are at least correlated with later economic success, in part because they predict success in later schooling. (Several tests—including the SAT— are specifically designed to predict success in college or later schooling.) Perhaps more significantly, standardized test scores have recently become a popular barometer of the basic health of our schools. The sharp fall in average SAT scores between 1963 and 1979 is widely viewed as irrefutable proof of the decline of American educational standards. Specialists and even nonspecialists have also become aware of scores obtained on tests administered to younger students than those taking the SAT. During the late 1960s and early 1970s, the trend in these test scores was negative, too.[4] The falloff in standardized test scores was larger and longer lasting in higher grades and in tests of higher-order reasoning ability. Even in grades four and five, however, educators observed a modest decline in average performance.

For a decade or more, it appeared that school achievement as measured by standardized tests was slipping at virtually every rung in the educational ladder, from elementary school through college. Performance on the tests has subsequently improved, though few in the general public seem aware of the fact. The improvement occurred earlier and was larger in the lower grades. Recent fourth and fifth graders have achieved average scores that often surpass the previous peak scores registered in the mid-1960s. At the high school level, however, average performance continues to lag behind levels achieved during the 1960s.

The test score decline, which began in the mid-1960s, coincided strikingly with the onset of the decline in U.S. productivity growth. This coincidence in timing led some observers to infer a connection between the two developments. The two trends may be linked, but it is doubtful that any failure of our schools "caused" the sudden slowdown in productivity improvement. The fact that both test scores and productivity growth declined at the same time actually casts doubt on the proposition. The failure of the school system to educate youngsters can only be reflected in productivity as poorly schooled cohorts move into the job market. Because virtually none of the early student cohorts that performed poorly on tests had entered the work force when the productivity slowdown began, there is a little reason to believe that their inferior performance on the tests could have affected average productivity.

Productivity performance continued to slide as cohorts with low test scores entered the work force in the early 1970s. But the abruptness of the slide casts further doubt on the idea that poor schooling played much of a role. Multifactor productivity growth rose at an annual pace of 2.02 percent from 1948 to 1965, 1.04 percent from 1965 to 1973, and just 0.21 percent from 1973 to 1987. Lagging school performance could only cause this kind of deterioration if young labor force entrants played an extraordinary role in determining average productivity. As Bishop (1989, pp. 178-197) has pointed out, this is highly unlikely: teenagers earn only about 2 percent of all wages. A final argument against the view that school failure is an important source of our productivity problems is the fact that productivity woes have not been confined to our shores. Virtually all industrialized countries suffered abrupt declines in productivity growth in the early 1970s, and in most countries the falloff was even larger than the one experienced by the United States.

To maintain that lagging schooling performance cannot account for the sudden fall in productivity growth is not the same as arguing that schools have played no part in productivity trends. Bishop (1989) has made a convincing case that the test score declines are measuring a genuine change in the general mental ability of school graduates and that this decline may be contributing significantly to slow productivity growth in the 1980s and 1990s. He argues that students graduating from high school in 1980 learned about 1.25 grade-level equivalents less than students who graduated in 1967. If students learned less, human capital theory suggests that their subsequent productivity should reflect this fact. Bishop estimates that the decline in general mental ability reflected in the tests can explain a relative deterioration as large as 0.24 percent a year in average labor quality between 1980 and 1987. Though this deterioration is not nearly large enough to explain the drop in U.S. productivity growth since the late 1960s, it is worrisome nonetheless.

The perception that average school quality is slipping, as well as the suspicion that the slippage may explain deteriorating productivity performance, has pushed educators and policymakers to ask whether changes in school policy can reverse the trends. In fact, as we have already seen, the depressing achievement trends of the late 1960s and early 1970s were largely reversed in the 1980s. Many test scores, except at the highest schooling levels, had already begun to rebound by the late 1970s. American students nonetheless continue to rank low in international comparisons of student knowledge and ability. In science and mathematics, for example, junior and senior high school students fare dismally on international tests of achievement. The average scores of American seventeen-year-olds are below the average for students in nearly all other countries surveyed on tests of mathematics competence (Chubb and Hanushek 1990).

It is not obvious how this performance can be improved, however. The simplest suggestion—to spend more money—may be attractive to educators and students but is not guaranteed to yield improved results. If better performance automatically followed higher spending, the deterioration in average achievement would not have occurred. Calculations by John Chubb and Eric Hanushek show that average U.S. spending per student, controlling for the effect of inflation, rose more than 60 percent between 1966 and 1980, when most of the test score decline occurred. Since 1960 spending per pupil has nearly tripled, as the pupil/teacher ratio has fallen one-third and teachers' salaries have risen almost a third in comparison with average U.S. wages (Chubb and Hanushek 1990). These improvements in school inputs have not obviously bolstered school performance.

It is possible, of course, that increases in school inputs have helped offset what would have been even larger achievement declines in the absence of greater spending. Hence, aggregate time series trends cannot be used by themselves to draw strong conclusions about the efficacy of boosting school inputs. But evidence from microanalytical studies is not much more promising than the recent time series evidence.

Since the preparation of *Equality of Educational Opportunity* in 1966, education analysts have invested heavily in gathering data on detailed characteristics of schools, teachers, and students that might help explain individual student performance. Many data sets have been statistically analyzed in an effort to measure precisely the impact of school inputs and teacher, student, and parental characteristics on a variety of measures of student performance, including scores on standardized tests, school attendance, promotion, and graduation.

Most analysts, including the authors of *Equality of Educational Opportunity*, agree that family background is very important in explaining achievement differences (Coleman 1966; Hanushek 1986). Children with well-to-do, well-educated parents tend to outperform children attending the same school who are raised in less prosperous families. The studies do not agree, however, in finding a consistent and powerful effect of school inputs on student performance.

In recent surveys of this literature, Hanushek (1989, pp. 45-51) concludes that there is no evidence that teacher/pupil ratios, teacher education, teacher experience, teacher pay, or spending per pupil have a consistent or significant effect in improving school achievement. Table 1 shows Hanushek's tabulation of the findings from 187 studies of the effect of school inputs on student performance. The first column shows the total number of studies examining a particular input. The second shows the number concluding that the input has the expected positive effect on performance and that the effect is statistically significant. The third shows the number concluding that the effect has an unexpected *negative* effect on performance and that the effect is statistically significant. The remaining columns show the number of studies that find the factor is insignificant in explaining performance. Where possible, Hanushek has indicated the number of studies showing the factor has a positive or negative effect, even where that effect has been determined to be statistically insignificant. (Not all analysts report the sign of a statistically insignificant coefficient.)

My reading of the evidence in Table 1 is slightly less pessimistic than Hanushek's. He is almost certainly correct that the teacher/pupil ratio, teacher education, and teacher salary can be shown to have no consistent effect on student performance. A more formal statistical analysis of the data might reveal, however, that spending per pupil and teacher experience contribute to student achievement at some barely tolerable significance level.[5] Nonetheless, the case for added school inputs is hardly overwhelming. For some of the inputs—including additional teachers and more highly trained teachers—there is literally no case at all.

One notable conclusion of recent studies is that, even though measurable teacher and school characteristics have little observable impact on student performance, *un*observed characteristics appear to matter a great deal. To quote Hanushek: *"Teachers and schools differ dramatically in their effectiveness"* (1986, p. 1159). After controlling for characteristics of students and their parents that affect student achievement, as well as observable characteristics of schools and teachers, analysts find that students in particular schools or enrolled in particular teachers' classes consistently perform better than average. Some unobserved characteristic of the skilled teachers causes

Table 1. Results of 187 Studies of the Effects of School Inputs on Student Achievement

Input	Number of Studies	Statistically Significant		Total	Statistically Insignificant		
		Increases Achievement	*Decreases Achievement*		*Increases Achievement*	*Decreases Achievement*	*Unknown*
Teacher-pupil ratio	152	14	13	125	34	46	45
Teacher education	113	8	5	100	31	32	37
Teacher experience	140	40	10	90	44	31	15
Teacher salary	69	11	4	54	16	14	24
Expenditures per pupil	65	13	3	49	25	13	11

Source: Chubb and Hanushek (1990, p. 220).

them consistently to outperform teachers who achieve only mediocre results with their students. Similarly, some unmeasured aspect of an effective school causes it to be more productive than other schools in raising student performance.

This finding has opened up a relatively new field of educational research. Using a case study approach, analysts study only a handful of schools in an attempt to discover those special, unmeasurable aspects of schools that make some more effective than others. The literature on this subject has identified several aspects of effective schools that make them distinctive. They have strong educational leadership. They have a clear sense of academic purpose and well articulated educational goals. And they have a highly professional teaching staff. Unfortunately, these admirable qualities are difficult to attain. If it were simple to secure them, the nation would be blessed with a much more effective school system.

EFFECTS OF SCHOOL REFORM

The recent research on the effect of school inputs on student performance holds little promise that spending money on additional or more costly inputs will improve student achievement. The prospect of smaller class size might be pleasing to teacher and student alike, but there is no convincing evidence it raises student learning. Higher salaries could improve teacher morale and raise the quality of entrants into the teaching profession, but proof is lacking that it will boost standardized test scores.

The gloomy verdict reached by analysts of school performance stands in marked contrast to the conclusions reached in the human capital literature. While school performance researchers have concluded that observable teacher and school characteristics make little difference, scholars working in the human capital tradition find that school characteristics have a noticeable impact on the economic benefits workers derive from their schooling. Students educated in more costly schools receive a higher earnings gain per year spent in school.

The contradiction between the two sets of findings is deeply puzzling. If both sets of conclusions are accepted at face value they imply that public spending on more costly school inputs can raise productivity in two or three decades but cannot affect student achievement anytime in the foreseeable future. Two explanations of the apparent contradiction have been offered. Card and Krueger (1990, pp. 2-3) argue that the aspects of schooling that raise labor market earnings are poorly measured by standardized test scores. Consequently, better schools could succeed in improving students' capacity to earn even though they apparently do not succeed in raising academic achievement.

Hanushek (1986, pp. 1153, 1172) suggests that data limitations have prevented analysts from estimating well-specified models of the effect of school quality on subsequent earnings. Schooling quality, as measured in a typical human capital study, is correlated with unobservable characteristics of family background which, because they are unmeasured, must be excluded from the analysis. The correlation between measured school quality and unobservable parental inputs leads to a spurious finding that school quality—as measured by school inputs—affects subsequent earnings.

I find neither of these explanations particularly convincing. Card and Krueger's argument implies that schools efficiently utilize resources to achieve a goal they cannot measure—post-school economic success. Perversely, however, they are very inefficient in achieving improvements in the only outcomes they seem to care about and can actually observe, namely, those related to achievement of students in school. Arguably, schools ought to try to maximize the earnings gains their graduates can obtain as a result of school attendance. As a practical matter, it is very difficult to know how to accomplish this. I know of no school that even tries. Few schools seem interested in what happens to their graduates after they leave. Most do not even know whether school leavers find jobs. By contrast, all schools have a passable idea of the scholastic accomplishments of students in their care. Scholastic achievement is, after all, the main goal most educators set for their students. Yet the school performance literature suggests that given more resources (or better paid teachers, or smaller class sizes, or greater teacher experience) educators cannot reliably organize the resources to improve student achievement. It would be astonishing if they could organize them to improve post-school earnings.

I find Hanushek's argument equally unpersuasive. Although some human capital analysts have ignored the influence of family background variables when estimating the effect of school quality on returns to schooling, other analysts have not. No set of control variables is perfect. Yet the effects of school quality on subsequent earnings have been found to be significant in a wide variety of specifications.

A simpler explanation for the paradox may be that variations in U.S. school inputs once made an important difference in terms of both in-school achievement *and* post-school earnings. The variations in school inputs are now small enough so that their practical significance for current school achievement is small and swamped by other factors. However, the historical variations were quite wide, so the effects of past input differences continue to be observable in the personal income distribution.

Studies of the relationship between school inputs and American educational achievement rely on data collected after the early 1960s. Studies of the relationship between school inputs and U.S. labor market performance rely on earnings data collected during the past three decades. They are based, however, on the experiences of people who received their schooling before 1960.

Until the Second World War there were wide differences between states in the resources invested in education. According to Card and Krueger (1990, Table 1), the student/teacher ratio facing students born between 1920 and 1929 was 34 in South Carolina, 36 in North Carolina, Alabama, and Arkansas, and 38 in Mississippi. It was only 28 in New York, Rhode Island, and Massachusetts. The school year lasted 154 days in Georgia, 150 days in Alabama, and just 139 days in Mississippi. In New York, New Jersey, and several midwestern states, the average school year had already reached 180 or more days. Teachers were paid only 65-70 percent of the average state wage in several southern states; in the mid-Atlantic and southern New England states, teachers were paid substantially more than the average wage.

These differences are quite wide, especially when one considers that they reflect the average conditions in an entire state or region. Many students in the most disadvantaged regions presumably attended schools that had even higher class sizes, even shorter school years, and even lower teacher pay. For black pupils in the south, conditions were especially grim. Welch (1966, pp. 59, 65-66) notes that black students in Georgia in 1920 faced a student/teacher ratio of 56. In 1930, 38 percent of the teaching staff of black southern schools had not graduated from high school; only 9 percent had obtained four or more years of college. It is easy to believe that a year of schooling received under these conditions would not be worth as much as a year of schooling received in New York or New England.

However, by the 1950s school inputs grew more nearly equal across the states. Black schooling was significantly improved, even before desegregation occurred in the 1950s. The Coleman Report, issued in 1966, concluded that there were no sizable differences between the educational resources available to black and white students. The statistics tabulated by Card and Krueger show a tremendous equalization in school inputs, even for students born in the thirty-year period between 1920 and 1949. A reasonable inference might be that as school resources in the poorest regions approach those in the average region, the payoff to extra investment in school inputs decreases substantially. Unfortunately, this conjecture cannot be confirmed until sometime in the future when lifetime earnings patterns of students educated in the 1960s and 1970s become available. The data assembled by Card and Krueger, although more extensive than those collected by any other researcher, are probably insufficient to detect nonlinearities in the relationship between school inputs and the rate of return to schooling.[6]

If it is true that additional investment in school inputs cannot reliably raise the school performance or lifetime earnings of American students, the most promising route to reform must involve reorganization of the resources we currently invest. One promising conclusion of the school performance literature is the finding that school principals can identify the effective teachers on their staffs. According to Murnane (1975) and Hanushek (1986), among others, principals' evaluations of individual teachers are highly correlated with researchers' estimates of the teachers' overall effectiveness. Thus, even though the qualities that raise teacher effectiveness are not observable to the social science researcher, the effective teachers are apparently known to principals.

If principals were given authority to hire, promote, and discharge the teachers on their staff, and if they used this authority to recruit and retain the most effective teachers, school performance would evidently improve. When principals have little discretion in choosing their staff, the effectiveness of teachers will depend largely on the rules governing teacher recruitment and on the voluntary choices of teachers to remain in teaching or find more attractive employment elsewhere. Where principals have discretion to select their staff, but little inducement to exercise it, the result for teacher effectiveness is probably similar.

One promising reform would be to confer on principals greater authority to select and discharge their teachers. At the same time, principals should be given strong incentives to hire and retain an effective staff. This might be accomplished within a public school system by tying principals' employment and pay to the average educational progress of students in their school. Student progress would be measured by standardized test scores, and each school's educational goals would be adjusted to reflect the social and economic circumstances of the student body.

There is of course strong resistance in the teaching profession to reforms that tie teacher pay or employment to evaluations of teacher performance. Teacher representatives correctly argue that social science can provide no objective and consistent method for assessing the performance of individual teachers. Principals' evaluations could therefore be subverted to achieve personal or political rather than educational goals. In addition, teaching is said to be a cooperative undertaking. By reducing teachers' job security or tying their pay to performance, teachers would be placed in competition with one another, thus reducing the effectiveness of the cooperative educational enterprise.

The first argument certainly has merit. Relying on principals' evaluations to determine teacher promotion and retention leaves open the possibility that principals' decisions will not always be fair according to absolute or easily verified educational criteria. On the other hand, the goal of absolute fairness toward teachers must be weighed against the ultimate goal of schools, which is to instruct students in a commonly accepted curriculum. A wealth of evidence demonstrates that teacher effectiveness varies widely. This evidence suggests that it can be worthwhile to reduce the job security of teachers in order to allow the removal of ineffective teachers from the classroom. The loss of job security should certainly be compensated by an increase in average teacher pay. This combination of reforms—higher pay in exchange for reduced job security—will yield a far greater improvement in school performance than salary increases alone.

The argument that teacher competition would fatally interfere with cooperation that is essential to learning seems to me illogical and probably insupportable. In the great majority of classrooms in the United States there is only a single instructor; instruction does not occur in a team environment. The educational progress of students in these classrooms appears to depend to an important degree on the quality of their instructors. Whatever help teachers give one another outside the classroom, many teachers remain singularly ineffective in helping their students to progress. Under these circumstances, perhaps it is better to lose some cooperation outside the classroom in exchange for greater ability to remove those teachers who appear not to benefit from the current level of cooperation. Other college-educated workers, engaged in professions where the necessity for cooperation and teamwork is much more obvious, will not be sympathetic to teachers' complaints about increased competition with their peers. After all, managers and industrial designers, who are engaged in highly cooperative occupations, are forced from the beginning of their careers to compete as well as cooperate with their professional colleagues.

Even if it is useful to offer principals the authority to recruit and discharge teachers, such authority will not improve schools' effectiveness unless principals can be persuaded to exercise it. Economists worry that current institutional arrangements do not provide public school principals with strong incentives to undertake the unpopular measures needed to remove ineffective teachers, even if they were given the power to do so. Political scientists Chubb and Moe (1990) argue that democratic control makes it difficult if not impossible for public schools to offer the proper environment and administrative incentives for effective schools to flourish. Because of this kind of pessimism, critics of the public school system have suggested a variety of ways to reform the structure of the school system. One of these is greater emphasis on magnet schools. Another is the introduction of the concept of merit schools.

Magnet schools are simply schools in the regular school system that have been given extra resources or a distinctive curriculum or teaching staff. The student body is drawn, at least in part, from across normal school boundaries and on the basis of parent or student choice. Magnet schools can spur educational innovation in an entire school system by demonstrating the feasibility or superiority of new techniques. Students who attend these schools can receive an improved education compared with that they would receive in neighborhood schools.

On balance, however, it seems doubtful that magnet schools can significantly improve the average effectiveness of a district's schools. Even if magnet schools achieve demonstrably superior results, other schools in the district face no strong incentives to emulate their methods. Demand for entrance into good magnet schools often far outstrips the available number of places, and there is no obvious pressure anywhere in the system to increase the number of places to match demand. Even more disturbing, children not lucky enough to obtain a place in magnet schools may be even more disadvantaged after the introduction of the reform than they were before. Better teachers and students from standard schools may be siphoned off to the magnets, thus reducing the average quality of instruction for luckless students forced to remain in standard schools.

As an inducement for individual schools to improve their performance, it is sometimes suggested that additional resources should be provided to schools achieving superior results (merit schools) while resources are taken away from schools that are less effective. This proposal is not very sensible unless students are added to more effective schools at the same time that resources are added. If a school is already achieving above-average results with average resources, it hardly seems equitable to permit its students to achieve even better results with increased resources at the same time that performance in other schools is permitted to languish. The opposite policy—pouring additional resources into failing schools in order to promote equity—is no more sensible. As shown in the earlier discussion, there is no firm evidence that additional resources will consistently or reliably raise student achievement.

To move both students and resources toward more effective schools while moving them away from less effective schools, some reformers now advocate public school choice. Parents and students would be permitted to cross school boundaries, and possibly school district boundaries, to select the school that most closely matches their preferences. Money, in the form of a public tuition payment, would follow the student to the new school, bringing extra resources into those public schools that attract pupils and reducing resources available to less popular schools. Under a hopeful interpretation of parent and student motivations, parents would seek out more effective public schools for their children, thus depriving the less effective schools of both students and money.

This proposal could improve average school performance if enough parents care enough about school effectiveness to try to send their children to effective schools and if district administrators permit popular schools to expand and the least popular ones to close. I suspect, however, that added choice among existing public schools will not greatly improve school performance unless district administrators also give far more latitude to principals and their teaching staffs to develop their own distinctive approaches to instruction and curriculum. Otherwise, parents would be given a choice among essentially identical alternatives. If all public school alternatives looked similar, I expect that parents would select schools on the basis of convenience, thus causing little shift in the current distribution of students.

Greater choice among public schools would also yield little benefit if current personnel practices are preserved. In particular, if ineffective teachers in shrinking or closed schools retain their right to employment somewhere in the district school system, it is hard to see what system-wide benefit would be derived from permitting parents greater choice in selecting public schools. Students would be sorted into different classrooms, with some students obtaining a better instructor while other pupils obtained a worse one. Better informed parents would presumably seek out the schools with the most effective instructors, but children of less well informed parents would be stuck with mediocre or ineffective teachers. On balance, no gain in performance would be achieved.

Chubb and Moe argue that it is unrealistic to expect that public school administrators or politicians who currently influence school policy would voluntarily surrender their authority to control what goes on inside public schools. Public schooling in this country suffers from poor average performance precisely because authorities and special interests outside the school seek to maintain excessive bureaucratic control over details of school operation they are in a poor position to oversee. Any structural reform that depends on the good will of these administrators, politicians, or special interests for successful implementation is doomed to fail. Even if parents are permitted to choose public schools, bureaucrats or politicians will so circumscribe their power of choice that its impact on school performance will be slight. Vested interests like teachers unions and district school boards will undercut essential elements of reform, primarily to protect the tenure or power of their members.

To circumvent these problems of democratic control, Chubb and Moe (1990) suggest greater reliance on markets in the distribution of school resources. They propose to offer parents full subsidies, vouchers, or scholarships that are redeemable at any public or publicly accredited school, including most private and parochial schools. This reform would vastly expand the range of school choice and greatly diminish the influence of politicians and central school administrators in the detailed operation of schools. Politicians and state accrediting agencies would retain their influence on curriculum and teacher training through their power to determine school accreditation criteria. In addition, they could prevent racial or other kinds of discrimination in private schools through the simple expedient of withholding voucher payments to schools deemed to be discriminatory. But their influence on a wide range of school administrative decisions would be greatly reduced. If they sought to impose seriously counterproductive requirements on the public schools, disgruntled parents in those schools could take their children (and voucher payments) out of the public school system. In the competition to survive, public schools would have to improve in order to flourish.

Contrary to a popular misconception, it is not necessary that all parents become well informed about school effectiveness in order for a school choice plan to improve average school performance and student achievement. Even if only a minority of parents spend the time and effort to find the best school for their children, the characteristics of average schools could eventually change quite dramatically. The decisions of well informed parents to withdraw their children from less effective schools and place them in more effective schools not only has an immediate effect on the percentage of pupils being educated in more successful schools, it also places strong pressure on the declining schools to improve the effectiveness of their instruction. Few people seriously believe that more than a handful of consumers are well informed about automobiles or telephone service. Yet most U.S. economists confidently expect that introduction of competition in these markets must eventually result in improvement in the quality or cost of products available to the consumer. In my view, this expectation is usually justified by experience.

The problem with applying this insight to education is that few people would be satisfied with an improvement in the average performance of schools if the improvement yielded a substantial rise in inequality. We know from research on the determinants of school performance that children of better educated and wealthier parents do better in school, presumably because their home environments are more supportive of scholastic achievement. It seems reasonable to expect that highly educated, affluent parents would also make more effort to find good schools for their children if wide school choice were offered to them. It thus seems likely that many of the benefits of school choice will be obtained by the children of economically successful parents.

I do not believe children from poor families will fail to benefit at all from greater school choice. The parents of many of these children care deeply about the quality of schooling available to their children. Under the current system, these concerned parents have few affordable options outside of the neighborhood public school. With publicly funded choice, their options would expand, and many parents would take advantage of the improved choice. In addition, children in other poor families may eventually benefit as an indirect result of greater competition among public and private schools (just as poor and perhaps ill-informed car buyers benefited from increased auto competition in the 1970s and 1980s). In practice, however, fewer children from poor than from affluent backgrounds are likely to benefit from greater schooling choice. If the gains enjoyed by affluent children far outstrip those obtained by the poor, the reform could contribute to the trend toward greater economic inequality, which has been a disturbing trend of American life since the early 1970s.

To improve the chances of poor families under a school choice system, it would be desirable to offer additional subsidies or more generous voucher payments to schools providing education to economically disadvantaged children. The school performance literature indicates that pouring extra resources into schools does not yield reliable or consistent gains in student achievement. But this finding was obtained in the context of noncompeting public schools. The purpose of extra subsidies in a school choice environment is to make it more attractive for the better schools to enroll disadvantaged students. If the extra subsidy were large enough, good schools might find it to their advantage to seek out disadvantaged children. These children would thus enjoy a larger share of the educational benefit from added school choice.

Two decades of historical experience and social science research suggest that school performance is more likely to be improved through better management than from additional resources. The organizational reforms needed to improve school performance are not easy to achieve. In the short run, politically powerful groups are asked to make tangible sacrifices for diffuse, distant, and uncertain benefits. The only likely benefit of these reforms is improved school achievement, as measured by standardized test scores. It is not at all certain that higher scores translate into substantially higher earnings, and it is still less certain whether individual earnings gains from improved schooling result in equivalent gains to the wider economy. We do not know whether lower educational performance was a major or minor contributor to recent productivity performance. So we cannot be certain whether a robust improvement in schools will lead to a strong rebound in productivity growth or an uptick that is too slight to notice.

Even if we cannot be certain that school reform will have a big payoff in improved economic performance, the struggle to improve the organization of schools is worth waging. The country asks its citizens to invest no fewer than twelve years in formal schooling. At a minimum we should expect current American students to equal the achievement levels reached in this country in the 1960s and perhaps the achievement of average European and East Asian students today. To reach either goal requires a major effort—and probably a political miracle.

ACKNOWLEDGMENT

Eric Hanushek, Alan B. Krueger, Laurel McFarland, Richard J. Murnane, and Robert J. Thornton kindly provided suggestions and comments on an earlier version of this paper. I gratefully acknowledge the financial support of Lehigh University's Martindale Center. The views expressed are the author's alone and should not be ascribed to the Brookings Institution or the Martindale Center.

NOTES

1. See Burtless (1990, pp. 8-10) and Blackburn, Bloom, and Freeman (1990, pp. 31-43).
2. Studies of the impact of U.S. school quality include Morgan and Sirageldin (1968); and Johnson and Stafford (1973). A study based on a similar methodology for the case of Brazil is described in Behrman and Birdsall (1983). All three studies find significant and meaningfully large impacts of school quality—as measured by the cost of school inputs—on the earnings impact of an added year of education.

3. Researchers sometimes report that an aptitude test score is a better predictor than educational attainment of productivity on a specific job. This does not imply, however, that it is a better predictor of earnings in the general population. The low correlation of educational attainment and productivity in a particular job might simply reflect the peculiar character of applicants for that job. Consider, for example, the idiosyncratic nature of college graduates who work as burger flippers in a fast food franchise.

4. For an excellent survey, see Congressional Budget Office (1986).

5. For example, if Hanushek had performed a formal meta-analysis of the findings from the studies included in Table 1, he might have found that increases in spending per pupil, on balance, contribute to improvements in student achievement. The methodology of meta-analysis is described in Bangert-Drowns (1986).

6. It is necessary to test for nonlinear effects in order to determine whether the payoff to additional school resources drops off after some threshold point representing resource adequacy.

REFERENCES

Aaron, H.J. 1978. *Politics and the Professors: The Great Society in Perspective.* Washington, DC: The Brookings Institution.

Bangert-Drowns, R.L. 1986. "Review of Developments in Meta-Analytic Method." *Psychological Bulletin* 99, 388-399.

Behrman, J.R. and N. Birdsall. 1983. "The Quality of Schooling: Quantity Alone is Misleading." *American Economic Review* 73 (5): 928-946.

Bishop, J. 1987. "Information Externalities and the Social Payoff to Academic Achievement." Center for Advanced Human Resource Studies, Working Paper. No. 87-06. Ithaca, NY: Cornell University.

————. 1989. "Is the Test Score Decline Responsible for the Productivity Growth Decline?" *American Economic Review* 79 (1): 178-197.

Blackburn, M. L., D. E. Bloom, and R. B. Freeman. 1990. "The Declining Economic Position of Less Skilled American Men." Pp. 31-67 in *A Future of Lousy Jobs? The Changing Structure of U.S. Wages,* edited by G. Burtless. Washington DC: The Brookings Institution.

Card, D. and A. Krueger. 1990. "Does Schooling Quality Matter? Returns to Education and the Characteristics of Public Schools in the United States." N.B.E.R. Working Paper No. 3358. Cambridge, MA: National Bureau of Economic Research.

Chubb, J.E. and E.A. Hanushek. 1990. "Reforming Educational Reform." P. 215 in *Setting National Priorities: Policy for the Nineties,* edited by H.J. Aaron. Washington, DC: The Brookings Institution.

Chubb, J.E. and T. M. Moe. 1990. *Politics, Markets, and America's Schools.* Washington, DC: The Brookings Institution.

Coleman, J.S. 1966. *Equality of Educational Opportunity.* Washington, DC: U.S. Government Printing Office.

Congressional Budget Office. 1986. *Trends in Educational Achievement.* Washington, DC: Congressional Budget Office.

Denison, E.F. 1985. *Trends in American Economic Growth, 1929-1982.* Washington DC: The Brookings Institution.

Griliches Z. and W. M. Mason. 1972. "Education, Income, and Ability." *Journal of Political Economy* 80 (3): S74-S103.

Hanushek, E.A. 1986. "The Economics of Schooling: Production and Efficiency in Public Schools." *Journal of Economic Literature* 24 (3): 1141-1177.

_____. 1989. "The Impact of Differential Expenditures on School Performance." *Educational Researcher* 18, 45-51.

Hunter, J.E. 1986. "Cognitive Ability, Cognitive Aptitudes, Job Knowledge, and Job Performance." *Journal of Vocational Behavior* 29 (3): 340-362.

Johnsn, G.E. and F.P. Stafford. 1973. "Social Returns to Quantity and Quality of Schooling." *Journal of Human Resources* 8 (2): 139-155.

Johnston, W.B. 1987. *Workforce 2000: Work and Workers for the 21st Century.* Indianapolis, IN: Hudson Institute.

Morgan, J. and I. Sirageldin. 1968. "A Note on the Quality Dimension in Education." *Journal of Political Economy* 76 (5): 1069-1077.

Murnane, R.J. 1975. *Impact of School Resources on the Learning of Inner City Children.* Cambridge, MA: Ballinger.

National Governors' Association. 1990. *National Educational Goals.* Washington, DC: National Governors' Association.

Schmidt, F.L. 1988. "The Problem of Group Differences in Ability Test Scores in Employment Selection." *Journal of Vocational Behavior* 33 (3): 272-292.

Spence, M. 1974. *Market Signalling: Informational Transfer in Hiring and Related Screening Processes.* Cambridge, MA: Harvard University Press.

Welch, F. 1966. "Measurement of the Quality of Education." *American Economic Review* 56 (2): 379-392.

_____. 1967. "Labor-Market Discrimination: An Interpretation of Income Differences in the Rural South." *Journal of Political Economy* 75 (3):225-240.

_____. 1973a. "Black-White Differences in the Returns to Schooling." *American Economic Review* 63 (5): 189-204

_____. 1973b. "Education and Racial Discrimination." Pp. 43-81 in *Discrimination in Labor Markets,* edited by O. Ashenfelter and A. Rees. Princeton, NJ: Princeton University Press.

INDEX